# DANGER IN THE FIELD

The nature of qualitative inquiry means that researchers constantly have to deal with the unexpected, and all too often this includes coping with the presence of danger or risk. *Danger in the Field* is an innovative and lively analysis of the experience of different forms of danger in various qualitative research settings. Made up of researchers' reflexive accounts of their own encounters with 'danger' while carrying out research, this book expands our common sense use of the term to encompass not just physical danger, but emotional, ethical and professional danger too. In addition the authors pay special attention to the gendered forms of danger implicit in the research process.

From the physical danger of researching the night club 'bouncer' scene to the ethical dangers of participant observation in a home for older people, these contributions provide researchers and students with thought-provoking insights into the importance of a well-chosen research design.

**Geraldine Lee-Treweek** is Lecturer in Sociology at the Department of Applied Social Science, Stirling University. **Stephanie Linkogle** is Lecturer in Sociology at the School of African and Asian Studies, University of Sussex.

# DANGER IN THE FIELD

Risk and ethics in social research

*Edited by*
*Geraldine Lee-Treweek and*
*Stephanie Linkogle*

London and New York

First published 2000
by Routledge
11 New Fetter Lane, London EC4P 4EE

Simultaneously published in the USA and Canada
by Routledge
29 West 35th Street, New York, NY 10001

*Routledge is an imprint of the Taylor & Francis Group*

Typeset in Perpetua by Taylor & Francis Books Ltd
Printed and bound in Great Britain by Clays Ltd, St Ives PLC

*British Library Cataloguing in Publication Data*
A catalogue record for this book is available from the British Library

*Library of Congress Cataloging in Publication Data*
Lee-Treweek, Geraldine, 1969–
Danger in the field: risk and ethics in social research / Geraldine Lee-Treweek and
Stephanie Linkogle. p. cm.
Includes bibliographical references and index.
1. Social scientists–Vocational guidance. 2. Social scientists–Professional ethics. 3.
Social sciences–Research–Moral and ethical aspects.
I. Linkogle, Stephanie. II. Title.
H62.L419 2000
300'.7'2–dc21     00–035278

ISBN 0–415–19321–4 (hbk)
ISBN 0–415–19322–2 (pbk)

# CONTENTS

v

# CONTENTS

# CONTRIBUTORS

**David Calvey** is a Research Fellow at CRIC (ESRC Centre for Research on Innovation and Competition) and an Honorary Fellow in the Sociology Department at Manchester University. His research interests are in critical organisation studies, popular cultural studies, ethnomethodology and ethnography. He has held various lecturing and research positions at the Universities of Manchester, UMIST, Manchester Metropolitan University, Liverpool John Moores University and the University of Queensland, Australia.

**John Gabriel** is Professor of Sociology and Head of Department of Sociology and Applied Social Studies at London Guildhall University. His recent publications include *Racism, Culture, Markets* (Routledge, 1994) and *Whitewash* (Routledge, 1998).

**Janet Jamieson** is a Research Fellow at the Social Work Research Centre, University of Stirling. Working in the field of Social Work and Criminal Justice she has conducted research exploring young people's understanding of offending, evaluative studies of four intensive probation projects and contributed to a study on the Scottish Children's Hearing System. Her current research interests include young people and offending, women offenders, community and crime and the perspective and experiences of ethnic-minority young people in Glasgow on offending and victimisation.

**Arthur J. Jipson** is Assistant Professor of Sociology at Miami University in Oxford, Ohio. His research interests include white 'racialism', hate crime, the American labour movement, Internet communication, the recording industry, and corporate crime. He has been conducting research on white 'racialists', militia members, and the American Patriot movement since 1993 and his current research projects include re-examining the State of Indiana versus Ford Motor Company case and the construction and utility of hate crime legislation. Dr Jipson has been published in Popular Music and Society and ChildNews and also has appeared on CNN, TBS and National Public Radio's 'All Things Considered'.

**Gloria Lankshear** is a Research Fellow in Sociology at the University of Plymouth. She gained a degree in Social Policy and Administration and an MSc in Research Methods before undertaking research about community care. Her PhD focused on the barriers to the implementation of new technology in the National Health Service and this has led to her current research interest in new technology and its surveillance capabilities.

**Geraldine Lee-Treweek** is Lecturer in Sociology at Stirling University with teaching and research interests in the fields of the sociology of health and illness and qualitative methodologies. Her current research focus is the study of the rehabilitation of people with back pain and she has an ongoing interest in the study of emotional labour in a variety of work settings.

**Gayle Letherby** is Senior Lecturer in Sociology at Coventry University. Her research and writing interests include all things methodological including auto/biography and feminist research in theory and practice, motherhood/non-motherhood, kinship and the family and working and learning in higher education.

**Stephanie Linkogle** is Lecturer in Sociology at the University of Sussex in the School of African and Asian Studies. Her research interests include women's popular movements in Central America, feminist movements, sociology of religion, research methodology, cultural studies and the media. Her publications include *Gender, Practice and Faith in Nicaragua: Constructing the Popular and Making Common Sense* (Avebury, 1996), and articles in *Bulletin of Latin American Research, Race and Class* and *Sociological Research Online*.

**Chad E. Litton** is Assistant Professor of Sociology at South-Eastern Oklahoma State University. His primary interests lie in the study of new religious movements, ideology development, commodification of sexuality, extremist ideology, rural culture, and undergraduate education.

**Jeff D. Peterson** is Assistant Professor of Sociology at Linfield College in McMinnville, Oregon. His research includes work on squatters in the United States and urban social movements in Mexico. His most recently published article is 'La Lucha Por El Ciudadano: Movimientos Sociales, Pronasol, y La Teoria de Nuevos Movimientos Sociales en Guadalajara, Mexico' in *Espiral* No. 15 (May–Aug) 1999, University of Guadalajara. He also has an ongoing research project on transitions in Latino cultural identity in Oregon.

**Louise Westmarland** is Lecturer in Criminology at the University of Teesside. Her PhD was an ethnographic study of gender and operational policing. She is interested in the ways force and strength interact with embodied authority in terms of the enactment of power, social control and masculinity. At present she is working on a book about gender and the covert worlds of surveillance teams and detective work.

# ACKNOWLEDGEMENTS

The editors would like to acknowledge the help and support provided by the following people during the writing of this book: Bethan Benwell, Johnston Birchall and Kate Thomson. Special mention must be made of the contributions of Roger Homan, David Morgan and Rik Scarce, all of whom provided invaluable advice to the project. Finally we would like to thank Mari Shullaw at Routledge for her belief in our ideas in the first place and for fighting our corner at numerous points along the way.

# OVERVIEW

*Geraldine Lee-Treweek and Stephanie Linkogle*

Are you in danger? This is a question not often asked within social science research, but we argue that there are a range of dangers involved in investigating social life of which researchers should be more aware. These dangers have often not been explored, or in many cases even identified, in methodological literature. Here, and in the contributions which follow, we aim to remedy this gap by making danger visible and explaining its relationship to data collection and the understanding of social phenomena. Throughout this book, the term danger will be used in relation to the experience of threat or risk with serious negative consequences that may affect the researcher, participants and other groups in society. This is not a book about the general problems of research; indeed we draw a line between dangerous aspects of research and aspects of the research process which are merely challenging or difficult.

This text is concerned predominantly with researcher risk. The rationale for this focus is that there are several contemporary texts which address research ethics and which are concerned, in the main, with risk to participants of social research (Bulmer 1982; Homan 1991). We would argue that concern for participants has been a focus of debate in the social sciences for some time. Consequently, researchers are often well versed in outlining the importance of protecting participants, the ways they intend to do this and the possible consequences of the research process upon the lives of those being studied. They may also have had to submit proposals and plans to ethics committees or funding bodies to explain in detail how they will manage any possible risks to those they are hoping to study, prior to gaining access or funding. However, the issue of their own or their co-researchers' safety and welfare needs is often thought through in a cursory manner or in an *ad hoc* contingent fashion once in the field. This book places the risk to the researcher centre stage and is designed to complement the debates around protecting participants.

Indeed, in many of the chapters that follow, threats to the researcher and to participants are shown to be connected. Our experience of risk as researchers

1

frequently parallel those of the people we are studying. In the case of studying dangerous occupations, danger and risk may be part of the participants' world as an everyday reality and defining feature of the work. In other situations the experience of an unusual dangerous event, such as a disaster or bout of disease, may allow the researcher to see how participants mobilise against the threat. In other research situations, the dangers of the field come specifically from the processes involved in collecting data, for instance managing relationships with groups who may behave in a threatening manner, or the basic practicalities of getting to research sites. For instance, Sam Punch (personal communication) experienced physical threat when researching childhood in rural Bolivia, when she was attacked by village dogs as she tried to reach remote households on foot. Some dangers rely on a contingent approach to management; however, this is no excuse for complacency in the prior evaluation of possible threat.

Currently, social science is becoming more aware of the importance of re-searcher safety and well-being. In Britain this is being driven, in part, by a general tightening-up of health and safety procedures within universities. In the United States, fear of litigation is focusing attention on the need for rigorous evaluation of research proposals and safety arrangements prior to entry to the field. Various disciplines within social science have also begun to recognise the need for researcher safety too. So, for instance, the Social Policy Association (Britain) is developing guidelines for fieldwork safety procedures. These changes indicate that it is no longer acceptable to apply different standards of care to participants and those carrying out research, whether they be seasoned researchers, students or contract researchers brought in to undertake a specific task in the research process. The chapters that follow aim to contribute to this growing interest in researcher safety by presenting reflexive views that discuss the experience of danger. Furthermore, the contributions attempt to go beyond being a set of interesting 'stories' of threat and danger in the field, and aim to analyse the ways that risk serves a useful purpose in understanding social life but can also be managed or minimised through planning and forethought.

The first chapter invites the reader to consider the various aspects of danger and risk that researchers encounter in the field and presents a framework for categorising these dangers. Using the headings of physical, emotional, ethical and professional danger, the chapter provides a basic organising structure for the subsequent contributions and maps out the way these threats have been conceptualised in the past. Emphasis is placed on the fact that, although risk in the field is a frightening experience for the researcher, it does on many occasions enrich our understandings of the research site and enables us to think and write about social life as insiders. Each chapter contributes a reflexive case study of research danger to present illustrations of the key forms. Although each is chiefly concerned with one particular type of danger, our framework is not intended to be discrete. Therefore many contributions discuss more than one form of research risk and make reference to the way that different risks are often interconnected in the field.

Chapters 2, 3 and 4 are concerned primarily with physical danger and threat to the researcher. In Chapter 2 by Westmarland, participant observational research in an overtly dangerous and masculinised setting (the British police force) is examined. In this case, physical danger is both a research topic and an experiential resource, which allows a clearer understanding of how police work is carried out. Westmarland studied the relationship between danger, risk and heroism in police culture by accompanying armed response vehicles and being present during the day-to-day work of police officers in inner city areas. Her chapter charts her transformation from being constructed by officers as 'at risk', to being one of the team at critical incidents involving firearms. Westmarland argues that sharing the experience of serious danger with her participants permitted an in-depth understanding of the highly gendered world of policing. Chapter 3, contributed by Calvey, is concerned with the physically challenging world of night club door work. In this he reflects upon the experience of covertly taking employment as a 'bouncer' to access a social world which would be out of bounds to overt study. Bouncing is an occupation faced with attempts to professionalise and clean up its image but which, on the ground, Calvey contends, is still involved with managing violence, drug gangs and public disorder. Calvey advocates a lived experience of the setting as the best means to understanding the pressures of doing this dangerous job. At the same time, he discusses the necessity of careful planning to protect the researcher from the very real possibility of sustaining physical injury.

Jamieson's contribution (Chapter 4) examines the practicalities of ensuring safety in the field by discussing research into young people and crime in Scotland. In this study, Jamieson was involved in interviewing a potentially 'dangerous' group (young men), often in their own homes. She argues that safeguards and precautions should be built into any research strategy and emphasises the importance of planning, team work and colleague support in countering physical risk. Although Jamieson recognises the practical and financial constraints upon research projects that make the provision of support difficult, she contends that communication with one's co-researchers and mutual support is essential to countering physical danger in the field and providing a de-brief to threatening experiences. Lastly, Jamieson notes that the contemporary practice of contract research makes it more difficult for researchers to ask for basic safety procedures and equipment (such as mobile phones) and less likely that funding bodies and research managers will be told of problems experienced in the field. She argues that personal safety considerations need to become a composite part of research design.

In Chapters 5, 6 and 7 we turn to the issue of emotional danger in social research. By emotional danger we mean serious threat or danger to researchers brought on by negative feeling states induced by the research process. In these chapters, the concept of emotional danger is developed to show that it can affect researchers in two ways: first, through destabilising personal identity and second, through providing greater insight into the research process. We argue that these two processes overlap and often serve to generate new levels of understanding for the researcher. In Chapter 5 Lankshear outlines how contract research, focusing upon the implementation of new health care technology, took her into two very different research settings in which she experienced diverse dangers. The first, a hospital pathology laboratory, is rife with physical threats that were completely unanticipated prior to entering the field. Interestingly, Lankshear notes that whilst her participants were well prepared for the threat of disease, in the form of inoculations and training, threats to her own health as a participant observer were overlooked. The second half of the chapter examines another piece of hospital ethnography but on this occasion in a maternity suite. Here, Lankshear discusses prior personal experiences that were brought to the fore whilst undertaking the fieldwork, causing her great distress. Despite this, she does not argue that personal experience should debar researchers from studying topics that overlap with negative experiences in their own biographies. Rather, she illustrates that insight came from seeing the setting from the dual perspective of being an ethnographer (and current participant observer) and former participant.

Lankshear's chapter addresses the threat to emotional well-being brought on by studying an area defined by research managers or external bodies. As she notes, for the contract researcher this can mean researching topics which, if they had a choice, they might avoid. In contrast, Chapter 6 by Letherby focuses attention upon the emotional threat that can arise out of taking an autobiographical approach to a topic of choice. Letherby's research is in the field of involuntary childlessness and New Reproductive Technologies. As an involuntarily childless woman herself, Letherby argues that there are great benefits to using one's own experience as a starting point for research and as a resource throughout the research process. However, there are emotional risks in scrutinising one's own experience and being able to identify directly with that of participants. Letherby's chapter explains the ways that such feelings are useful as data and also how she managed negative emotions by seeking support from kin and colleagues. Her final points address the issue of writing the self into one's academic work and the threats involved with taking what is a new and developing approach. Letherby recounts how her work has been received by some members of the academy as 'sloppy sociology'. She argues that the autobiographical approach challenges the accepted mainstream academic division between self and participant, which underpins ideas of valid knowledge. Thus, the chapter highlights the professional dangers which researchers can experience when challenging the traditional boundaries of research practice or writing.

In Chapter 7, the final chapter focusing primarily upon emotional danger, Lee-Treweek examines the way such dangers are often a feature of a setting and are shared by a researcher and his/her participants. Using her experience of carrying out ethnographic research in Bracken Court, a nursing home for older people, she relates the way that researching the home had a substantial negative impact upon her emotional well-being. Admitting to not being well prepared for her fieldwork experience overall, she describes her confusion at some of the feelings that arose in the setting and her attempt to write them away by over-zealous note taking. The second half of the chapter discusses how these feelings were transformed into insight through analysis and recognition of the connections between the researcher and participants' experiences. The chapter finally discusses the importance of seeking support and guidance on the emotional impact of research when fieldwork experiences are very distressing. Lee-Treweek notes the interrelationship between a researcher experiencing emotional danger and the existence of ethical dilemmas in the field. She argues that her distress was, in part, caused by not knowing what to do in the face of ethical problems. The use of colleague support, personal counselling and specialised study groups is discussed as a means of coping, and the need for thorough planning and ethical considera-tion is presented as a prerequisite to managing emotional threats.

Chapters 8, 9 and 10 broadly address ethical danger. By ethical danger we mean the serious risks associated with making judgements in the field. Making the wrong judgements about what to study or how to study social life has consequences for how one's research is seen by others in the academy and beyond. Ethical danger ties together the experience of the researcher and the researched by recognising the wider effects of carrying out unethical research, including the impact upon both participants and the researcher. This area has already been touched upon in Calvey's, Letherby's and Lee-Treweek's contribu-tions but is further developed here. In Chapter 8, Linkogle discusses Santo Domingo, the Nicaraguan popular religious festival, as a dangerous terrain both for participants and researcher. Her chapter is framed by a consideration of both the general physical risk of conducting research in Nicaragua and the ethical dangers presented by cross-cultural research. She highlights the problems of interpreting meaning when studying other societies through the cultural lens of the researcher.

Jipson and Litton continue this theme in Chapter 9 in their discussion of the dangers of studying extremist groups. Their ethnographic research has been in the field of self-identified 'Racialists' and members of New Religious Movements (NRMs), such as the Branch Davidians. However, the points raised within the chapter can be generalised, by and large, to the study of all dangerous groups.

Jipson and Litton note that extremists usually advocate non-tolerance towards other groups within society and this makes studying them risky for researchers in a myriad of ways. A major area of concern is the 'positive' effects that research can have upon the group being studied. Jipson and Litton comment that participating in the research process is sometimes seen by extremist organisations as legitimisation and can be used as propaganda to support extremist ideologies. Whilst supporting the idea that 'Racialist' and NRM groups are as valid an area of study as any other group, they maintain that researchers must remain mindful of the negative impact of research upon the wider community or those who are targets of racism, intimidation or violence. Finally, Jipson and Litton contend that they have found that ethical dangers are intertwined with professional dangers. They argue that their field of study has often been interpreted by colleagues, other academics and the general public as reflecting a personal interest and persuasion towards extremism. Their chapter indicates the importance of planning in social research and of the maintenance of a clear position whilst in the field. It is evident from their chapter that social researchers cannot allow themselves to be manipulated to the detriment of other members of the community, or to themselves.

Gabriel's chapter, in contrast to Jipson and Litton's, focuses specifically upon the experiences of an anti-racist researcher studying racism. He stresses that research should contribute to challenging racism and the privileges of being white. How such research is framed and conducted is not just the decision of the individual researcher but is tied to changing forms of political mobilisation and academic debate. Reflecting on his decision to focus on less extreme but more pervasive and significant forms of racism, Gabriel contends that research on extremist groups, in many cases, raises unavoidable and unacceptable ethical risks.

In Chapter 11 Peterson reflects upon a dimension of danger that is unexplored in the other contributions, that is the professional dangers of managing other people's experiences of risk in the field. Peterson uses his experience of running 'urban plunges' (courses which involve students and staff members living down-and-out on the streets) as an undergraduate course in the United States, and of teaching research methods on site in Nicaragua, to explain the difficulties of catering for others' experiences of risk. Despite the dangers that are necessarily involved in undertaking such supervision and teaching, he is positive about the nature of danger and threat as an educational tool in the research process. He notes that a measured degree of risk in the field allows students and researchers, at all levels of expertise, to become more aware of the differences between their own and other cultures. For instance, situations which we, as researchers, perceive to involve risk are sometimes seen in a very different way by the researched. In other situations the sharing of experiences that are felt by everybody in the field to be dangerous can lead to the development of greater trust and understanding between the ethnographer and participants. Thus Peterson draws our attention to the pedagogic and informative properties of danger in the field.

The grouping of chapters by type of danger is a functional device, aimed to provide structure to the range of experiences that the contributors discuss. However, because we do not intend to simplify researchers' experiences of risk, our framework is not designed to be compartmentalised. Each contribution, whilst predominantly focusing upon one type of danger, generally touches upon more than one within the overall examination. It could be argued that there are many aspects of danger, and substantive research topics, which are absent; however, the book is not intended to cover every type of calamity which a social researcher may face in the field. Neither is it intended to frighten away potential social researchers or, indeed, to make qualitative research look heroic. It aims to be a starting point for further debate and discussion about safety in the field and sets out to advocate the careful consideration of the health and well-being of the researcher (as well as, and with equal importance to, the researched). Finally, we want to highlight the need for forethought and planning, discussion and support amongst researchers; and the careful analysis of how risk provides insight within the field. By the end we hope that you will be able to answer the question posed at the beginning of this overview. In addition, you will also have been presented with the various ways in which the contributors addressed experiences of danger in the field and we hope this will help you plan for, identify and cope with any threats that you face when undertaking qualitative research of your own.

# Bibliography

Bulmer, M. (1982) *Social Research Ethics*, London: Macmillan.

Homan, R. (1991) *The Ethics of Social Research*, London: Longman.

# 1

# PUTTING DANGER IN THE FRAME

*Geraldine Lee-Treweek and Stephanie Linkogle*

## Introduction

The role of this chapter is to present a framework for conceptualising the dangers which qualitative researchers must negotiate in their work. The framework identifies four key areas of danger: physical, emotional, ethical and professional. These are illustrated in the chapters that follow. This scheme of dangers can be seen to have an ideal-type quality, as it simplifies and separates out experiences of serious danger. It is important to note that, although, for ease of discussion, we deal in this chapter with each form of danger in a distinct manner, in the contributions the interconnectedness of research risks is highlighted. We seek to demonstrate the robustness of this framework as a device for categorising the experience of danger and risk in research. As this is a possibility within all research settings, our discussion is of pertinence to all qualitative social science researchers. The chapter intends to turn the spotlight on both the conspicuous and the hidden dangers of research and to initiate debate about how researchers can plan for, mitigate and cope with a range of dangers within the field.

We argue that, traditionally, danger for the social researcher has been narrowly understood as immediate physical threat. Whilst it is important to acknowledge this dimension, we attempt here to expand the notion of danger to encompass other forms of risk. Consider this simple example: two researchers are carrying out research involving participant observation, one into white-water rafting and another into the work of nurses in hospital accident and emergency departments. White-water rafting may appear to be more dangerous as the researcher has to engage in a physically challenging pursuit in which injury might occur. The researcher, or those who are in receipt of funding and employ him or her, would possibly assess the dangers of data collection and (perhaps) try to mitigate risk by making decisions about safety equipment and training. In comparison, the risks of the hospital study may seem tame, as although the consideration of ethical issues around protecting participants will almost certainly have played a major role in preparations for the research, a hospital setting does not seem as risky to the researcher as the potentially physically dangerous pursuit of rafting.

On closer investigation, however, the hospital is revealed as the site of different types of physical danger to our example of rafting. Staff working in accident and emergency departments increasingly find themselves the target of physical assault; in the same way the researcher, observing and participating in this setting, may also be placing themselves in physical jeopardy. Accidental exposure to disease, contaminating body fluids or needle-point injuries are other potential sources of physical danger a researcher may encounter in this setting. There are also emotional and ethical stresses which may arise from studying hospital work. For instance, the researcher may witness fatally injured patients at the hospital, which could induce severe emotional distress, either at the research site or perhaps later at home. The threats involved in studying hospital work are less likely to have been anticipated because of the way we conventionally divide up research settings in terms of safety and danger. But the consequences of such dangers are no less real than those faced by the researcher observing rafting. Furthermore, the emotional aspect of this setting may have insidious long-term effects of a psychological nature.

We argue that risk and danger are often concealed aspects of social research. This book aims to address these lacunae. Throughout the text, a focus is placed on reflexive experience to highlight the ways in which the authors managed danger as an aspect of their work.

## Social research in 'risk society'

Ulrich Beck (1992) argues that attempts to minimise and measure risk have become defining features of contemporary societies.[1] This concern has arisen out of the emergence of new risks, which are the by-products of the information age and an enhanced capacity to estimate and contain previous threats, such as certain types of disease (Beck 1992; Beck et al.1994). However, although there is a shift towards controlling threat in general society, the workplace and the home, in an unequal society some individuals and social groups have more access to knowledge about risk, and greater agency to limit their exposure to it, than do other groups. We would add that there are also issues arising out of risk management for academics and researchers, for instance we often study the risks to society, from ill health or crime, etc., yet we rarely consider the dangers involved in carrying out research.

Social science researchers are oddly placed within risk society. Public and private sector institutions are held responsible for performing relevant risk assessments for the constituencies they serve and society at large. For instance, in most countries, employers are under an obligation to protect the health and safety of their workers by taking appropriate steps to identify and minimise workplace hazards. Ultimately, however, the benefits of minimising risk are weighed up in relation to the financial costs of compensation. The social researcher, whilst covered on campus or in the research centre by risk assessments carried out on the safety of offices and corridors, workstations and electrical goods, etc., are not in the same situation outside of them. Although employers still have obligations towards employees who are on business outside the workplace, assessing risk becomes more difficult and, to some extent, researchers themselves are expected to make choices about the risks they face. Social research involves us entering other people's workplaces, homes and communities and we are often unaware of the threats of the field until we have been there for some time. Moreover, the traditional view of research as an individual vocation and craft has meant that the occupational risks of doing research have not been recognised. Even though many, if not most, social researchers are linked to academic institutions, either as employees or as students, the risks they take are frequently seen as exclusively their own. In fact research 'excellence' is traditionally bound up with the notion of a researcher striking out and breaking new ground. In this formulation, the researcher must take risks to expand the parameters of social science knowledge and to do so implies a strategic choice.

Therefore, we posit that all qualitative research is to some extent potentially dangerous. In highlighting the need for researchers to be more aware of the risks they are taking and for greater responsibility on the part of relevant institutions, we are not, however, arguing that such risk is intrinsically negative. The nature of qualitative inquiry means that researchers encounter the unexpected and threatening as part of their attempt to understand the world of participants. Quite often such experience provides insight as it is a normal part of the range of threats experienced by participants themselves. It would not be realistic to remove all threat involved in social researching. This does not obviate the need to prepare for the potential risks one might encounter in the field.

## Physical danger

Physical danger has featured in research accounts from early anthropological literature through to the Chicago School and modern urban ethnographies (Fielding 1981). One might argue that Chicago School sociology was built upon the elevation of the endurance of physical danger. Fieldworkers studied aspects of everyday life in the city, often focusing upon street life, male work cultures and gangs (Anderson 1923; Wirth 1928; Whyte 1955; Becker 1966, 1970). It is not surprising that such accounts are popular, they provide vivid and alluring descriptions of risky researcher/participant encounters and of aspects of social life with which the majority of people have little contact. This type of research (quite literally) provides us with a view of another world with different rules, values and experiences of risk. Moreover, the researcher's account of narrow escapes and nerve in the face of danger have often been taken to indicate commitment to the pursuit of knowledge. For example, James's (1973) study of Glasgow street gangs can be interpreted as a demonstration of how a researcher's toughness in the face of adversity served as a passport into the world of male subcultures. The danger James encounters is a gripping feature of his description of life in the field.

Research on communities under threat, for example in high crime areas, war zones and in situations where torture and political repression occur, also presents obvious and immediate dangers to researchers. For instance, anthropologist Myrna Mack Chang, one of the first researchers to study and document the appalling situation of internally displaced people in Guatemala, was brutally murdered by individuals with strong connections to the Guatemalan military (Menchú 1998). In such cases the consideration of the consequences of physical threat is of paramount importance to staying alive in the field. However, the practical day-to-day work of researching within less politically charged settings can also be physically dangerous. In this volume, for instance, Westmarland and Calvey discuss the study of physically dangerous occupations: police work and night-club door work respectively. To groups engaged in illegal activities, social research may be perceived as a threat and consequently group members may act in violent ways to protect themselves from exposure and punishment. At the same time, the researcher may be at risk from others, such as law enforcement or rival dangerous groups (Williams et al. 1992).

One may also be at personal risk when carrying out mundane research-related duties, such as travelling on foot to people's homes to carry out interviews. This type of risk is often low priority when planning research yet many researchers face it whilst carrying out projects. There are other types of physical danger which do not involve violence or the threat of violence, but do carry the potential of physical harm. For example, contributor Gloria Lankshear came into contact with highly dangerous biological material whilst conducting research in a hospital. She notes that workers at the research site were warned of the dangers and protected via inoculation, whereas she was only offered protection halfway through her observation. Researchers who carry out fieldwork in developing countries, where there is little provision of hygienic drinking water and infectious disease is common, may risk serious adverse health consequences. For instance, as described in this collection, Linkogle suffered a number of debilitating health problems whilst conducting research in Nicaragua. These problems ranged from contracting intestinal parasites to having an adverse reaction to anti-malaria medication. The threat of disease in the field is more usually, and more easily, associated with researching other cultures, but Lankshear's chapter illustrates the need for the issue of protection of health to include potential risk in our own societies.

In seeking to expand the concept of physical danger within the research process it is clear that experiences of risk or actual danger are not evenly distributed. We need to consider the gender dynamics of physical threat. Although it is possible for both male and female researchers to experience physical risk, gender often shapes the forms such dangers take, as well as the ways in which researchers are able to counter these threats. In this book, both Louise Westmarland and David Calvey reflect on their different experiences of physical danger whilst conducting research on exclusive, male-dominated occupational settings. In part, these differences arise from the nature of the masculinised setting under study; masculinity is exhibited in different ways in the police force and the occupation of night-club door work. However, Westmarland and Calvey's respective genders also had a significant impact on how they were able to navigate their research terrain. Although not directly discussed within this text, women researchers may also face the threat of sexual harassment and assault (Warren 1988).

In this volume, Jeff Peterson notes that prevailing constructions of masculinity and femininity meant that when he was threatened with a knife in the Mexican village in which he lived and was conducting fieldwork he received an unexpected response from villagers. His encounter was laughed off and it was assumed that as a man he would possess the skills and the courage to defend himself. At the same time increased security measures were recommended for his wife, who was his co-researcher and who, as a woman, was seen to be far more vulnerable if attacked. It is evident that a lack of awareness of gender systems in the field they are entering can be hazardous to researchers when their norms and expectations of gender are not shared by their participants.

We argue that certain dangers have traditionally been hidden within research accounts. Reflexive accounts are important in drawing out and making explicit the dangerous character of research. Furthermore, we maintain that physical danger has itself been characterised too narrowly. More mundane experiences of danger may not be as immediately compelling as the image of the intrepid researcher facing imminent physical violence. However, they constitute a significant and under-explored area of danger for researchers. Physical dangers often cannot be removed from research sites and we are not suggesting that the researcher's response to them should necessarily be to abandon their research. The risk of physical threat is often shared by participants and researchers alike. Understanding these situated threats can provide a greater appreciation of participants' lives and experiences. However, the safety and well-being of the researcher should always be placed as equal to protecting participants when planning research.

## Emotional danger

Serious threats to a researcher's emotional stability and sense of self are often involved when undertaking qualitative research with participants undergoing stressful life events. We would like to invite you to think about the possible emotional implications of this recent job advertisement for a qualitative researcher. One section of the advertisement has been included below but it is paraphrased to conceal the identity of the institution and study. The research project was to involve in-depth interviews with terminally ill patients and their carers:

> The researcher will have daily interaction with patients who are dying and their kin, thus awareness of the issues these groups may experience and the capability to cope with this kind of setting are essential. When required, support will be available.

This example provides an illustration of research work which would involve obvious emotional stress to the individual researcher. The work would entail gathering potentially distressing data on the experience of serious illness and could require the researcher witnessing participants in states of pain, fear or anxiety. Relationships with the research participants may sometimes demand emotional support work which could threaten the researcher's own mental well-being. In this case the possibility of damage to the researcher, through handling and managing threatening emotions, can be quite easily identified.

It is not necessary to carry out research with the dying to experience feelings of emotional threat in the field. Qualitative researchers experience a myriad of feelings ranging from extreme fear and anxiety to warmth and joy. This collection is, in part, concerned with the ways that negative emotions can affect the researcher's sense of self and, in the long run, the quality of their research. We define emotional danger as the experience of severe threat due to negative 'feeling states' induced by the research process. Therefore, we are not talking about just feeling uncomfortable but real distress which can spill over into other areas of the researcher's life, such as their family and personal relationships or connections with colleagues at work. Emotional danger is a complex subject because research settings may produce diverse emotions in researchers and participants. Indeed, individual life experience always mediates how one responds to a setting. This point is clearly illustrated in this collection by Letherby's discussion of autobiographical research and Lankshear's chapter on the different

13

dangers in a pathology laboratory and hospital maternity suite. Lankshear expresses her surprise at the way carrying out research in a maternity suite led her to recall, and question, her own experiences of childbirth and motherhood. This chapter highlights the way research often affects the everyday and taken-for-granted meanings of our lives, causing us to examine our assumptions and seek new interpretations of events.

The emotional side of social life was, until recently, perceived to be outside the remit of social research. In parallel, traditional research methodologies have generally excluded the emotions of the researcher from the research process (Kleinman and Copp 1993: 23). The inclusion of emotion was considered to be unacceptable and at odds with the construction of social science as akin to the natural sciences. Within the normative model of research, investigation and discovery were only possible if untainted by feeling states and other intangible aspects of human experience. Later, with the development of symbolic interactionism and ethnographic methods of inquiry, emotions were still often absent from discussion with perhaps only a passing mention of them within the reflexive sections, which were clearly differentiated from the main body of the text.

In many ways the inclusion of feelings in early qualitative studies was deemed useful only as part of the proof that one had actually been in the setting and carried out the research. For instance, early Chicago School sociologists, such as Anderson (1923), Wirth (1928) and Zorbaugh (1929), and the second wave of Chicago interactionists (sometimes termed the neo-Chicagoans), such as W. F. Whyte (1955) and Becker (1963), produced works which contain data of an emotional nature. To research and create their ethnographies these researchers must have been embroiled in emotional relationships and gathered emotional data in the field. However, this aspect of the fieldwork is not overtly discussed and is made invisible through the selective and exclusionary processes of writing. How fascinating it would be if we could call up the accounts of emotional effort and skill which these ethnographic texts represent. Perhaps then we could gain an understanding of how these experiences are transformed into meaning for the researcher. Without such accounts, we are left to assume that there is an imperceptible shift from the researcher's experience of emotion during research, to its contribution to understanding. This kind of writing has helped create the mystique of ethnographic methods, concealing the components of undertaking such research and minimising its emotional and self-engaging aspects.

From the avoidance of the emotional, much contemporary qualitative sociol-ogy can now be said to have become overtly 'emotionally aware'. This manifests itself in two ways. First, researchers are far more aware of the emotions of participants. According to the British Sociological Association's Statement of Ethical Practice (1992: 704), one of the researcher's key priorities is to prevent the distress of participants. Homan (1991) has noted that the model for statements of ethical practice, which are now part of organisations like the British and American Sociological Associations, were developed from medical and scientific ones. Within these models the participant was given primacy in terms of protection from negative consequences and this is reflected in statements developed by the social sciences such as: 'members should consider carefully the possibility that the research experience may be a disturbing one and, normally, should attempt to minimise disturbance to those participant in research' (British Sociological Association 1992: 705). The statement adds that this might include threat to participants from having to face self-knowledge or being made to dwell on distressing aspects of social life that they would normally avoid. Although the guidelines are not rules and cannot legislate for all experiences, they advise caution, planning and forethought by the researcher on the possible consequences of research. One of the difficulties faced by social researchers is that consequences can be difficult to predict and the definition of what is distressing differs from person to person and may also change over time and life course events.

In addition to pre-existing statements of ethical practice, professional organisations such as the British Sociological Association and American Anthropological Association have been affected by dynamic methodological developments within the disciplines they represent. For instance, the development of feminist debates around the treatment of research participants was initially concerned with the vulnerability of women within the research process (Oakley 1981; Finch 1984). However, this has broadened into a discussion of the management of research relationships in general and has highlighted the need for consideration of the risks to all participants and those affected by research. At the same time, there has been a move towards a greater emphasis on the study of personal and sensitive aspects of social life. Within this research agenda, the need to protect participants and engage in debates around the ethics of talking people through painful experience becomes of prime importance. A central concern is the need to manage the emotions of research participants and not leave them with painful baggage from the research experience. Researchers such as Cannon (1989), who researched women's experience of breast cancer, have been able to illustrate clearly the mutual interchange of both information and feeling which occur when interviewing on sensitive topics. This is a more intense experience when both parties share aspects of their biographies, such as losing a loved one or having experienced illness.

Although shared researcher/participant experience can be used positively, in some situations the researcher can be made to feel that they are a poor substitute for other services. Unlike a social worker or qualified counsellor, a researcher is rarely trained in such issues as managing distress, ending difficult interactions and identifying ways in which a person could be helped or encouraged to help themselves. However, the research situation and individual participants may push researchers into taking on these types of activities. The dangers to the interviewee can be severe in these cases, but what also becomes clear is the psychological threat to the researcher, as the manager of someone else's dangerous emotions and possibly also their own.

The pressure upon the researcher from emotions in the field has begun to be recognised within the social sciences. From a predominant focus upon managing and protecting the emotions of participants, the discussion and analysis of the management of researchers' emotions has become more important. This type of analysis is no longer the preserve of specialist texts of reflexive accounts, such as Bell and Newby (1977) and Bell and Encel (1978). Increasingly, emotional aspects of research are beginning to impact upon mainstream methodological discussion. The notion of emotional danger draws upon the emerging sub-discipline of the sociology of emotions (Karp and Yoels 1993; Young and Lee 1997). In terms of the unsettling effect that a setting can have on a researcher's sense of self, it could reasonably be suggested that this is particularly likely in the case of 'sensitive' topics such as the body, sexuality, ageing, disability and abuse. In these situations, the researcher may find themselves confronted with difficult data to gather, distressed research participants and threatening images of the body. Emotional danger can also be particularly acute when the area under study relates directly to the biography of the researcher. Feminist research has reconstructed our understanding of the role of the self in the research process, arguing that 'objective', depersonalised research denies the subjective character of social inquiry and ignores the insight that reflexivity, as a methodological tool, can bring to the research process (Stanley 1992).

The emotions experienced by the social researcher can shape their analysis and understanding of a setting in a positive way. Nevertheless, we note that the practice of using the self as a resource can be emotionally dangerous. In this collection, Letherby's chapter on involuntary childlessness and autobiographical research indicates the double-edged character of using and exposing the self in social research; and Lankshear's reflexive account emphasises the stress of researching a field which has personal meanings. In a sense, Lankshear is an example of a 'statistic' studying the social production of other statistics and bringing to the study important insider information. Lee-Treweek's chapter provides an account of undertaking research in a home for older people. She discusses how she was able to use her own feelings of threat and fear to understand the work of auxiliary care staff who initially appeared thoughtless and detached from the needs of those they cared for. These chapters illustrate the way that emotional danger can destabilise personal identity but at the same time provide greater insight into the world of research participants.

## Ethical danger

There is a substantial body of social science methodology literature which considers the issue of research ethics. This has focused primarily on the protection and welfare of participants (Bulmer 1982; Homan 1991; Lee 1993). The history of debates on research ethics can be traced to the post-World War II period. As the full horror of Nazi medical experiments on unwilling participants became known there was a destabilising of the scientist's right to the 'pursuit of knowledge' at any cost, and primacy was given to the rights of participants in research. These developments underpinned the emergence of ethical codes of practice in the natural sciences, but such codes were slower to develop in the social sciences. In part this was due to the fact that the dangers posed to participants were generally not acutely physical. However, there are some infamous cases of unethical practice in the social sciences, such as the research of Milgram (1963). A social psychologist interested in social compliance, Milgram encouraged research participants to give electric shocks to a human 'victim' in another room. While no shocks were in fact administered, everything was done to make the participants believe that they were inflicting pain on another person. The consequence for some participants was severe, with a number of them shaking and crying as they administered the shocks. Milgram's research has universally been condemned as unethical. Other cases of unethical research include Humphreys (1970), who carried out observational research of public toilets without informed consent and Wallis (1976), who researched Scientology, initially in a covert manner. These cases have become landmarks in the development of ethical principles for social science research. In a sense they served as tests of the boundaries of ethical principles and now informed consent, confidentiality and protection of participants are central to most social science codes of ethics.

However, whilst informed consent can be seen as a benchmark for ethical practice, the issue has not been definitively resolved and some researchers continue to work in this tradition. David Calvey in this volume, for instance, defends his decision to conduct covert research on night-club bouncers, arguing that gaining access to the field would not be feasible by other means. This controversial stance seems more palatable when the social group under investigation is engaged in violence and other criminal behaviour. However, such an approach begs important questions including: would such a covert approach be equally justified in conducting research on other hard-to-access groups such as cloistered nuns? Does the moral character of participants lessen their right to choose whether or not to participate in research, and is the value to society of the research so great that it outweighs this right? The issue of covert study remains the subject of great debate in the social sciences and, although funding bodies on the whole will not fund such research, the use of covert methods continues.

Even in situations where researchers do not intend to conceal their identity, gaining informed consent can be more complex than it might immediately appear. For example, in this volume Linkogle notes that when researching the Santo Domingo festival in Nicaragua, several thousand people were in attendance. It was clearly impossible to gain informed consent from such a large number of participants. Beyond such practical difficulties, the notion of informed consent itself is potentially problematic as researchers may not be able to provide participants with sufficient information about the consequences of their involvement. This may be because the shape of the research is not entirely clear but also because the consequence of the fieldwork and its wider dissemination may be difficult to predict.

We argue that researchers have an ethical responsibility to undertake an assessment of the risks that participants and society at large may face as a consequence of their work. Yet we realise that ethical danger to participants is often difficult to predict, especially when social research is reinterpreted by other institutions such as political parties, pressure groups and the media. Although David Morgan's research on female factory labourers offered participants anonymity, the British press exposed the research site and reinterpreted his findings in a way which mocked and trivialised the lives of the women (Morgan 1972). David Morgan (in personal communication) has since noted that he has become increasingly wary of the dangers of research being misconstrued in the public arena and the damage that this can cause to participants. In particular he argues that we have little control over the use of our findings once in the public domain and that protecting individuals can become impossible once the media are involved in following a story.

Sometimes protecting participants demands a high degree of professionalism and personal loss on the part of the researcher. A case in point is that of Rik Scarce, who was the first sociologist to be jailed for refusing to breach the American Sociological Association Code of Ethics on confidentiality. In 1991 Scarce was a doctoral student studying ecological movements at Washington State University in the United States. As part of his research Scarce had contact with numerous activists in radical ecological organisations and was well known for his research on campus. During a trip away with his family, a laboratory at Washington State University was raided by Animal Liberation Front activists. Scarce found himself involved in a court case in which law enforcement demanded that he release any information about the crime he had gathered during his research. Scarce argued that the American Sociological Association's code of ethics stated that where assurances of confidentiality had been given to participants it should be honoured even when 'legal force is applied' (American

Sociological Association 1984: 3). He argued that the code prevented him even from revealing whether he had interviewed particular activists. Scarce was subpoenaed but fought against providing evidence until he was finally jailed for five months in 1993. His incarceration had profound implications for social researchers in the United States. Essentially it means that a researcher cannot provide total assurance of confidentiality to any participant unless they are prepared (in a worst case scenario) to go to jail to protect this assurance.

The case of Rik Scarce is an example of the importance given to protecting participants within ethical guidelines and by individual social science researchers. Although the impact of research on participants is the centrepiece of social scientific ethical codes, an ethical danger which can be of equal importance is the consequence of research on communities beyond the direct research participants. Arthur Jipson and Chad Litton in this volume acknowledge that their research posed potential dangers to the social groups that were targeted by the racist movements under investigation. Research on racist groups can serve to highlight the profile of these organisations, further disseminating their views. As a consequence, racial violence may become more likely and the movements themselves may gain enhanced status and legitimacy. The piece is unsettling because the authors attempt to avoid presenting these movements as 'deviant', arguing that a more neutral social movement perspective can better provide a sense of how these movements see themselves and how they rationalise their horrifying actions. In contrast, contributor John Gabriel is concerned to explore the ethical dilemmas entailed in researching anti-racist activism. He reflects on how changing notions of race and ethnicity have presented a shifting set of ethical dangers for researchers working in this area.

Another set of ethical dangers spring from the unequal and potentially ex-ploitative power relations amongst researchers. We reiterate the point made by both Sue Scott (1984) and Roger Homan (1991) that research projects are often staffed by postgraduate students and junior and temporary staff, many of whom are women. This raises important issues about the ways in which ethical concerns about power disparities cannot be restricted merely to an analysis of researchers and participants. The management of research project staff and temporary members of faculty is an ethical issue that is not often considered. Equally, issues around the treatment of students, especially postgraduate students, have an ethical dimension. Fully tenured members of staff are often able to buy out teaching whilst undertaking research duties. This work tends to be given to relatively poorly paid postgraduate students. This may well be of benefit to students as it enables them to gain teaching experience that will enhance their career prospects. However, in some cases it can be an exploitative relationship where postgraduates find themselves out of their depth, working long hours without financial compensation and ultimately damaging their own research and, hence, future employment.

Therefore, we are arguing that ethical dangers should be considered in a broad manner, ranging from the way we treat research participants, to the methodologies we choose in the field, and the way we treat each other as researchers. At the same time, new topics within social research such as embodiment, emotions and death are also likely to change current social science ethical structures and guidelines, such that the development of research ethics can be seen as an emergent, empirically informed and continuous process within the social sciences.

## Professional danger

Within the social sciences there are conventional and accepted methodologies, theoretical perspectives and values. For this reason, researchers can face what might be called professional danger when they break with established theoretical and methodological conventions. We define professional danger as serious risk associated with the consequences of challenging or deviating from existing occupational dynamics and collegial preoccupations. Different academic or theoretical discourses may be in fashion or powerful at one time but may go out of vogue in another. For instance, Scott (1984), in her well-known article on power relations and research, argues that leftist and feminist researchers have in the past been 'red-listed' for their political perspectives. Although the types of theory or method favoured by the majority of researchers may change there will always be 'unfashionable' topics and emerging or unpopular methodologies which find themselves on the margins of academic acceptability. This type of danger has significant consequences for the academics involved, who may experience serious problems in publishing their research and in securing respect and support from their colleagues. Furthermore, in an increasingly competitive academic climate professional dangers are often centred around the difficulties of obtaining and securing employment within the academy or other research settings. Also, the professional dangers an individual might face are magnified when they are at the start of their academic or research career and are therefore less established. In this way professional danger can be seen as an insidious threat to social science and the development of social research, as it threatens to quell innovation, emergent ideas and the diversity of academic thought.

The boundaries of acceptable methodology have certainly changed over the last thirty years. It is important to bear in mind that up until comparatively recently, interpretative approaches were negatively compared to the normative paradigm of quantitative methodologies. Despite the impact of symbolic interactionism and prominent qualitative schools of sociological study, qualitative methodologies have a secondary status to quantitative approaches in many social science disciplines. Qualitative accounts have been seen – and continue to be seen in some disciplines – as unreliable, lacking validity, open to value judgements, personal or political ideologies and misinterpretations. Feminist scholarship has been a major player in defending qualitative methods and pivotal in the attack upon normative notions of what studying society should be about. Although the boundaries of acceptability are always shifting in relation to emerging qualitative research methods, methodologies such as interviewing, document analysis and observation have been generally accepted as valid by all the social science disciplines, the health services and major funding bodies. Indeed, the use of qualitative and quantitative approaches together in the same project is now commonplace.

However, as new and innovative qualitative methods emerge, such as the use of autobiography, participatory research and collective memory work, the older debates about what constitutes knowledge, how we judge various accounts of social life and issues around reliability and validity, re-emerge. It is in these circumstances that conflict becomes visible in the academic and research community. This is a subject addressed in Letherby's chapter in this collection on autobiography and involuntary childlessness. She discusses the problems of this type of method and the responses she receives to her work from various audiences. Letherby argues that one's motives in using the self in this way are often questioned and that autobiographical research has sometimes been constructed by (quite powerful) voices in the academic community as indicating a lack of academic rigour. Furthermore, she notes that this impacts negatively upon one's career by, for instance, reducing one's chance of publishing in mainstream books and journals.

All academics who threaten academic convention in some way may find themselves in danger of negatively affecting their employability or being labelled informally as a troublemaker. One way of placing oneself in professional jeopardy is to criticise the structures which maintain power relations in the academy. Although mainstream social science is involved in the detailed analysis of social life, it is not known for applying self-reflection and criticism to its own structure, composition and attitudes. However, for those who work in academia with low status and little power the threat of marginalisation within the profession can profoundly shape their experiences of danger and research risk. Lack of job stability and the existence of very short-term contracts in academic and research work (three-month contracts are not unheard of in many institutions) severely curtail the likelihood of direct attacks on power in these settings. Scott's (1984) scathing article on power relations and research remains an important critique of the way lower-status workers, often women, are treated within the academic hierarchy. Using her own experience of research work and academic power

21

relations, she highlighted the way that young researchers often found themselves undertaking the face-to-face interview work for higher-status colleagues and fund-holders. Scott argued that she and her peers who were engaged in postgraduate or contract research work had little status, space or power of their own within their institution.

Sue Scott (in personal communication) notes that her article (Scott 1984) caused consternation and anger within certain groups of higher-status staff, who interpreted the article as a member of the lower-levels of the hierarchy breaking rank. Furthermore, she feels that the repercussions of her critique of academic power and protocol, along with her feminist approach, have represented an obstacle to her career. Despite this, Scott has used active strategies to circumvent the problems and power imbalances she has faced. For instance, she was enabled and supported by networking and gaining encouragement from others in a similar position, such as women academics in the British Sociological Association Women's Caucus. Joining and being active within the British Sociological Association committee system has, she argues, served the same function. Scott (in personal communication) notes that women are in a better position now than when she wrote her article as there are now more women making it to higher-status positions within the ranks of academia. Women in these higher-status roles are more likely, due to their own experiences of marginality, to empathise with those who are currently on the margins of the academy and to encourage their integration.

Publication is increasingly important to all those involved in academia or research. In Britain, where university departments are rated, in part, by their production of quality publications, it is seriously damaging if an academic, for whatever reason, is unable to produce refereed pieces of written work. The seriously marginalised academic, working within an unpopular or unfashionable research paradigm, may not be able to publish at all or only publish in a restricted range of lower-status publications. It is fairly common knowledge within academia, as noted by Jamieson in this volume, that the social sciences go through phases of interest in particular research topics and these are often related to the fads of funding bodies. So, for instance, older age may be highly prioritised at one time but at another may be low on the funding agenda. This can have severe consequences for career progression and networking within a discipline and is more threatening to those early in their career who may not have full tenure. Thus what you study, as well as how you study it, can pose professional dangers to researchers.

Under the rubric of professional danger we also place some of the risks that may be encountered by those who undertake controversial research on powerful and often litigious groups. The repercussions of Roy Wallis's (1976) work on the Scientology movement provide a cautionary tale. Wallis carried out work on this religious group, initially covertly, by attending a course as a potential recruit. Although he revealed his intentions later, and the Church of Scientology gave permission for publication, they insisted on a high level of editorial control. Unfortunately, Wallis's publications on the Church caused them offence and a campaign of threats and intimidation against him ensued and continued for some years. Many of these incidents were personally malevolent, such as the sending of letters to his department about his sexuality and professionalism as a lecturer. This case illustrates well that the professional danger arising from one piece of research can 'menace' a researcher for years after completion. It may be impossible to think through completely the range of professional dangers a paper might provoke. Once published, research findings assume a life of their own with the researcher often having little control over their use or interpretation.

Professional danger is therefore one of the most insidious dangers in the research process because it can constrain what social science researchers feel able to study, to say or to challenge. Deviating from established types of research, theory or method, challenging established power structures within the academy, or enraging groups outside, can have serious consequences for the individual's ability to publish, gain permanent tenure and engage with their peers on an equal level. Ultimately, many forms of professional danger impact upon the integrity and vitality of the social science disciplines as a whole, damaging their ability to be emergent, innovative and exciting.

## Conclusion

In conclusion, we would invite you to examine the importance of this aspect of qualitative research, which has been obscured and marginalised by traditional debates on methods. In particular we would like you to consider our framework, and the dangers we identify, in relation either to your own research experiences or to those of researchers you have read about. We would like the risks of carrying out your work, which perhaps did not cross your mind before, to be the object of examination and reflection. To this end we have presented you with a framework of dangers which encompasses all the types of danger that researchers may experience. This typology is necessarily simplistic due to the range of experiences we are trying to bring together. We are not arguing that there are distinct categories and, as illustrated by the chapters which follow, researchers often experience a range of dangers simultaneously. The interesting thing is that some of these dangers are more visible and acceptable than others. So, as we have argued above, serious physical risk has often been the only form acknowledged in accounts of qualitative research. We argue that all forms of serious risk to the researcher are of equal interest and importance to those carrying out research or thinking about the research process. By bringing all of these into the spotlight as real and central issues, not just of personal experience and interest, but of analysis and meaning, we hope to challenge the invisibility of danger within academic discourse. Finally, after this lengthy discussion of the range of dangers one may experience in the field, perhaps we should provide a little reassurance about our aim here. We do not want readers to conclude that research is too dangerous to carry out. Research, like other areas of life, can be risk-managed to minimise the dangers one may experience. At the same time, threats can arise in an *ad hoc* manner and as such are not just a negative feature of the research process but can be methodologically and theoretically productive. Rather than put people off, we want researchers to become more aware of possible risks and for this to filter into academic debate about how we can address this important aspect of researching social life.

## Note

1   Individuals, for example, can access their predicted risk of being murdered or assaulted through a test on the Internet, devised by Ken Pence of the Metro Nashville Police Department.

## Bibliography

American Sociological Association (1984) *Code of Ethics*, Washington, DC: American Sociological Association.

Anderson, N. (1923) *The Hobo: the Sociology of the Homeless Man*, Chicago: University of Chicago Press.

Beck, U. (1992) *Risk Society: Towards a New Modernity*, London: Sage.

Beck, U., Giddens, A. and Lash, S. (1994) *Reflexive Modernization*, Cambridge: Polity.

Becker, H. S. (1966) *Outsiders: Studies in the Sociology of Deviance*, London: Collier Macmillan.

—— (1970) *Sociological Work: Method and Substance*, Chicago: Aldine Publishing.

Bell, C. and Encel, S. (1978) *Inside the Whale: Ten Personal Accounts of Social Research*, Oxford: Pergamon.

Bell, C. and Newby, H. (1977) *Doing Sociological Research*, London: Allen & Unwin.

British Sociological Association (1992) 'BSA Statement of Ethical Practice', *Sociology, The Journal of the British Sociological Association* 26, 4: 703–7.

Bulmer, M. (1982) *Social Research Ethics*, London: Macmillan.

Cannon, S. (1989) 'Social research in stressful settings: difficulties for the sociologist studying the treatment of breast cancer', *Sociology of Health and Illness* 11, 2: 66–77.

Fielding, N. (1981) *The National Front*, London: Routledge & Kegan Paul.

Finch, J. (1984) ' "It's Great to Have Someone to Talk to": The Ethics and Politics of Interviewing Women' in C. Bell and H. Roberts (eds) *Social Researching: Politics, Problems, Practice*, London: Routledge & Kegan Paul.

Fine, G. A. (1993) 'Ten lies of ethnography: moral dilemmas of field research', *Journal of Contemporary Ethnography* 22: 267–94.

Giddens, A. (1990) *The Consequences of Modernity*, Cambridge: Polity.

Homan, R. (1991) *The Ethics of Social Research*, London: Longman.

Humphreys, L. (1970) *Tearoom Trade: A Study of Homosexual Encounters in Public Places*, London: Duckworth.

James, P. (1973) *A Glasgow Gang Observed*, London: Eyre Methuen.

Karp, D. and Yoels, W. (1993) *Sociology and Everyday Life*, Itasca, Ill: Peacock.

Kleinman, S. and Copp, M. A. (1993) *Emotions and Fieldwork*, London: Sage.

Lee, R. (1993) *Doing Research on Sensitive Topics*, London: Sage.

—— (1995) *Dangerous Fieldwork*, London: Sage.

Menchú, R. (1998) *Crossing Borders*, London: Verso.

Milgram, S. (1963) 'A behavioural study of obedience', *Journal of Abnormal and Social Psychology*, 67, 4: 94–117.

Morgan, D. H. J. (1972) 'The British Association Scandal: the affect of publication on a sociological investigation', *Sociological Research*, 20, 2: 185–206.

Oakley, A. (1981) 'Interviewing Women: A Contradiction in Terms' in H. Roberts (ed.) *Doing Feminist Research*, London: Routledge & Kegan Paul.

Rosaldo, R. (1993) *Culture and Truth: The Remaking of Social Analysis*, London: Routledge.

Scarce, R. (1994) '(No) trial (but) tribulations: when courts and ethnography conflict', *Journal of Contemporary Ethnography*, 23, Part 2.

—— (1995) 'Scholarly ethics and courtroom antics: where researchers stand in the eyes of the law', *The American Sociologist*, 26, Part 1.

Scott, S. (1984) 'The Personable and the Powerful: Gender and Status in Sociological Research' in C. Bell and H. Roberts (eds) *Social Researching, Politics, Problems, Practice*, London: Routledge & Kegan Paul.

Stanley, L. (1992) *The Auto/biographical I: The Theory and Practice of Feminist Autobiography*, Manchester: Manchester University Press.

Wallis, R. (1976) *The Road to Total Freedom: A Sociological Analysis of Scientology*, London: Heinemann Educational.

—— (1977) 'The Moral Career of a Research Project' in C. Bell and H. Roberts (eds) *Social Researching: Politics, Problems, Practice*, London: Routledge & Kegan Paul.

Warren, C. (1988) *Gender Issues in Field Research*, Newbury Park, CA: Sage.

Whyte, W.F. (1955) *Street Corner Society: the Social Structure of an Italian Slum*, Chicago and London: University of Chicago Press.

Williams, T., Dunlap, E., Johnson, B. D. and Hamid, A. (1992) 'Personal safety in dangerous places', *Journal of Contemporary Ethnography* 21, 3, October: 343–74.

Wirth, L. (1928) *The Ghetto*, Chicago: University of Chicago Press.

Young, E. and Lee, R. (1997) 'Fieldworker feeling as data: emotion work in first person accounts of sociological fieldwork' in V. James and J. Gabe (eds) *Health and the Sociology of Emotions*, Oxford: Blackwell.

Zorbaugh, H. W. (1929) *The Gold Coast and the Slum: a Sociological Study of Chicago's Near North Side*, Chicago: University of Chicago Press.

# 2

# TAKING THE FLAK

## Operational policing, fear and violence

*Louise Westmarland*

## Introduction

The study of policing would appear to be a field where threats to personal physical safety are inevitable. However, rarely are the field experiences of researchers studying the police discussed in terms of how the encounters with danger positively inform the research. In this chapter physical danger and risk are examined as a composite aspect of understanding police work and police identities. It argues that 'where the action is' is often where the insight lies. Therefore, as researchers we should not perceive the experience of danger in the field as an obstacle to understanding the worlds of participants but as an opportunity to examine how risk enters their lives. For many members of society physical risk is an everyday part of their lives or occupations, therefore trying to exclude the possibility of researcher-risk is not possible if one is taking an ethnographic approach. In the case of my observation of police work, gender identities were found to be important to how the police understood and worked with risk and danger. It was only through experiencing danger with police officers that I was able to theorise about the role of threat to the shaping of identities.

The chapter discusses ethnographic research concerning gender and operational policing in the North-East of England (Westmarland 1998). A number of different police environments such as street patrols, police canteens and specialist departments were used to compare and contrast the ways in which gender identities at work can be dependent upon notions of competence, sexuality and, in the case of the police, their 'heroic function'. I would contend that the experience of threat and danger is not only a commonplace part of the work of policing but it is also central to police officers' work identities. In undertaking this research it would have been impossible to exclude the possibility of risk to the researcher and, I would argue, counterproductive to the ethnographic endeavour. In order to understand the risk involved it had to be encountered with

26

the participants. Also, I will argue later, the way police officers around me changed as they re-evaluated my ability to cope in 'risky' situations was important data in itself. When studying occupational groups which face personal threat on a regular basis, we (social researchers) need to attend closely to changing notions of risk and danger in the field and the ways in which participants understand us in relation to these risks. Therefore, physical dangers should not merely be understood as negative aspects of research but, in some situations, as opportunities for greater insight into participants' worlds.

## The variety of research sites

Two periods of fieldwork, each lasting approximately six months, were carried out with two contrasting forces: one a rural 'county' force, the other a large, urban, metropolitan one. From these investigations it seems that gender identities are reinforced by a number of activities that are core to the police mandate. Furthermore, the findings of the study revealed some of the ways in which categories such as 'masculinity' and 'femininity' are defined within police occupational cultures.

Variety of research site was an important aspect of the observation as it allowed me to view interaction in different settings between different groups of officers. My aim was to study these settings by attempting to become an 'insider'. For example, the night-shift officers from a particular subdivision were asked by their inspector if I could accompany them at various intervals, perhaps each time they came back on nights. These officers would be ordinary 'street cops' patrolling a number of differing inner-city areas – some 'hard' police districts and some 'softer' less busy beats. In addition, some specialist departments such as the mounted, marine and firearms teams were accompanied on training exercises and also 'live' operations. The focus of this chapter will be the way my data-gathering methods, broadly based within an ethnographic tradition, were used to elicit information and led to danger being employed within an analytic framework. As the study from which this data is drawn was conducted in a largely 'male' police culture, interrelationships between gender, fear and social control were also addressed. It is noteworthy that this is the first ethnography with full and extensive access to police activities and culture focusing on gender to be conducted by a woman researcher on the streets of Britain.

## Policing danger

In the past, studies of 'cop culture' have illustrated the way group solidarity is reinforced in policing due to concerns for the physical safety of their colleagues. Several 'insider' accounts such as those by Holdaway (1983) and Young (1991), for example, have suggested that violence plays a fundamental part in the daily lives of officers. Studies by 'outsiders' (Uildriks and van Mastrigt 1991; Punch 1993) have described the way this may also apply to those conducting field observations. Similarly, articles and research manuals which provide guidance for the unwary and uninitiated, such as Lee's *Dangerous Fieldwork* (1995), tend to warn about potential dangers which may be encountered in the field (see also Peritore 1990; Sluka 1990; Lee 1993; Hockey 1996). In general, such advice concentrates upon three areas of potential risk, namely people, places and social situations. In other words, these warnings concern the way that danger will be encountered by researchers as 'outsiders' to the unknown worlds they are approaching.

A limited number of studies have accounted for the way individual researchers have dealt with frightening situations. In his description of the research he conducted in Northern Ireland, Sluka argues that 'anthropological fieldwork is more dangerous than in the past' and given that most researchers are not prepared to regard death as an acceptable occupational hazard, he outlines a number of strategies, including withdrawal from the research site, as 'methods of managing these problems' (Sluka 1990: 114). Similarly, Peritore argues that Latin America is a dangerous place to conduct research because 'North Americans frequently carry a set of implicit assumptions regarding their legal and civil rights' (Peritore 1990: 359). As a result, he recommends that '(t)he researcher must work to minimise his or her own or others' exposure to violence' (Peritore 1990: 359). In another ethnographic study conducted in Northern Ireland, in which Hockey confesses to be so 'scared shitless' (1996: 23) that he almost did not return to the base in Crossmaglen where he was observing the activities of foot patrol soldiers, he reports that it was often a struggle to control his emotions. His strategy for coping with his anxiety, prior to his return to South Armagh, was to keep himself 'hyper-busy, analysing field notes from the previous periods of field work and teaching numerous undergraduate classes' (Hockey 1996: 22).

Similarly, in conducting the study from which this chapter draws its data, a number of 'dangerous' people and places and difficult, frightening situations were encountered. As an outsider in terms of police occupational culture and, it might be argued, also 'other' in terms of gender identity, certain arrangements regarding my personal safety had to be almost continuously re-negotiated. Indeed, one of the most worrying aspects, from my experience during extensive periods observing operational police officers, is the sheer volatility of people's emotions, particularly during police interactions with the public. In the past it has been argued that a major determinant of police culture is the way officers have to control their reactions to being constantly under threat of 'unexpected' violence (Reiner 1992). As ethnographers generally have to be prepared to be in the 'thick' of the action, this was an occupational hazard, while at the same time a useful research tool. In the following example one of the officers comments that he thought I had been rather blasé at an incident we had attended earlier that night, saying, 'I hope you don't mind me saying this, but you were a bit too close when we arrested those two lads tonight, we were worried you were going to catch it' (Male Police Constable (PC) 1995). His concern was echoed by another officer one evening as we were preparing to go out on patrol, 'You'd better put this on [a protective anti-stab vest]. The town could kick off tonight and it's better to be safe than sorry' (Male PC 1995). On another occasion, driving at full speed to a reportedly 'serious' disturbance in a public house, I was told, 'You'll have to stay in the car when we get there, there'll be guns, knives and baseball bats, it's a real prigs' pub' (Male PC 1994).

As these examples illustrate, conducting police work ethnography can be physically hazardous but also fraught with difficulties regarding 'protectiveness' and gendered expectations of the suitability of some situations for 'outsiders'. Indeed, in addition to Lee's warnings about certain places and situations being risky, he notes that a number of dangerous groups, such as 'gangs and outlaws', drug dealers, terrorists and the police, are sites of potential 'occupational hazards' (Lee 1995: 48–52). To avoid 'mishaps', therefore, he lists a number of precautions which should be taken to maximise personal safety. Such advice includes fostering 'a rapport with local informants' and generally 'developing a sensitivity to potentially hazardous situations and utilising preventative strategies for avoiding them' (ibid.: 28). He goes on to outline a number of methods to reduce risk in the field, including safety awareness, policy changes to specify 'precautionary guidelines', 'good practice', and training by role playing (ibid.: 64–72).

Although the desire to avoid certain pitfalls and events which may lead to death, injury or termination of the study is understandable, in this chapter it will be argued that to 'design out' danger can in some cases make the exercise pointless. As ethnography relies upon experiencing the world of the cultural group which is the focus of the study, to avoid danger where fear, 'showing bottle' and being emotionally and physically 'tough' are central elements of that environment, would be counterproductive. In reality, it seems that the only way to gain access to crucial data is to be 'where the action is' when working with groups of police officers.

## Enduring fieldwork

In order to experience the 'gritty reality' of spending time as a participant observer with the police, it is essential to have attempted to live the life of the 'ordinary cop'. In many cases this means enduring considerable boredom, accompanying them as they carry out apparently pointless orders given by

29

supervisory officers and suffering endless shift work without proper sleep, basic warmth or access to a reasonably healthy diet. All of this must be completed with the appropriate level of complaint, as a display of solidarity with the researched. In other words, voicing the opinion that policing is difficult and tiring is acceptable, but to compare it with the cosy world of academia, is not. Furthermore, to make remarks about any particular difficulties associated with 'being a woman' in such an environment, or to claim special treatment, would be ethnographic suicide.

With regard to this I was faced with successfully completing a number of informal initiation tests, the results of which were disseminated to other groups of officers I might encounter. It seems that these tests were designed to calculate whether I could be trusted not to act inappropriately or to communicate certain information up the rank structure, and, more importantly, whether I had 'bottle'. As the following examples from the fieldwork show, these tests of courage were a combination of physical and emotional strength.

## *Just testing ...*

In the first couple of cases, tests of trust were simple ones, involving a number of occasions when jobs were 'cuffed'[1] in favour of taking an informal tea break or giving a friend or relative a lift somewhere in the police car. In the second type of test, more serious errors were made in my presence with no attempt at concealment, such as minor road accidents or 'near misses' in which the police car was damaged; paperwork was lost and general rule-bending occurred such as allowing certain misdemeanours by members of the public to pass them by without taking any action. All of this has been reported as standard procedure in the business of being a police ethnographer and to a certain extent replicates the process through which probationer police officers have to pass. Similarly, there comes a point in police operational experience where those accompanying a new officer or researcher become aware of the latter's feelings and reactions when physically threatened. It seems that this is a process which is often hastened or at least not actively prevented by more experienced officers, who in turn have been subjected to it earlier in their careers. Many police officers are adept at frightening people and feel that it is 'good' for probationers, researchers and anyone they feel has not been 'tested', to be toughened up using such techniques.

My capacity to withstand physical discomfort and threat to life was tested on a number of occasions when a message would come over the police radio that there was a suspect 'brandishing a weapon, possibly a shotgun'. During these situations, of which there was an average of one per fortnight in the six months' fieldwork at the metropolitan police force I researched, a number of elements of the 'bottle' test could be observed, including: not making a fuss; keeping still and quiet on the way to the incident; not breathing loudly or showing anxiety; following orders exactly and without comment and getting into a flak jacket in a moving vehicle in time for arrival at the incident. On the way to a call where a man was reported to be threatening his wife with a shotgun, which involved being driven at high speed in a police personnel carrier, the sergeant in charge shouted over his shoulder: 'Everyone in the back get your fucking flak jackets – right now, and I mean everyone' (Male Sergeant 1994). In order to emphasise my potential involvement in the forthcoming incident he made sure the order was unambiguous. Being 'one of the lads' in this type of situation means taking orders like everyone else, with no special considerations. Furthermore, to complain about the physical difficulties of standing up in a van that is speeding along a dual carriageway, taking sudden turns to negotiate roundabouts and avoid collisions with other vehicles, whilst struggling into a protective vest, would be seen as ungrateful, naive and disrespectful by the officers on the shift.

It has been argued by those who have had close contact with the police at work, that for some male officers the basis of their occupational cultural beliefs and narrative traditions (Holdaway 1983) is fighting and violence, sexual conquests and feats of drinking. These elements of their working lives have been said to 'all combine together into a kind of cult of masculinity' (Smith and Gray 1983: 87). Therefore remaining steadfast in the face of adversity and danger is clearly important for the credibility of the researcher who needs to be accepted into the group. In his discussion of male behaviour and attitudes in the police, Fielding argues that the values of 'cop canteen culture' can be seen as 'an almost pure form of hegemonic masculinity' (1994: 47). Similarly, although Reiner admits he has not included gender in his considerations to date, he discusses the way 'danger and authority are thus interdependent elements in the police world, to which police culture develops a set of adaptive rules, recipes and rites' (Reiner 1992: 110). In addition, Reiner (1992) and Holdaway (1983) describe at length the way police officers often discuss their sense of separation and isolation from the members of general society, the so-called 'civvies', due to the danger they face and the unpleasant tasks with which they have to cope.

One of the ways police officers support this assertion about their 'special' status is by arguing that they have to endure situations which 'normal' members of the public will never encounter. Violent and sudden death is an example of this. Their cultural knowledge, they believe, is a result of seeing the 'unpleasant' side of life, and the 'worst' sections of society, as part of their daily work. In the course of my fieldwork there were a number of disturbing instances in which people died in circumstances which could be regarded as gruesome. One of these was a road accident in which a serious head injury resulted in some of the contents of a skull being left on the pavement after the injured person had been removed to the ambulance. As I was standing looking down at this, one of the police officers came over with a large torch and said to me, 'See that, that means they're dead when that comes out' (Male PC 1994). He shone his torch on the pile of claret-coloured, jelly-like substance, whilst searching my face for a reaction. Later, back at the police station canteen, after we were delayed getting in for our evening meal due to the road being cordoned off to record the accident scene, one of the male officers passed me in the queue saying, 'Couldn't face your dinner earlier, eh? Nothing like a head injury to put you off your chicken jalfrazi is there?' (Male PC 1994).

I am arguing here, therefore, that danger and fear are interdependent parts of the police environment which can be encountered by ethnographers who enter their world. As a powerful emotion, fear can control the way we behave and researchers faced with some situations would normally tend to avoid certain experiences. In order to use danger within the research process, however, as a means of better understanding cultures such as that of the alleged 'macho cop', it is an important precursor for understanding the rules, rites and rituals of policing. Accordingly, it appears that a new approach is needed to threats to personal safety by examining the positive aspects of danger in the field. In order to reflect upon the usefulness of placing the researcher in the metaphorical line of fire, two potential areas of danger will be examined here. First, threats to the body, with the potential for causing physical injury, and second, dangers which give rise to emotions such as fear but are not, in terms of physical damage, necessarily 'real'. It is, of course, impossible to analyse these two aspects of fear and danger without reference to each other. Since researchers act as embodied agents, an examination of the process which avoids 'both bodily essentialist and social constructionist analyses of the body' (Maynard 1997: 9) is warranted. Indeed, numerous theoretical studies that have examined the significance of the body in sociology, such as Shilling (1993), Turner (1996), Mackenzie (1998) and Scott (1997), have argued for the study of the body as 'an agent in its own right rather than as unintelligent, static and passive' (Maynard 1997: 9). It has recently been asserted that this will lead to the 'rejection of Cartesian binary or dichotomous categories as supposed descriptions of social life' (Stanley and Wise 1993: 187). With these approaches to the body in mind, therefore, this chapter will now explore the effect of 'gendered' bodies in terms of the corporeal aspect of 'lived experience' and the potential benefit of 'bringing the body back in' (Frank 1990). In this way the gendered body will be regarded as a research tool or element, in order to propose a new approach based upon the vitally important role of danger in the research process.

## Experiencing fear

In the discussion which follows, a series of examples from the research will be analysed with regard to gender, embodiment and participant observation. It will be clear from these incidents, drawn from extensive periods on patrol with a range of officers from two contrasting police forces, that perceptions of danger were important determinants of the study. It is apparent that there is an absence of applicable 'rules' to deal with numerous situations arising in the field. It would be difficult, if not impossible, to anticipate all the situations one might encounter in research within research training courses, departmental or professional academic body guidelines. Indeed, as a newly-funded PhD student, finding myself hiding behind a tree in the course of a police firearms containment, and facing the threat of being shot, I did wonder whether the potential attractions of ethnographic tradition, of 'telling it like it is', were worth the risk. As Hobbs suggests, however, a certain status is attached to ethnographers because '(M)achismo, as well as a veil of eccentricity, is responsible for the cult of field-work, as some of the grime of "real life" is brought back to the office' (Hobbs 1993: 62).

In terms of my own research it was essential, and central to the research process, that emotions such as fear were experienced in order to understand the 'world view' of the officers being observed. As it was an ethnography which concentrated upon the role of gendered identities in the police, with particular emphasis upon the 'force and strength' debate,[2] it was crucially important to analyse whether men and women differ in their experiencing of fear. In effect, I was concerned with the way men and women use their bodies in the course of their duties, and how perceptions about gendered identities, in terms of erotic, genital identities, which take 'genitalia to be the definitive "sign" of sex' (Butler 1990: 109), and socially constructed roles at work, is significant.

Examples that illustrate this approach are detailed in the study from which this chapter is drawn and include police officers assuming that there are 'male' and 'female' tasks. For instance, jobs which involve under-age sex, rape and allegations of indecency are shunned by male officers who assume that a woman who has been raped will 'not want to give her statement to a male police officer'. On the other hand, domestic violence incidents, which give them the chance to be 'heroes' triumphing over bullying partners to protect 'weaker' women are considered appropriately 'masculine' work. In the past it has been accepted that this 'differential deployment' of women in the police has stunted their progress in terms of promotion (Jones 1986; Brown et al. 1993; Heidensohn 1992) and movement into specialist posts. As a male-dominated occupation, it has been alleged that for years women have been 'ghettoised' (Walklate 1995: 119), constrained in their career choices, made to work in departments concerned with 'women and children' and prevented from achieving a high-profile 'arrest portfolio'. One of the reasons this has been perpetuated, it is alleged, is due to selection procedures and 'assumptions about the ways in which large males deploy their strength' (Her Majesty's Inspector of Constabulary 1995: 22). To what extent this can be substantiated empirically, however, had not been tested prior to the study which is being discussed here.

### Showing 'bottle'

'Right you two, get over there behind that car, but keep out of the line of fire as you go across the road. You two, round the back of the house, find some trees and get behind them for protection. When the ARV [Armed Response Team] gets here, we'll loud hail the house and hopefully they'll decide to give themselves up. If anyone comes running out, keep your fucking heads down.'

(Male Inspector 1995)

Although the instructions being issued to a group of officers at a 'stake out', reproduced above, cannot be classed as a regular occurrence in the general course of daily policing, it is an eventuality which many 'ordinary cops' have to be prepared to face. As Reiner observes, one of the features of the police role is the way officers are not necessarily encountering danger constantly, but they are 'unique in regularly being required to face situations where the risk lies in the unpredictable outcome of encounters with other people' (Reiner 1992: 110). One of the areas which was chosen for the fieldwork was a residential suburb to the west of a large northern city in England, where levels of violent crime are notoriously high, leading to it being dubbed 'West Beirut' by the officers working there. This was characterised by the fact that a number of 'criminal families' lived in the area, and as one of the officers observed: 'In most places, if there's a "threat to kill" call, it's usually some idle remark over the garden hedge about the kids annoying the people next door, but round here, the next week you find them blowing bits out of each other' (Male PC 1995).

Similarly, calls from members of the public reporting the sound of gunshots were not regarded as lightly in this subdivision as they might be elsewhere. In these cases, houses in the locality would be visited, possibly searched, and incidents closely logged and entered on the crime report system for future intelligence purposes. At a 'drive-by' incident which occurred in the course of the fieldwork, a shotgun was used to blow a hole through the front window of a house where a family was sitting watching television, with the ammunition peppering the rear wall of the room. A couple of weeks later, the body of an occupant of the house was found lying at the end of the street, the victim of a dispute about the owning of 'doors'[3] in the town.

As the 'drive-by' was being investigated, in the early hours of a freezing cold morning, I was standing with a group of officers near the scene. Due to the noise generated by the police pulling up in their vehicles neighbours were soon out of their houses asking what had happened. As the scene was regarded as an 'exclusion zone' until the area had been 'contained', in case the assailant was still in the vicinity, they were asked to go back inside their houses. At this point, a number of shotgun cartridges were discovered on the front doorstep, suggesting that there might be someone with a gun inside the house and the senior officer was distracted for a moment. Almost simultaneously a car came screaming round the corner of the street, and everyone had to duck behind any available wall or recess, fearing that the gang had come back to continue their work. In situations such as this, researchers are as vulnerable as anyone else at the scene. Due to the high level of gun-related incidents and serious woundings in the area, officers wear body protection, so-called 'flak jackets', especially for evening and night shifts, and ask for updates from control room staff regarding the possibility of guns being at the incidents they are attending. At one call I attended an officer requested an intelligence report over the radio on the way to a 'robbery in progress' at a 'known address'.[4] On asking whether there was any intelligence of importance, the control room replied that there were 'twelve pages', to which the officer travelling to the scene replied, 'Well if it's not too much trouble, could you look to see if he's likely to have a fucking gun?' (Male PC 1995).

Tension would be running high at times such as this and travelling to incidents where experienced, competent and apparently 'fearless' police officers were plainly worried, was unnerving. In terms of the research process, it is impossible for the ethnographer to remain outside the scene, physically or emotionally, as they are no more protected than with the same ineffectual body armour worn by the officers under observation. Furthermore, one of the dangers for 'outsider' participant observers is that they generally lack the training the police receive, and yet can be seen as legitimate targets by those who aim to injure them. To all intents and purposes, wearing a flak jacket, standing with the police at the scene of a stake out, typified by the one described above, the researcher feels, and probably becomes, one of the more vulnerable people at the scene. Participant observers accompanying the police can hardly expect to be shielded from events which may involve physical danger facing the officers themselves and to do so would lead to loss of 'face' and solidarity, leading to general ridicule, perhaps making the research relationship untenable.

Given this type of situation, where relatively covert studies of 'deviance' are being conducted, it would clearly be very difficult, as Pearson observes (1993), to build up relations with the local population as a safety measure. For example, in the case study of cannabis dealers conducted by Fountain (1993), this would have been counterproductive because she would have had to reveal her identity. Indeed, most police ethnographies would be impossible to conduct if the 'local', so-called 'prig' population (Young 1991: 111) were to be approached in order to develop the 'rapport' that Peritore recommends (1990: 359). In essence, to conduct a valid ethnography, which involves significant periods in the field, observing certain groups for whom violence is a daily occurrence, danger in the research process is a largely unavoidable and necessary element of the process. In the case of a woman researcher this is especially relevant because the police regard themselves, in the main, as the protectors of vulnerable groups. As female bodies are believed to be 'weaker' and more vulnerable, it is clear they would be seen as in need of protection. On a number of occasions I was told, for example, not to walk about outside the police station or in the city by myself. One inspector asked in horror, having seen me on the closed-circuit television monitor earlier that night, 'You haven't been going out on your own, have you?' (Male Inspector 1995). On another occasion officers I was accompanying arrested two young men and there was no room for me in the patrol car. As we were only a couple of hundred yards from the police station I volunteered to walk back to meet them after they had 'booked in' their suspects, but was told, 'Oh, no, no, you can't walk about around here. I'm not being funny, but anyone could have seen you out with us tonight. It's much too dangerous' (Male PC 1994).

An illustration of the way researchers have to display solidarity with the group they are studying, sometimes against their better judgement, is contained in the following example. It occurred towards the end of a six-month period of fieldwork and synthesises two central ideas discussed in this chapter. First, that danger is a central element of police research and second, that the gendered body is a significant determinant of that process. It happened one evening in a custody suite in one of the busiest stations in the division. A young man of about sixteen years old had been arrested on suspicion of burglary. He had previous convictions, was on bail for similar offences and had failed to appear at court when requested on a couple of occasions. His mother was waiting in the custody area as he was being formally charged, and both were expecting that on completion of the paperwork he would be released and they could go home. In a discussion with his inspector, however, the custody sergeant had decided that certain criteria had been fulfilled meaning that their prisoner could be 'kept overnight for court' rather than given bail. As it was a Saturday night, this would entail a longish stint in custody until Monday morning. Upon hearing this news, the boy's mother burst into tears and the suspect himself was not far from doing the same. Suddenly, however, he made a lunge for a small gap in the officers surrounding him and came running towards where I was standing in the doorway. He crashed into me and I put my hands out for protection, grabbing his jacket, at which point the police officers sprang into action, pulled him off me and dragged him bodily into a cell. To the accompaniment of his cries of protest and pain he was roughly stripped of his belt and shoes and berated for 'attacking a woman' and someone who was not 'even one of us'.

In the course of physically threatening incidents such as the one described above and those mentioned earlier, where guns were involved, a number of interesting methodological issues are available for analysis. Although the police themselves are not usually the intended direct target of violence – it is more likely that they have simply got in the way of someone using a gun on a third party – the researcher is 'with' the police and cannot be distinguished from them by potential assailants. It is important therefore to explore the idea of the researcher as 'innocent' or 'passive' observer of a cultural scene. In some cases, as described above, where the suspect attempted to escape, people may regard the researcher as the 'softer option' in their bid for freedom. As these types of incident tend to lead to the group expressing concern for the 'outsider' who has 'shown bottle' in displaying police-like behaviour, confirmatory remarks such as 'You're one of us now' and 'Well done, we'll be awarding you danger money next', and so on, are made. As a result, deeper levels of trust and friendship can be fostered, leading to a feeling of mutual solidarity, facilitating a more in-depth level of experiential confidence sharing. Furthermore, it allows a common criticism that is levelled at ethnographers, particularly those with access to powerful and hard-to-reach groups such as the police, that the behaviour these groups display does not represent their normal practices, to be refuted to some extent. In other words, the allegation that the police will act in ways which they believe the researcher wants, finds acceptable or will lead to their activities being reported in a more favourable manner, are more difficult to support. As some of the incidents here described tend to suggest, when bullets, escapees and threats to kill are flying, there is little time for officers to consider whether their actions are being observed or to modify their behaviour.

## Danger from above

On some occasions in the course of the fieldwork, there was another aspect of threat that I shared with the officers whom I accompanied on duty. It was perceived to be the result of certain actions at dangerous incidents, such as those described above, where a message would come over the car radio, simply announcing an address or general location and requesting officers 'to attend the report of a shooting'. Calls such as these would be eagerly attended by everyone on duty, often at speed, but were made apparently more hazardous by actions or orders given by supervisors once everyone had arrived. From my point of view, perhaps more acutely due to my relative 'outsider' status, it seemed that danger was often precipitated by supervisors who failed to take some aspect of risk into account. As a result of their cavalier attitude, sometimes a greater sense of fear, danger and frustration would be experienced by officers. Two such examples during the fieldwork were firearms incidents where spent cartridges were discovered outside houses following reports by neighbours of gunshots. On both occasions, police officers I was accompanying were horrified and extremely frightened when the officer-in-charge, without bullet-proof protection, simply went up to the front door and knocked, calling out to the potential occupants, 'It's the police, have you got a gun in there?' As one of the officers remarked to his colleagues during this risky endeavour, 'What an idiot – he's putting us all at risk. Get the experts out, the firearms team, for God's sake. We're all going to get blown to bits' (Male PC 1995).

On another occasion I witnessed an inspector take charge of a firearms incident, in order to contain a house where a man had been seen at a window with a gun. He did this by attempting to disguise himself as a taxi driver to entice the assailant into a car, after which he said he would drive him to the police station and arrest him. Only the 'insubordinate' actions of a sergeant who used a mobile phone to alert the firearms team leader at home on call, prevented the inspector's plan from going ahead.

As described earlier, in other studies it has often been reported that police 'canteen' culture fosters high levels of group solidarity. In order to feel protected police officers need to confirm each other's 'insider' status by excluding 'outsiders' who lack specialist police training or experience. Researchers, to be afforded the same levels of protection and access to the site, need to be accepted as part of the team. This means fitting in with the cultural milieu, being trusted, looked after, warned of dangers, and, as Morgan (1987) has argued, in certain situations threatened with social ostracism. In his discussion of the way he became one of the 'men' whilst doing his national service, he explains that certain sacrifices have to be made because, 'Fear of exclusion from the group became perhaps an even more powerful force than wishing to join it and be accepted' (Morgan 1987: 48). As he suggests, adjusting to belonging to some groups may involve certain compromises, especially in the case of a 'non-macho' or woman fieldworker in a predominantly male setting. To remain outside, however, and failing to join the 'team' could be even more unpleasant, and in terms of ethnographic research, a self-defeating process. In order to construct an account of police work, life and culture which can claim for itself a reasonable measure of plausibility or 'vraisemblance' as Atkinson describes it (1990:39), it seems that certain risks have to be taken. As mentioned above in the discussion about the mind/body dichotomy, this can take the form of not only risking the status of one's sense of 'self' but also direct danger to the body. Indeed, as Van Maanen explains, ethnographers can provide 'personal, first-hand experience of the culture in question' from the 'native's point of view' and can contribute another perspective to the detached 'scientific' status of observation studies within the discipline (Van Maanen 1988 in Atkinson 1990: 34).

Furthermore, as a woman, it is advantageous to observe certain behaviour which Brittan (Brittan 1989: 27) argued leads to the constant necessity to negotiate one's gender identity in the 'obstacle race', which has to be run according to rules that are continually being rewritten and reinterpreted. Men, he argues, have lost their 'gender certainty' due to the 'erosion of male power in the workplace' and are therefore facing a 'crisis of masculinity' (1989: 25). Arguably, using insider/outsider status, the boundaries of which are constantly being renegotiated, can be a convenient vehicle for observing and experiencing the contradictions and difficulties of 'macho cop' culture. In other words, as an outside 'other' I felt it was possible to observe such behaviour and yet remain on the edge of the world of policing. At the same time, as an outside/insider,[5] in terms of my role as a participant observer, it was possible to experience danger, fear and associated emotions leading to a deeper understanding of the police world.

As the researcher is the 'primary research instrument' as a participant observer, ethnographies are based upon the premise that supposedly rational ' "facts" of society and culture belong to a different order to those of nature' (Walsh 1998: 217–18). It has been argued here that fear and danger and the reflective nature of the gendered body can be used to substantiate and throw light upon the nature of the police work and its associated cultural beliefs. As Hammersley and Atkinson suggest, ethnography 'involves the ethnographer participating overtly or covertly in people's daily lives for an extended period of time' (1995: 1), which may lead to problems with the plausibility and credibility of the claims made by the research. Consequently, the ethnographer is 'especially dependent upon discursive formats to inform and pursue the reader' (Atkinson 1990: 11) and as a 'factual' as opposed to fictional work, it has to have arguments which are capable of supporting the claims it makes. As Atkinson suggests, '(T)he mere declaration on the part of the author that the account is "true" is no guarantee that a text will be read in that way' (Atkinson 1990: 36). In essence, ethnography has tended to suffer from a lack of validity in terms of its non-positivist stance. It does not usually provide the generalisable findings of large-scale studies, nor the categories of coded replies from in-depth interviews. On the other hand, the strength of ethnographic research is that through participant observation it provides a view of social life which can lead to the understanding of the hopes, fears and beliefs of certain cultural groupings which would be inaccessible by other means.

## Conclusion

In terms of the empirical examination of what has been called the 'study of the body' in sociology, police research, which employs fear, risk and danger as part of the process, can extend our understanding of what it is to be part of their cultural world. By reading signs of acceptance by the group, the researcher can reflect on the way they have been taken into the confidence of the team. In addition, by comparing the 'insider' knowledge gained as part of the research process, with their innocence and naiveté at the beginning of the project, it is possible to begin to analyse the role of danger in the field. Researchers have to learn when to reach for the flak jacket, when to duck and how to deal with a prisoner who views them as a potential escape route, in order to 'survive' with their personal credibility intact. Members of the shift begin by overtly protecting the 'outsider' in order to 'watch the back' of their 'civvy' charge, but as experience grows, the researcher learns to realise as quickly as they do that the car that is pulling up may be the gunmen returning to the scene of a 'drive-by'. Frustrations at the incompetence of supervisory officers and fear of the consequences are felt equally by the researcher and the police officers and police behaviour 'under fire' is especially understandable as it is experienced personally.

Reflecting upon danger in the field can therefore provide a starting point for the understanding of the way men and women use their bodies 'in action' and the significance of gender on the streets in the police. In the fieldwork discussed in this chapter, some of the more dangerous incidents provided evidence of the importance of gender in the research process. In addition, relatively insignificant 'dangerous' occurrences, such as traffic accidents and 'near misses' in patrol cars, are opportunities for discussions of police culture.

In reflecting upon dangerous situations in the field it is clearly not recommended or useful to seek risk and danger. Also the presence or likelihood of danger in the field means that careful planning is needed and the relevant safety procedures, recommended and/or used by the researched, should be followed at all times. However, where the group under study experience risk on a regular basis the ethnographer is necessarily going to become involved in it in some way as the research progresses. In the case of the research discussed here I was involved with studying a work culture that is said to be based upon 'acting tough' (Uildriks and van Mastrigt 1991: 160) and being able to 'handle' violence. It would have been pointless to withdraw, ignore or invoke strategies to avoid this important aspect of the officers' daily experience. Conducted in a reflexive way, studies which analyse dangerous lives and working environments can provide valid and plausible understandings of social worlds which would otherwise be inaccessible. Danger and fear contribute to this process as an indicator of cultural knowledge, acceptance by the researched and evidence of the researcher having seen the world as it is for them. In essence, when the 'flak' is flying, the ethnographer needs to be around to catch it.

## Notes

1  'Cuffing' means ignoring a job to which they are directed.
2  See for example Heidensohn (1992) for a full discussion.
3  Owning of 'doors' is the protection racket which allegedly provides cover for drug dealing at night-clubs.
4  A 'known address' is one to which the police have been called regularly and might imply some suspected activities such as drug dealing.
5  See Brown (1996) for a detailed discussion of this aspect of police research.

## Bibliography

Atkinson, P. (1990) *The Ethnographic Imagination: Textual Constructions of Reality*, London: Routledge.

Brittan, A. (1989) *Masculinity and Power*, Oxford: Basil Blackwell.

Brown, J. (1996) 'Police research: some critical issues' in F. Leishman, B. Loveday and S. P. Savage (eds) *Core Issues in Policing*, London: Longman.

Brown, J., Anderson, R. and Campbell, E. (1993) *Aspects of Discrimination within the Police Service in England and Wales*, London: Home Office.

Butler, J. (1990) *Gender Trouble: Feminism and the Subversion of Identity*, London: Routledge.

Fielding, N. (1994) *Cop Canteen Culture. Just Boys Doing Business? Men, Masculinities and Crime*, London: Routledge.

Fountain, J. (1993) 'Dealing with data' in May, T. and Hobbs, D. (eds) *Interpreting the Field. Accounts of Ethnography*, Oxford: Clarendon Press.

Frank, A. (1990) 'Bringing the body back in: a decade review', *Theory, Culture and Society* 7: 131–62.

Hammersley, M. and Atkinson, P. (1995) *Ethnography: Principles in Practice*, 2nd edition, London: Routledge.

Heidensohn, F. (1992) *Women in Control? The Role of Women in Law Enforcement*, Oxford: Clarendon Press.

Her Majesty's Inspector of Constabulary (1995) *Developing Diversity in the Police Service: Equal Opportunities Thematic Inspection Report*, London: HMSO.

Holdaway, S. (1983) *Inside the British Police: A Force at Work*, Oxford: Blackwell Press.

Hockey, J. (1996) 'Putting down smoke: emotion and engagement in participant observation' in K. Carter and S. Delamont (eds) *Qualitative Research: The Emotional Dimension*, Aldershot: Avebury.

Hobbs, D. (1993) 'Peers, careers and academic fears: writing as field-work' in D. Hobbs and T. May (eds) *Interpreting the Field: Accounts of Ethnography*, Oxford: Clarendon Press.

Hobbs, D. and May, T. (eds) (1993) *Interpreting the Field: Accounts of Ethnography*, Oxford: Clarendon Press.

Jones, S. (1986) *Policewomen and Equality*, London: Macmillan.

Lee, R. M. (1993) *Doing Research on Sensitive Topics*, London: Sage.

—— (1995) *Dangerous Fieldwork*, London: Sage.

Mackenzie, C. (1998) 'A certain lack of symmetry: Beauvoir on autonomous agency and women's embodiment' in R. Evans (ed.) *Simone de Beauvoir's* The Second Sex: *New Interdisciplinary Essays*, Manchester: Manchester University Press.

McNay, L. (1992) *Foucault and Feminism: Power, Gender and the Self*, Cambridge: Polity Press.

Maynard, M. (ed.) (1997) *Science and the Construction of Women*, London: University College London Press.

Morgan, D. (1987) '*It will make a man of you': Notes on National Service, Masculinity and Autobiography. Studies in Sexual Politics*, Manchester: Manchester University Press.

Pearson, G. (1993) 'Talking a good fight: authenticity and distance in the ethnographer's craft' in D. Hobbs and T. May (eds) *Interpreting the Field: Accounts of Ethnography*, Oxford: Clarendon Press.

Peritore, N. P. (1990) 'Reflections on dangerous fieldwork', *American Sociologist* 21: 359–72.

Punch, M. (1993) 'Observation and the police: the research experience' in M. Hammersley (ed.) *Social Research: Philosophy, Politics and Practice*, London: Sage.

Reiner, R. (1992) *The Politics of the Police*, London: Harvester Wheatsheaf.

Scott, A. (1997) 'The knowledge in our bones: standpoint theory, alternative health and the quantum model of the body' in M. Maynard (ed.) *Science and the Construction of Women*, London: University College London Press.

Shilling, C. (1993) *The Body and Social Theory*, London: Sage.

Sluka, J. A. (1990) 'Participant observation in violent social contexts', *Human Organisation* 49, 2: 114–26.

Smith, D. J. and Gray, J. (1983) *The Police and People in London. Volume 4: The Police in Action*, London: Policy Studies Institute.

Stanley, L. and Wise, S. (1993) *Breaking Out Again*, London: Routledge.

Turner, B. S. (1992) *Regulating Bodies: Essays in Medical Sociology*, London: Routledge.

—— (1996) *The Body and Society: Explorations in Social Theory*, 2nd edition, London: Sage.

Uildriks, N. and van Mastrigt, H. (1991) *Policing Police Violence*, Boston: Kluwer Law and Taxation Publishers.

Walklate, S. (1995) *Gender and Crime: An Introduction*, London: Prentice Hall.

Walsh, D. (1998) 'Doing ethnography' in C. Seale (ed.) *Researching Society and Culture*, London: Sage.

Westmarland, L. (1998) 'An Ethnography of Gendered Policing', unpublished PhD thesis, University of Durham.

Young, M. (1991) *An Inside Job*, Oxford: Oxford University Press.

# 3

# GETTING ON THE DOOR AND STAYING THERE

## A covert participant observational study of bouncers

*David Calvey*

## Introduction

This chapter discusses a covert participant observational study of door supervisors, or bouncers as they are more traditionally called, in the leisure and entertainment sector of Manchester, England. The fieldwork was conducted between January and June 1996. Similar to Westmarland's experience of police work (Chapter 2), the research involved substantial physical threat to the researcher. However, unlike Westmarland's experience, mine was a covert study, carried out without the knowledge of bouncers, club and pub owners and customers. This chapter discusses my experience of physical threat and highlights the ways in which bouncer/researcher relationships were enhanced by shared experience. However, at the same time there were important ethical issues involved in the research. The implications of the covert nature of the research are still ongoing and I have deliberately allowed some years to pass between the completion of the fieldwork and publication, as I feared recrimination by the door community if my research role was discovered. The experience of threat continuing after the fieldwork is completed and when one may be working in totally unrelated research areas is not uncommon or indeed new. Wallis's (1976, 1977) experience of studying Scientology followed him for years after the work was completed. This chapter contributes a recognition of the need to be aware of the longer-term consequences of research upon researchers themselves in terms of physical risk and threat.

The research discussed in this chapter was a sociological ethnography of door work that explored cultural practice, work culture and social organisation. My interest in studying this area grew out of being employed as a working bouncer for a local 'door' agency in pubs and clubs throughout the Manchester region. I had trained in martial arts for several years prior to undertaking the research and so was physically equipped to study this field. Due to recently completing a local authority DoorSafe (door staff training) course I had made a number of useful initial contacts and had negotiated access to a local door agency. Throughout the study other contacts were made which allowed greater access to this occupational setting. The chapter is organised into five broad sections. The first section is concerned with outlining the backdrop to the study by examining the professionalisation and occupational imagery of bouncers and bouncing and the regulation of door work. The second section discusses the intellectual orientation of the approach adopted in the study and the third section describes two key ethnographic episodes from the fieldwork. The penultimate section reviews the dual concepts of nomadic ethnography and the covert research role as strategies that articulate the management of research danger. The final section offers some reflections on ethical dangers and proposes a reflexive position for ethnographic research. In this way the chapter raises issues which are relevant beyond the study of door work to all research involving fieldwork in physically threatening contexts with potentially physically dangerous groups.

## The professionalisation and regulation of door work: from folklore and mythology to big business

Bouncers are often typified as aggressive and unintelligent heavies and this image can be seen as part of their mythologisation as icons of masculinity. The categorisation and typification of bouncers in this way conventionally frames their perception and interpretation by others. Classically, they are the 'men of honour' when on your side and the 'heavies' when not on your side. Doors can be both opened and slammed shut. Put simply, bouncers can make or break your night out, with the club or pub effectively becoming their monopoly. However, in the United Kingdom, an occupational transformation is currently occurring: job title, job description and occupational image have shifted from that of bouncer to door supervisor, door steward and door security operative. As an occupational group the people who do this work are beginning to present themselves as undertaking a trained and professional form of labour, one which shuns the previously mythologised notion of 'bouncer'.

Bouncers have both traditional and contemporary associations with criminality in the shape of organised criminal gang activities and, particularly in the contemporary context, the sale of popular 'dance drugs' throughout the entertainment and leisure industries. At the same time, the 'night-time economy' and 'cultural industries' (Lovatt and O'Conner 1995) of many cities have experienced a boom, evidenced in the number of new pubs and clubs opening.

Dance culture is now an integral part of the cultural industries and the lifestyle of a significant section of some communities. As a result, large numbers of door staff are in demand, dramatically increasing the number of private security agencies providing this service. The 'bouncing classes' currently represent by far the biggest private security operation in the UK. In 1996 an estimated 2,000 security companies were recorded with 50,000 door personnel. These figures are an estimate by the GMB union, quoted in the *Guardian*, April and May 1996.

The bouncing classes are composed primarily of males, although the proportion of female bouncers is increasing. If these men were the 'lads' of the counter school culture (Willis 1977), now that they are grown up they are doing door work. Most commonly, door work forms part of the informal economy, although professionalisation of the industry aims to reduce that. The drive for professionalisation, however, has evolved simultaneously with the rise of gangsterism and the widespread sale of 'dance drugs'. Bouncing has become an important source of employment and 'doing the doors' is now big business.

In an attempt to regulate door work, local authority door supervisor registration schemes are organised collaboratively by city councils to enable door staff to work in premises licensed for public entertainment throughout the United Kingdom. There are also attempts by unions to unionise the group and provide in-service training. Part of the rationale behind regulation is to make the work less dangerous and more open to scrutiny. However, the professionalisation of door work has gone hand-in-hand with its criminalisation. So widespread are the connections between club culture, drugs and door work that the Home Office conducted policy research into the area by the Police Research Group (Morris 1998). This research highlighted the way that door supervision was subverted by organised criminal factions involved in drug dealing in the dance culture, summed up in the commonly-used phrase 'control the doors, control the floors'.

The regulation of door work was started in the early 1990s. The implementation of Manchester DoorSafe happened in 1994. Many of the bouncers I had contact with during the study viewed the scheme ritualistically as a bureaucratic requirement to get 'badged up'. Employment was restricted by the City Council if you failed to display a DoorSafe badge when doing the doors. Such a process is part of the wider surveillance of both door work and the use of city spaces. However, there are still concerns over the trustworthiness of door staff among several club and pub owners in Manchester, who want police to act as door staff, as they do in parts of the United States, to deter drug dealers and violent thugs. Currently, police chiefs in Britain are opposed to the idea, but the debate continues.

The European-style reshaping of the leisure and entertainment sectors of Manchester has, ironically, brought with it gangsterism. The extension of licensing laws and the development of a café society provides opportunities for door agencies to monopolise doors and develop drug within venues. It has long been the case that bouncers, affiliated to organised criminal fraternities, have colluded with drug dealers, but this has become more acute due to the recent growth of the dance drug scene, which in turn is linked to the internationalisation of club culture. There has been much local, and indeed national, press interest in bouncers and bouncing in Manchester. Various popular dance clubs have closed in Manchester city centre due, in part, to drug and gang problems. Others have opened up with new, supposedly strict, door systems. This environment of cultural, social and occupational change makes the study of bouncing an interesting, rich and emergent area. The bouncer is at the centre of these changes, managing the door, managing their own role and monitoring their own occupational transformation. To study this area is to step into a dangerous world where attempts at regulation have not been as successful as was hoped.

## Methodological concerns and bouncing: ethnomethodologically-inspired ethnography and covert participant observation

The objective of this section is to ground the version of participant observation that I practised in the study, within my intellectual orientation. Participant observation can usefully be seen as a tool embedded within an ethnomethodologically-inspired ethnography (Calvey 1993). Such an approach uses ethnography, and in this case a covert style, as a basic methodological strategy while departing from traditional styles. My ethnography, in terms of logic and reasoning, is inspired by an ethnomethodological program (Garfinkel 1996) on which there is a dedicated literature.[1] Briefly, this approach involves taking the issue of description seriously. It starts and stays with the research participant's perspective and is grounded in the 'lived experiences' of the participants. Thus the central objectives of this ethnography are to describe as faithfully as possible the natural setting of door work in a manner which does not trivialise, diminish or caricature the observed phenomena. This ethnographic mode is one of a wide range of styles.[2] This means of studying the social world utilises participant observation as its main methodological tool.[3] The important point here is less about method than about methodology. Namely, the researcher is embedded within the setting and the socially interactive nature of his/her role is explicitly accepted. It is the very character of this method that produces the duality of the research role and the dilemma of being simultaneously an insider and an outsider.

In terms of taking a covert role, some argue that such a stance is ethically indefensible. However, given my concern with authenticity and the lived experience of this dangerous work, it would have been nearly impossible to gain

46

access any other way. My defence of the methodology adopted in the study revolves around certain premises being taken seriously. First, my central concern is with attempting adequately to describe, understand and explicate participants' accounts of their world in a spontaneous and emergent manner. Second, this examination is done whilst abstaining from, bracketing or being indifferent to, all corrective moral judgments of the adequacy, value or success in the way participants perform their work. What needs to be kept in mind is the difference between academic and street ethics and the corrective tendencies of the former on the latter. Third, immersion is a condition in this type of embedded role and, last, ethnography is a temporal, contingent and practical matter. An overt role would have been inappropriate for this topic as the participants are reluctant to give any information about their work activities to external agencies. Even if they did it would be highly selective and artificial. Covert participant observation was the richest way to engage with the participants in any meaningful sense. To get closer to and understand the experience of being a bouncer, one needed to do minimum damage to the natural settings of bouncing. The practical concerns, and the aim to understand the setting without disturbing it, problematised the issue of informed consent. From start to finish I was placed in an ethical dilemma and also in personal jeopardy, as a direct result of my use of covert methods. A key priority was to carry out the research with minimum damage to myself.

## Ethnographic episodes

The objective of this section is to outline two key ethnographic episodes that display and articulate the ethnographic condition and my experiences of physical risk during this study. The dominant source of data for the research was covertly tape-recorded conversations (a tape recorder was concealed in my jacket) and field notes of incidents which occurred as I worked alongside the bouncers. The two ethnographic episodes, one at a gay pub and the other a dance club, are drawn from a diverse range of door modes or contexts that I worked on during the six-month fieldwork period. The episodes are taken from the early and latter periods of the fieldwork respectively. It must be stressed at the outset that, although such ethnographic episodes form a rich picture of the fieldwork settings, they are limited in that they serve merely as snapshots or vignettes of that world. The episodes represent critical incidents on the door from which to analyse the concept of danger in the field and they can be understood as a routine part of door work. So while these particular events provide more insight than others they also capture the dangerous character of this fieldwork in general and its consequences.

## Ethnographic episode 1. Site X: a case of assaults, take-overs and swimming lessons

This research site was a recently-opened gay pub in the heart of the area of Manchester city centre known as 'the gay village'. It had six door staff and extended hours at the weekend until 2am. It has since become a popular venue in this fashionable area of the city. The area as a whole has experienced a boom of pubs, clubs and restaurants and has become economically strong as a business district. It has a 'gay friendly' door policy and selection process that has to be sensitively managed by door staff.

Here I recount my first night on this door which was carried out early on in my fieldwork. The experience of the night was an ethical baptism of fire in which I witnessed two assaults. The first involved a fellow bouncer punching a customer in the face after he refused entry to him. I was standing on the door alongside the action. The second assault followed on from the former. The customer who had been assaulted had a relationship with a gay bouncer who worked on the door of another club in the village. This bouncer was a senior member of a Manchester gang running the doors in the area. He took revenge on our member of staff, assisted by a team of eight other bouncers, by breaking his nose and throwing him in the canal. This assault was not resisted by our door team. Such a response was interpreted as a public demonstration of weakness resulting in a 'take-over bid' for our door. We had been seen to 'lose our bottle' in the face of conflict and hence our appropriateness for doing that door was questioned. The rival bouncers had clearly won the show of strength and put in an immediate offer to our management to run the door.

The fear for my team was of the door being perceived as an 'easy door' where other bouncers, gangs and aspiring local 'hard men' would impose pressure via a range of humiliation and intimidation tactics. Door respect was at stake. The police arrived, alerted by customers concerned by the enforced swimming lesson, but they gained no information or statements from the bouncers. Everyone, including me, had seen and heard nothing. Traditionally, information has never been given by bouncers to the police. One bouncer described one of the cardinal rules as, 'if the police are there nobody has seen fuck all'. It turned out that the dispute between the bouncers was deep rooted and linked to the assaulted bouncer attempting to gain membership in the dominant gang that controlled and monopolised the city-centre doors. The assaulted bouncer was removed from his post and the door agency found him work on another door away from the city centre. The management stated that he was temporarily suspended but he never returned. It was clear they were put under gang pressure to do this.

Such insider information would have been difficult for me to obtain by other methods, in particular overt ones. It was important that I was seen and treated as a working door person so I could understand the way the work was carried out and the constraints of the job. The feeling of physical danger was acute in terms of what I had witnessed and, marginally, been involved in. However, I resisted making a classic category mistake of conflating contexts and imposing corrective meanings. The work involved threat, violence and intimidation and the choices the bouncers made involved street values and ethics. This was people doing door work not in academia.

### Ethnographic episode 2. Site Y: a case of visits and vests

Working at Club Y was a high-status job because this was a dance-oriented club. Greater credibility and a door track record were required to gain employment here. The job gave me continued access to bouncing employment and was hence an important factor in securing continued access to the field. In essence, this door would open other doors. It took me a lot of canvassing of the door agency to get this one. The weekend I worked at the club was the occasion of its reopening after two weeks of intensive security precautions. The close-down had been due to successive take-over bids, violent incidents and intimidation tactics by various Manchester gangs, all interested as it was a new dance club in the city.

As a result the door staff had effectively lost control of the door. The club became a melting pot of gang interest and activity. The owners, a large multinational brewery chain, closed the club for two weeks to formulate a new security strategy. As part of these efforts £25,000 was spent on new measures including closed-circuit television. These measures were also intended to regain customer confidence after the close-down.

The owners of Club Y wanted a 'clean' door and were willing to recruit a new door team and enlist the full support of the police to stop the intimidation and halt gang infiltration on the doors. It was clear by the set-up of the door team that trouble was expected. All of the ten door staff, including myself, were fitted with bullet-proof vests. On fitting me with a vest the CID (Criminal Investigation Department) officer noted that it would stop bullets from most types of guns. One doorman later quipped that if guns were pulled 'he ain't gonna be around anyway'. This comment filled me with a certain amount of fear about my first night in the club but this gave way to my quest for richer data. However, there was an atmosphere of tension and apprehension all through the opening weekend. It became a question of when, rather than if, there was going to be gang interest and trouble over the re-opening.

Because my working knowledge of the gang structure, and particularly of the leaders or 'heads', was limited, I stressed to the head door person that I needed to be clearly told who had any form of privileged entry. I did not want to make mistakes on any door, but least of all on this door, on this night. At the same time I did not want the head door person to know too much about my concerns, so I had to be subtle in seeking advice. It is vital for door people to 'know the score' in terms of who controls the door so they can manage entry accordingly; the irony then being that to keep out gang members you need to employ gang members. Thus, being and staying on the door at such clubs requires a current working knowledge of gang organisation, including who are the leaders, and the ongoing gang ranking. This knowledge is part of the interactional management of respect enacted on the door between the door staff and the customers. Mismanagement could have severe repercussions for that individual and possibly for the whole door team.

The first night was generally regarded as uneventful. This was commonly perceived by the door team as the 'quiet before the storm'. The second night the club had a visit from a very senior Salford gang leader who monopolised doors throughout the Manchester area. All the door team, except me, recognised him. Their reactions told the story. When he arrived, one of the senior doormen hid behind the main door whilst nervously spying through the peek hole and firmly pronouncing that he was not going outside. The visit was a business one, made just before the club was due to open for the night. The gang leader arrived with his driver and parked outside the club. His driver then told the head door person to get into the car so the gang leader could talk with him. The other bouncers waited for the news inside the club and held an emergency meeting about the situation. Meanwhile customers had begun queuing outside. At this stage the safety of the door team was prioritised over that of the customers.

There was fear and apprehension building throughout the discussions held by the door team. The door buzzer started ringing more frequently as the customer queue grew. The team eventually agreed to open the doors of the club. It was a waiting game and the night suddenly started to turn into a very long one for everyone. The night continued without event until during the latter part of the night two young black men arrived at the front door. It was felt, after assessment of closed-circuit television, that they had guns in their possession. There was considerable panic and confusion amongst staff as to who they were and whether or not they actually had guns. There were certain significant assumptions made about the race of these men by the bouncers regarding their connection to dominant gangs in the city centre. These assumptions were illustrative of the racist nature of some of the door practices as young black men, mainly of Afro-Caribbean origin, were often discriminated against as a potential threat to the door team (Mungham 1976). Door teams are ethnically constructed according to which gang or coalition have an active interest in them. According to most of the door team the bravado with which the young men approached and demanded entry suggested that they were 'carrying'. Moreover, in terms of physical confrontation there were only two of them facing a full door team of ten. This convinced the door team of their intent. The front door was closed and temporarily locked with nobody, including customers, being allowed out. Indeed, one female customer, who needed to leave immediately, was flatly denied and allowed to vomit in the corner of the club. At this stage, most of the door team were huddled in the middle pay booth section trying to view the closed-circuit television monitor to see if they recognised the men. Indeed, for fear of possible shooting, nobody stood near the middle of the door but to either side. The head doorman was asked to go outside and investigate. He summed up the collective anxiety of the team by saying, 'I don't want to get no bullet over no bullshit.' The two men then left in a car. At no point were the police called. There is a traditional cynicism towards them amongst bouncers, and on this occasion there was a hesitancy to call the police as the club had just re-opened.

Despite the apparent dissipation of danger after the two men had left, the situation developed further when they returned to the club shortly after it had shut, demanding entry and attempting to force the front door open. At this point the club manager called a state of emergency, put the entire door team, remaining bar staff and DJs in a locked cellar and called the police for assistance on his mobile phone. Such was the level of intimidation that the club was abandoned in favour of personal safety. The intruders succeeded in damaging the front door but had left before the police arrived. The main question raised for the bouncers by this incident was whether these men were connected to the earlier visit of the Salford gang leader or were part of a rival gang displaying their interest.

The police stayed on site until everyone was off the premises. They suggested to the bouncers that we had better keep our vests on until we got home. Some of the door team were visibly shaken by the chain of events. Whilst the dangerous events were in progress I prioritised my own survival over sociology, but the tape was kept running throughout. Walking home with my vest on filled me with extreme anxiety about my personal safety and turned the brief journey home into a paranoid nightmare. Managing threats was a routine part of the job of being a bouncer but at this point I felt very vulnerable. Events had clearly illustrated that my role as a bouncer could result in serious injury and it took some time for my adrenalin and stress levels to subside when I returned home. Taking a side was one thing, the threat of being removed from one was another.

On reflection, to gain access to such observations it was vital that I had credibility as a working door person and had a door history. The concept of collective trust is integral to doing door work, encapsulated in the doorman's slogan 'watch my back'. More specifically, this trust is a fragile one involving high levels of suspicion and cynicism. This type of trust and risk management was not questioned or challenged by door staff, it was simply a condition of the work.

## Danger and all that: a case of the nomadic ethnographer

The nomadic role that I adopted arose from my need, driven in part by personal safety concerns, to move constantly around door settings. The rationale behind the nomadic role was two-fold. First, I wanted to draw on a wide range of settings for the research in order to do comparative analysis. Second, it diminished my chances of being discovered, as personal bonds were not given time to form, nor intimate biographical questions asked by door staff or regular customers. It was a paradox getting close to participants without allowing them to get too close to you. In short, the dangerous nature of this research necessitated that I adopt a nomadic ethnographic role. Thus I constantly engineered appropriate exits as I moved around various work sites. These self-created exits were usually based on issues of pay, personality conflicts with management and inappropriate hours. In the event that my cover was blown and my denial that I was anything other than an ordinary bouncer was rejected, I had rehearsed a cover story stating that I was linked to covert police surveillance. Merely stating that I was an academic would offer no or very little protection. When asked where I lived I had standard responses such as 'local', 'not that far away' or as a last resort 'the city centre'. I never provided a precise location. If I gave a phone number it was a mobile rather than home one.

This vagueness was rarely questioned. Strangely, this dangerous work was undertaken without knowing the surnames or addresses of your colleagues. But this did not matter and was taken as normal. As long as your colleagues were there to 'watch your back' when it mattered the rest was academic. That is not to say that friendships did not develop or that they were irrelevant. Indeed, door work features a lot of bonding and comradeship and due to the nature of the work close friendships develop, but it can also be a temporary line of work, in which one forms passing attachments to colleagues. In these circumstances I had to keep control of the information that my colleagues received about me. This meant limiting the opportunities for them to have access to personal information. For example, my partner kept a safe distance from the doors I worked. Such a distancing strategy was more problematic in the post-field experience but one which had to be sensibly maintained. After all, to the men on the doors, I had merely finished doing door work with them. Consequently, I was regularly asked when I was coming back or which door I was working.

Communication was kept on a first name basis only. Pay was in cash in an envelope with your first name on the front and no formal documentation. This suited me well because the less they knew about my biography the better for my personal safety. The flow of information from friends and students I knew also had to be controlled. Angst about my research role was compounded when I received some press coverage in the official newspaper of the University of Manchester Student Union. The article was titled 'Work Experience' and made reference to the first of the ethnographic episodes mentioned above. It read:

> Conscientious as ever, members of staff at the Sociology Department have been doing undercover research into the life of those much-maligned guardians of the door, Bouncers. At least, Biteback presumes that's why some tutors have been working on the door at Pub X in town. They wouldn't be moonlighting, would they ?
>
> (*Mancunion* Issue no. 13, 29/1/96)

As this newspaper had a large local student circulation and the piece was published in the early part of my fieldwork, I was concerned about my cover being blown by students. Fortunately this did not happen, although I was sensitised to the possibilities of such an occurrence.

During the fieldwork I maintained key contacts although I was involved in various shifting and temporary friendships with door staff. These relationships had to involve careful boundary maintenance. On the one hand it was necessary to display a bouncer's interaction rituals (Goffman 1967) including dress code, non-verbal codes and war stories in the appropriate argot – this is what I refer to as the 'bouncer self'. The constitution of a bouncer's subjectivity, self-image and identity is tied up in complex ways with these social practices that are expected and taken for granted in door work. The 'bouncer self' is embedded in masculinity and is accurately displayed in and through the interactional management of respect on the doors. On the other hand the duality of the research role is paramount. The difference between self and other must remain and not become blurred during the research process. By this nomadic fieldwork method I built an adequate picture of the field, wherein observations were drawn from various sites. A single ethnographic immersion at one door would have involved thick description but would have lacked analytic breadth. At the same time the nomadic approach also protected my personal safety and protected the boundaries between my bouncer and non-bouncer roles.

## Post-mortems, hangovers and reflections on ethical dangers

The research dangers I experienced were physical, emotional and ethical. The experience of physical danger and the routine management of conflict, both real and supposed, came with the research territory. It was more than simply a feature of the research setting. Importantly, it was integral to understanding the context of violence in which the participants lived and worked and which became normalised. A 'hardness passport' (James 1973) was required for entry into the bouncing game and once achieved was never questioned. In addition to the physical danger that I encountered, emotional risk was also an aspect of the research. These emotional dangers centered on the threat to my sense of self in the research process and the ongoing management of personal relationships, loyalties, obligations and confidences that developed. This became stressful the longer the fieldwork continued because I began to know more about the settings. Moreover, as time went on, the more participants assumed that I knew about the bouncing world. This is not sociological romanticism running riot, discovery would have meant 'door justice' in the shape of a 'good kicking'. Fortunately, this did not happen.

In terms of ethical dilemmas, I witnessed various criminal events such as assault, drug taking, theft of entrance money and the withholding of information from the police. It is difficult to plan for such events in the sense of taking legal advice and guidance beforehand but I became increasingly aware of the sensitive situations I was becoming embroiled in during the research. I was also offered, and refused, various drugs by doormen and frequently had to physically restrain customers. Such incidents were 'all in a night's work'. There was no time to stop and think about how to respond to them, except retrospectively. It is important to locate these ethical dangers as in the normal run of the job and my concern was in trying to understand the routine orientation of the participants to such events. As the ethnographic episodes display, the expectations of the role and my personal ethics could clash. This had to be negotiated in an occasioned and emergent manner by distancing myself as much as practically possible from such events whilst still performing the dual fieldwork role.

## The post-fieldwork experience and self-management

I would like to stress here that these multiple aspects of danger were experienced throughout the research, including during the post-fieldwork stage. Importantly, this shifts the picture of fieldwork away from a simplified chronology, often presented in traditional methodological literature, to a more complex and dynamic account. For me the research not only involved getting on and staying on the door but, once the study ended, staying out. After the fieldwork was completed, I was still treated as a bouncer by my erstwhile colleagues and was asked to work on doors, was queried as to where I was working and asked about old door relationships. The research role might have ended for the researcher but not for the researched. My story of who I was had to be sustained both throughout the study and after it. It was as if the study had no closing date.

Doing the door is a way of life and a lifestyle. By doing the job I had become part of the bouncers' community and in the post-fieldwork period many privileges were extended to me, including free entry into local clubs and pubs. These practices are seen by the door staff as legitimate social and economic fringe benefits (Mars 1994) of the job. You know you are distinguished from the crowd and observed as such. You are not just another punter but a punter who is also an ex- or current bouncer. Managing the post-fieldwork experience was not only a case of wearing two hats but also being competent at the impression management that goes with it. Moreover, because it was in a violent context the research involved more foresight, planning and skilful manoeuvre (Sluka 1995) than other contexts might have done. It could not be treated, and I certainly did not treat it, lightly. I partly enjoyed the seductive 'buzz' from working on doors from 'the inside' but I was simultaneously relieved eventually to melt back into the anonymous crowd. When one senior doorman of Manchester's largest night club, which was run by a dominant gang and has since closed down, stated I was now 'in the firm', as I picked up my wages, I definitely decided it was time to close the study. The double-edged character of my research, in simultaneously using and exposing the self, was a high-risk methodology. I refer to it as 'sub-aqua ethnography' – dangerous due to the constant fear of discovery. The field experience of getting on, staying on and leaving the door has been a powerful one.

In such a covert role there is also the issue of my over-identification, emotional attachment and collusion with the subject. However, this is only a serious problem if one holds on to a traditional concept of the objectivity of the fieldworker. For me, the issue is one of entitlement, in the sense of being able to talk adequately about bouncing and bouncers whilst, in my case, being a temporary and particular version of one. It is not to say that ethics can be relativised away or that professional codes of conduct need not apply. The question is in viewing ethics more broadly as situational and case contingent. A re-orientation is required that places ethics as part of the ethnographic condition. That is, ethics as part of the ethnographic setting rather than extracted from it and given honorific status.

This research account is a contribution to the developing literature on the dangers of research. It supports the attempts to de-marginalise danger and bring it from the periphery to the centre. It is my contention that research danger can be usefully conceptualised as a positively disruptive influence on traditional and conventional methodological accounts. It moves debates from simplified ideas of taking a side (Becker 1998) to issues of mixed loyalties and shifting identities in fieldwork. Ethical frameworks need to be understood as a dynamic and empirically-informed and continuous process. Codes of ethical practice are idealisations. In terms of my research I ran the risk of academic alienation because of the methodology which I employed, in spite of the pioneering nature of the investigation. Covert research always requires clear justification and explication as a research tool, but is nonetheless still criticised.

Ultimately, the topic dictated that the research be conducted covertly as the level of access, and hence analytic richness, which I gained would have been seriously diminished otherwise. Many sociologists would wholeheartedly reject all covert research on ethical grounds as violating the principles of informed consent, privacy and trust. Indeed, it is professionally frowned upon. However, it is one that I would vigorously defend on the grounds of both methodological necessity and appropriateness. Moreover, as with Fielding's (1981) contentious study of the National Front, topics need to be investigated analytically despite personal preferences and political tastes. In fact, more investigative social research should be done on controversial areas, although not blindly.

## Reflexive ethnography

My aim in this chapter is not to offer formulaic and prescriptive advice for the ethnographic research process but rather to reflect on some particular problems I encountered. My approach is neither to unify nor to integrate the varieties of sociological reflexivity (Slack 1993) into schematic meta-theories that gloss over serious differences. Rather it has been to frame and distinguish some of the features of a reflexive research position. My reflexive ethnography involves types of phenomenological and ethnomethodological engagement, immersion and participation. Reflections about the self and others in the study which I include here are deeply autobiographical. Such an approach serves to make the researcher less omniscient and more ordinary. Hence, part of the reflexive position is the application of scepticism throughout the process of inquiry.

Lovatt and Purkis (1996) stress that the duality of the research role produces a web of connections, tactics and identities, including autobiographical motives, which must be part of the foreground rather than relegated to the background. They add that the conventional sociological text is approaching its sell-by date and other creative modes of representation should be explored. I fully support such a diagnosis. In my work I have aimed to avoid the position of the privileged ethnographer. What is crucial is an understanding of the privileging game (Stanley and Wise 1993) and the resistance to it in social research.

This call for a reflexive position is about achieving a sensible and reasoned balance between 'desk work' and fieldwork, with the former emerging from the latter. What ethnographers practice and what they preach can vary significantly; there is plenty of methodological gesturing around. The reflexive nature of social research is a condition of the discipline and should not be used as a justification for academic introspection. My conception of reflexive research involves a certain type of democratisation. The spirit of experimentation can become self-regarding, pompous indulgence in which more is learned about the fieldworker than the field. In my opinion this tendency should be rigorously resisted throughout the fieldwork process. Instead we need to conceptualise and characterise the reflexive nature of the fieldwork process beyond the crude duality of taking sides.

## A final note

In terms of fieldwork strategies, a number of lessons can be learned from this case study about the safeguards needed when planning 'dangerous' research (for example the use of practical equipment like mobile phones, the careful choice of setting, letting someone know your whereabouts). Moreover, one has to become artful and skilled in impression management in the field (for example creating cover stories and exits when necessary, and coping with interaction rituals). Similarly, the ethical landscape needs to be contemplated before entry, although not in an obsessive way that would limit entry to the research setting. I have argued in this chapter that diverse and threatening topics and groups should not be ruled out because of ethical dilemmas. Such groups need to be understood as part of social life just as much as 'safer' groups and contexts. This chapter raises general issues which should be of use to researchers within general social research, popular cultural studies and criminology who are interested in observing other potentially dangerous groups or activities, such as football violence or gang culture. Similar personal safety concerns would be of importance in the planning process and in carrying out fieldwork.

The chapter may also be of more general use to social researchers or students thinking of undertaking ethnography in any field. In sum, my call here is for more types of reflexive ethnography, which involve a form of passionate sociology as an imaginative pursuit (Game and Metcalfe 1996; Morgan 1998). I hope to have presented door work not as exotica or subjugation but both as a type of work and an important part of popular culture. Although I was a professional stranger (Agar 1980), I have attempted to offer a brief glimpse of the reality which engages bouncers and to do so on their own terms. This has been done with a view to the research constituting a beginning and not an end in itself (James 1973). Ultimately, even if you have no intention of staying, you should at least be prepared to make the journey (Hobbs 1995). My journey was a rich one in many senses. The bouncer identity is constituted by and tied up with ideas about violence and masculinity that require exploration in future studies of the area.[4] My study has attempted to both demystify and de-romanticise the status and process of doing ethnography as well as to celebrate creative social research. The motivation was not to produce corrective analysis but to produce a faithful account of the rich social world of bouncers and bouncing.

As I was conducting the fieldwork my partner remarked: 'When you put that jacket on, your bouncer head comes on.' I reflected on this as an appropriate subtext for a description of my dualistic ethnographic journey. In saying this I am not being so naive as to claim that my temporary stay in their world entitles me to make uncontested claims on bouncers' behalf or, patronisingly, that I had become one of them. After all, bouncing was, and remains, a way of life and not just a sociological category. However, I have gained an empathy for and engaged with bouncers and bouncing. My approach is one sociological path amongst many. I hope that this study encourages others to take more risks and to be creative on their journeys.

## Notes

1 There is a wide literature on ethnomethodology including: Sharrock 1989; Garfinkel 1967, 1996.
2 There is a wide literature on ethnography that discusses its diversity and problematic issues: Van Maanen 1988; Atkinson1990; Stanley 1990.
3 There is an extensive prescriptive literature on participant observation: Whyte 1952, 1984. There is also a more limited literature that specifically discusses the problems of covert participant observation: Blumer 1986; Adler and Adler 1987; Lee 1995.
4 There is an interesting literature on violence mainly drawn from criminology, social psychology and gender studies: Short and Wolfgang 1972; McVicar 1974; Hobbs 1988, 1995. There is a growing literature on masculinity mainly drawn from various fields that can be related to this topic: Collinson 1996; Denby and Baker 1998.

## Bibliography

Adler, P. and Adler, P. (1987) 'The Past and Future of Ethnography', *Journal of Contemporary Ethnography* 16, 1: 17–86.
Agar, M. (1980) *The Professional Stranger*, London: Academic Press.
Atkinson, P. (1990) *The Ethnographic Imagination: textual constructions of reality*, London: Routledge.
Becker, H. S. (1998) *Tricks of the Trade: how to think about your research while you're doing it*, Chicago: Chicago University Press.

Bittner, E. (1973) 'Objectivity and realism in sociology' in G. Psathas (ed.) *Phenomenological Sociology*, New York: Wiley.

Blumer, H. (1986) *Symbolic Interactionism: perspective and method*, London: University of California Press.

Calvey, D. (1993) 'The Organisation of Work Culture: The case of a high-tech salesforce', unpublished PhD thesis, Department of Sociology, University of Manchester.

Collinson, D. (1996) *Men as Managers, Managers as Men: critical perspectives on men and masculinity*, London: Sage.

Denby, S. and Baker, C. (1998) 'How to be Masculine in the Block Area', *Childhood* 5, 2: 151–75.

Fielding, N. (1981) *The National Front*, London: Routledge & Kegan Paul.

Game, A. and Metcalfe, A. (1996) *Passionate Sociology*, London: Sage.

Garfinkel, H. (1967) *Studies in Ethnomethodology*, Englewood Cliffs: Prentice Hall.

—— (1996) 'An Overview of Ethnomethodology's Program', *Social Psychology Quarterly* 59: 5–21.

Goffman, E. (1967) *Interaction Rituals*, Chicago: Aldine.

Hertz, R. (1997) *Reflexivity and Voice*, London: Sage.

Hobbs, D. (1988) *Doing the Business*, Oxford: Clarendon Press.

—— (1995) *Bad Business*, Oxford: Oxford University Press.

James, P. (1973) *A Glasgow Gang Observed*, London: Eyre Methuen.

Lee, R. M. (1995) *Dangerous Fieldwork*, London: Sage.

Lovatt, A. and O'Conner, J. (1995) 'The City and the Night-time Economy', *Planning Practice and Research*, July.

Lovatt, A. and Purkis, J. (1996) 'Shouting in the street: popular culture, values and ethnography' in J. O'Conner and D. Wynne (eds) *From the Margins to the Centre*, Aldershot: Arena.

McVicar, J. (1974) *McVicar by Himself*, London: Arrow.

Mars, G. (1994) *Cheats at Work: an anthropology of workplace crime*, Aldershot: Dartmouth.

Morgan, D. (1998) 'Sociological Imaginings and Imagining Society', *Sociology* 32: 647–63.

Morris, S. (1998) *Clubs, Drugs and Doormen*, Paper 86, Crime, Detection and Prevention Series, London: Home Office.

Mungham, G. (1976) 'Youth in pursuit of itself' in G. Mungham and G. Pearson *Working Class Youth Culture*, London: Routledge & Kegan Paul.

Redhead, S., Wynne, D. and O'Conner, J. (1998) *Club Cultures Reader*, Oxford: Blackwell.

Reed-Danahay, D. E. (1997) *Auto/Ethnography: rewriting the self and the soul*, London: Berg.

Sharrock, W. (1989) 'Ethnomethodology', *British Journal of Sociology* 40: 657–77.

Short, J. F. and Wolfgang, M. E. (1972) *Collective Violence*, Chicago: Aldine.

Slack, R. (1993) 'Varieties of Sociological Reflexivity', unpublished PhD thesis, University of Manchester.

Sluka, J. A. (1995) 'Reflections on managing danger in fieldwork: dangerous anthropology in Belfast' in C. Nordstrom and A. Robben (eds) *Fieldwork Under Fire*, London: University of California Press.

Stanley, L. (1990) 'Doing ethnography, writing ethnography', *British Journal of Sociology* 24: 617–27.

Stanley, L. and Wise, S. (1993) *Breaking Out Again: feminist ontology and epistemology,* 2nd edition, London: Routledge.

Thompson, H. (1967) *Hell's Angels*, New York: Random House.

Twemlow, C. (1980) *The Tuxedo Warrior*, Chichester: Summersdale.

Van Maanen, J. (1988) *Tales of the Field: on writing ethnography*, London: University of Chicago Press.

Wallis, R. (1976) *The Road to Total Freedom: a sociological analysis of Scientology*, London: Heinemann Educational.

—— (1977) 'The moral career of a research project' in C. Bell and H. Roberts (eds) *Social Researching: Politics, Problems, Practice*, London: Routledge & Kegan Paul.

Whyte, W. F. (1952) *Street Corner Society*, Chicago: University of Chicago Press.

—— (1984) *Learning from the Field*, London: Sage.

Willis, P. (1977) *Learning to Labour: how working class kids get working class jobs*, Farnborough: Saxon House.

# 4

# NEGOTIATING DANGER IN
# FIELDWORK ON CRIME

## A researcher's tale

*Janet Jamieson*

## Introduction

Risk and danger to the personal security of the researcher is an issue gaining greater recognition within the social sciences (Renzetti and Lee 1993; Lawrinson and Harris 1994; Lee 1995). Renzetti and Lee (1993: 5), for example, emphasise that research can be threatening to the researcher as well as the participants and that researchers may be placed in situations in which their personal safety is jeopardised. However, to date researchers encountering and negotiating danger in the conduct of studies have been reliant on their own experience, judgement and common sense, a situation which is far from ideal for funding bodies, academic institutions, grant holders or indeed for those who actually conduct the fieldwork. Safeguards and precautions can be built into any research strategy but more attention needs to be given to how this is done and how *ad hoc* risk is dealt with in the field.

This chapter adds to the contributions on physical danger in this volume by focusing upon the importance of planning, team-working and colleague support in countering physical risk. It argues that risk control is particularly important in terms of short-term contract research work, in which research managers may not be aware of the threats researchers face when in the field until after the project is finished. Communication within a research team is central to countering physical danger in the field and goes hand in hand with assessing and planning for personal safety.

To examine these issues, the chapter discusses my experience of using qualitative methods to research the subject of young people and crime in Scotland. Although it is acknowledged that the study of crime may result in the disclosure of incriminating or emotionally upsetting information that may manifest itself as emotional threat to the researcher, in this particular study physical danger and the threat of physical danger were most pertinent to my experience of carrying out the research. The chapter discusses how the issue of danger was addressed in the development and day-to-day conduct of the study, my experiences of danger in respect of conducting research with a potentially 'dangerous' and unfamiliar sample (young men) in unfamiliar locales, and the challenges posed by the contractual basis of research funding.

In reflecting upon the study and developing this chapter, the concrete examples and incidences of danger seem minor. I recognise that it would be easy to overstate the extent to which danger is inherent to fieldwork. However, my experiences serve to illustrate that only a few threatening or dangerous incidences during a research project can have a substantial impact upon the researcher's sense of personal safety.

## Designing safe studies

Originally core funded by the Economic and Social Research Council and the University of Stirling, the Social Work Research Centre (SWRC) was formed to develop and undertake evaluative research on social work provision in Scotland within the themes of 'Community Care', 'Social Work and Criminal Justice' and 'Children and Young People'. This funding basis continued for ten years, until 1995, when the Centre secured continued funding for an additional five years from the Scottish Office and the University of Stirling. The Scottish Office contribution to the SWRC's funding required the Centre to undertake and complete four research studies within the themes of 'Community Care' and 'Social Work and Criminal Justice'. Within the latter theme we embarked on a study which addressed wider questions about young men and the choices they make with respect to involvement or non-involvement in offending (Jamieson et al. 1999). This study utilised both qualitative and quantitative methods to examine and explore young men's attitudes and experiences of offending in two Scottish towns.

The study was designed to address young men's resistance to, desistance from and persistence in offending. The study focused on three age cohorts: 14–15 years, 18–19 years and 21–26 years, with each respondent completing a self-report offending questionnaire to indicate if and how often they had committed a number of offences, either ever or within the last twelve months. The types of offences ranged from taking away a bicycle without the owner's permission to hurting someone with a knife, stick or other weapon. On the basis of this self-report data, or on the basis of discussion about offending during interviews, young men were divided into those who had never offended (resisters); those who had offended in the past but not within the previous twelve months (desisters); and those who had offended in the past and/or the previous twelve months (persisters). The aim was to interview equal numbers of young men in each of the offender categories and age cohorts. Those interviewed had all opted into this process. Interviews were conducted with a total of 138 boys and young men.

John Brewer (1993) comments that within research studies dangers mostly arise from everyday activities inherent to the research process and that such dangers are often quite incidental to the topic and geographical location of the research itself. In designing this particular research study it was recognised that some risks to the researcher were likely to emerge in the conduct of fieldwork. For instance, the interviews were to be undertaken with young people involved, to varying degrees, in 'risk' behaviour, in unfamiliar locations and at times outwith office hours. Thus, we developed a number of safety policies and precautions in an attempt to minimise the threat to researchers. For example, interviews were to be undertaken, as far as was possible, within office hours; mobile phones were carried; researchers had use of a car; office staff at the university were informed of the researchers' whereabouts and were alerted when the researcher was particularly concerned about a specific interview. The aim of these precautions was to provide backup or support in potentially vulnerable situations and to facilitate exit from the research site if necessary.

Overall, such precautions did in theory provide a measure of security and reassurance. However, the pressure of achieving the desired sample of participants within the time available meant that it was not always practical to adhere to all these safety-conscious practices. Another precaution considered and rejected as impossible was the use of partnered interviews. Resource implications as well as the more pragmatic concerns of getting the fieldwork completed made this impractical. However, towards the end of the project when safety considerations were more to the forefront of the fieldworkers' minds, I and another researcher did make efforts to be in the same town and, if possible, the same estate in order to minimise our fears around physical threat and actual risks.

## Vulnerability and the researcher

Perceptions of threat and danger within the field will obviously vary depending on who is undertaking the research and their ability to negotiate and deal with issues which arise. Mason (1996) comments that the real challenge of research is not only to identify important issues prior to embarking on the research, but also to resolve unanticipated issues as they arise. Those conducting research need to think and act holistically in ways which combine intellectual, philosophical, technical and practical concerns whilst facing new situations in the field. Fortunately, I was approaching this study from the relatively advantaged position of having substantial experience of interviewing a range of social work clients in previous studies. Therefore I was generally confident of my skills and abilities as a researcher to handle difficult situations and interviewees. However, as Sluka (1990) points out, dangers are never totally manageable and, just like anyone else, researchers can be unlucky. Thus, the researcher needs to make a 'concerted effort always to maximise skilful handling of the situation, while recognising that skill alone is no guarantee of success' (Sluka 1990: 124, quoted in Lee 1995: 9). Indeed, the challenge and ability to act in a manner appropriate to the demands of the research were heightened by the very real vulnerability I experienced as a result of the threats, felt and imagined, that I experienced in undertaking this fieldwork.

The fact that I am a female researcher, also small in height and build, had a major impact on the perceived threat of danger and felt danger I experienced in conducting interviews with an all-male sample in unfamiliar environments. Furthermore, a consequence of undertaking the interviews in respondents' homes necessitated my spending a considerable amount of time in socially and economically deprived local authority housing estates where the street culture made it difficult to remain inconspicuous and to feel safe. My anxiety and sense of threat in conducting the fieldwork also varied depending on who else was in the respondent's home when interviews were being undertaken. For example, parents, partners and children tended to be reassuring, whereas a room full of young men proved more alarming. In addition to personal vulnerabilities that may contribute to a heightened sense of threat and danger in conducting fieldwork, consideration must also be given to the overall theme of a particular research. In this case the discussion of sensitive issues with young men, some of whom were persistent offenders and drug users, obviously contributed to the anxiety and concerns I experienced.

## Researching potentially 'dangerous' groups

Political and media discourses of youth in Britain are often negative, identifying this age as a transitory period that is both troubled and troublesome (Muncie 1999). Indeed, the association of youth with crime in Britain can be traced from the fears and anxieties about youth cultures and movements in pre-industrial Britain up to modern concerns with persistent offenders and drug users (Pearson 1994). This enduring concern regarding the association between youth and crime appears to have some credence. A nationally representative self-report offending study of 14–25 year olds in England and Wales, undertaken in 1995, reported that one in five young men admitted to handling stolen goods; to shoplifting; and to participating in group fighting or disorder in a public place. One in ten young men admitted they had been involved in vandalism or theft from work (Graham and Bowling 1995). However, it also should be emphasised that studies of youth crime also demonstrate that involvement in serious crime and persistent offending are relatively rare (Hagell and Newburn 1994; Graham and Bowling 1995; Farrington 1996).

Despite the negative rhetoric often associated with young people, we did not anticipate or indeed experience the majority of interviews undertaken for the study as 'dangerous' or threatening. The young men opted into the research and were generally interviewed on a one-to-one basis. This minimised feelings of risk as the threat often associated with young people is the threat of the group rather than the individual. Furthermore, we recognised that involvement in offending is often an integral part of 'adolescence' for young people but that generally this offending is not serious. Also, the sampling process meant that many of the interviewees were not involved in offending or other associated 'risk' behaviours. However, in targeting and eliciting the participation of persistent offenders in the two older age groups, the majority of whom had an offending, drug-orientated and rather chaotic lifestyle, issues of researcher safety and perceptions of threats and dangers were often less incidental and very real.

The research approach and desired respondents in effect meant the use of an agency focus for the research was not appropriate. Many of the potential respondents were unlikely to be known to the statutory authorities or to be clients of social work criminal justice services. This research strategy meant the research lacked both gatekeepers and an agency base for undertaking fieldwork. This resulted in an increase in the risk of danger and 'felt' danger in both anticipated and unanticipated ways. For instance, although in one of the study sites office space was negotiated with two local projects working with young people, the majority of interviews were still undertaken in respondents' homes. In the other research site, lack of any office space necessitated that all the interviews were conducted in the respondent's home or choice of location. On a number of occasions this presented actual and felt threats because I was at the disadvantage of entering an unknown situation as a lone researcher.

The main safety precaution utilised when arranging interviews in respondents' homes was that of contacting them by telephone prior to interview. This meant that if there were any signs of problems or threat, for instance if the young person sounded high or confused, this could be followed up with further telephone contact. If I was still dissatisfied the young person could be excluded from the study on the grounds of researcher safety. In the event, only two situations were deemed threatening and, despite this, in both cases visits were made subsequently and interviews successfully completed. On both these occasions the interviews were conducted within office hours and colleagues had been alerted to my concern. If I had not been in contact within a specified time the secretarial staff would initially have tried to contact me on my mobile phone and if there had been no response they would have contacted the police. In one case, the interview was conducted without incident; in the other the home interview was indeed experienced as threatening to the researcher.

This latter interview was conducted with a male resister in his twenties who lived alone. On arrival at the address there was a delay in his opening the door of the flat and when I finally entered his home he insisted on locking the door from the inside. At this point he appeared very uncomfortable with my presence, but after explaining the study and asking if he was comfortable to continue it emerged that he preferred to sit in the chair on which I was sitting as it gave him a view of the flat door. As soon as the young man was settled in his preferred chair he relaxed sufficiently so that I was able to conduct the interview. During the course of the interview the young man acknowledged that he had mental health problems which, I felt, explained his edginess on initial contact and his obvious discomfort and agitation prior to, and to a lesser extent during, the interview. Furthermore, his locking of the door and his palpable discomfort when he could not see the external door were explained by the fact that he felt victimised by local residents in the area in which he lived. Despite knowing this information I was concerned and felt threatened and the interview was undertaken with as much brevity as possible. Thus, I balanced my own misgivings and anxiety with the need to complete the interview process and fulfil the demands of the research.

## The challenge of sampling and researching unfamiliar groups

We were able to identify suitable respondents for the youngest age group through local schools. The fieldwork with this age group did not cause any anxiety or concerns, probably because of their younger age in relation to the researcher and the fact that their parents were often in the vicinity when interviews were conducted. However, with the older participants there was no such convenient sampling framework and the lack of agency involvement meant that we were dealing with anonymous respondents, a factor which substantially increased the risk of researcher danger and 'felt' danger.

To identify suitable older interviewees a number of strategies were implemented. Initially we used the electoral register to contact young people of eighteen years old, in the hope that this would allow a sufficient base from which to snowball other participants. While this method met with some success it was not sufficient on its own to enable us to complete the desired sample. Therefore we placed an advertisement in the local paper in one of the study areas, enclosed flyers in the free weekly newspaper distributed to all homes, and contacted a range of local organisations and businesses in both study areas. However, each of these strategies produced a disappointing response. The final and most successful attempt to recruit a sample involved leafleting homes, local organisations and community groups and offering young people a modest financial incentive to participate in the study. We had found it particularly difficult to identify young men in the categories of desister and persister. However, when we were able to offer payment for interviews clients of a local probation project and drugs centre became more willing to participate in the research.

The probation project was extremely helpful and amenable to the study and provided office space for our research. Interviewees contacted through this project were obviously keen not to antagonise staff as they were either on probation or had chosen to retain contact with the project after their participation. Consequently, these interviews were not experienced as threatening, a stark contrast to the experience of interviewing clients on the drug project. The drug project ran a drop-in centre which operated as a place for young people to meet and get help and advice in relation to drugs. The drop-in centre was always well attended and the project offered us the opportunity to spend a few days in the facility to recruit potential interviewees. The project staff informed the young people using the facility of the days we would be there and the fact that payment would be forthcoming for interview. They also offered the use of office space to undertake interviews. In the main however we were left to our own devices, so we were in effect dealing with young people about whom we knew very little except that they were probably involved in various risk behaviours.

The response to payment for interviews within this project was overwhelming. In some respects the response was a researcher's dream in that we had people to choose between at a time when we were desperately needing to complete the fieldwork. However, difficulties did arise in that, having almost achieved the desired number of interviews, we were becoming more selective about who we interviewed and some of the young people putting themselves forward were not suitable. Lee (1995: 41) notes that inducements, especially in impoverished settings, often invite the attentions of ineligible respondents who may react in an angry or threatening way when they are turned down for inclusion in the study. Furthermore, he notes that strategies for 'cooling out' ineligibles may have to be devised. For our purposes we had to screen potential interviewees in such a way that they were not alerted to the fact that they may have talked themselves out of taking part in the study. Therefore we asked a number of questions, taking care not to say what we were looking for, and then had to be assertive in telling them that they were not suitable for inclusion. The apparent threat in this situation arose from the fact that these people had volunteered on the understanding they would be interviewed and that they would be paid for this. The potential participants were understandably disappointed when told they were unsuitable for interview; being turned down meant they were not getting money which many were relying on to help buy them their drugs for that day.

However, the negotiation of danger in this situation did not end with those who were unsuitable for the study, as further problems became apparent in relation to those who were suitable for inclusion. The time we had at the project to undertake interviews was fairly limited and the interviews themselves were quite lengthy, thus we were limited to the number of young people we could interview on each occasion. Negotiations had to be undertaken to decide which of the volunteers would be interviewed on that day, at which point heated arguments broke out among the participants as to who this should be. A strategy we found successful in dealing with this involved not engaging in their arguments, but interviewing one young person at random from each friendship group or couple and taking telephone numbers to facilitate the arrangement of interviews with the others.

Payment for interview also resulted in snowballing. Indeed, the prospect of payment for answering a few questions often led to my arriving at a respondent's home only to find two or three young male friends of the interviewee also wanting to be interviewed. Aside from the obvious discomfort of being in a room with a group of young men I did not know, some of whom were probably not suitable for interview, the situation was on occasion exacerbated by my tendency to arrange late-morning interviews with persisters. Experience suggested that late morning was a good time for interviewees, given that they were likely to be out of bed but not yet to have left home for the day. However, this often meant undertaking interviews with young men who, having just got out of bed, were in various states of undress.

Whilst visiting participants' homes the threat of attack or theft on the street was also of great concern. In addition to the actual interview payments, the study necessitated my carrying valuable equipment in the form of a tape recorder and laptop computer and I received numerous warnings from the participants about the threat of theft. These warnings were often given during the course of the interview, particularly when the young man was discussing his own or others' offending. I took some comfort in the assurances that there were certain types of offences which were considered unacceptable, one of which seemed to be stealing from women. There was also the general threat of carrying money and equipment about the research sites. Luckily for me I did not experience theft whilst in the field. Given that neither the money nor the equipment was my property, and the equipment was insured, I would have simply handed it over and extricated myself from the situation as quickly as possible.

## Professional danger

Like many researchers, I am employed on a contractual basis, albeit a fairly lengthy five-year contract. The lack of permanency of employment raises the stakes in terms of eliciting a sample and gathering data, especially as success may result in further funding and the potential for future employment. The funding mechanisms for research in higher education effectively mean that the pursuit of success and striving to overcome difficulties within funded studies may result in a researcher taking more and greater risks. For example, in the case of this research study my sense of personal threat may have been reduced if the fieldwork had not, by necessity, been so concentrated. This would have given me the opportunity to escape the field to the relative calm of the university environment more often and provided the opportunity to discharge and discuss anxieties with colleagues (Brown et al. 1986). This kind of colleague support and shared reflection upon field experiences can be very important in the assessment of perceived and actual risks to personal safety.

The funders of our study, when they became aware of the difficulties and anxieties encountered in conducting the fieldwork, proved extremely supportive. However, that was after the data collection was completed. Howell (1990) argues that researchers should push organisations involved in research, such as universities, colleges and government funding bodies, to think more seriously about researcher safety. Current research guidelines tend to give priority to participants and are wholly inadequate in respect of protecting the researcher. This is a viewpoint which deserves serious consideration given the increasingly competitive nature of the pursuit of research funding and the pressure to complete studies successfully once funds have been secured.

## Conclusion

This chapter has used the example of research on young people and crime in Scotland to discuss the way that research dangers should be anticipated and fully thought out before and during data collection. The necessary preparations for undertaking potentially dangerous fieldwork include: planning research thoroughly, working in a safety-conscious way, remaining constantly alert to potential risks, and being prepared to take action to respond to threat, even if this means leaving the field. However, this chapter has illustrated how the constraints of contract research can make such planning more difficult. In this case the researcher is usually working within a framework stipulated by outside bodies in which financial and time pressures can mean safety is given a lower priority than it should be. It is clear that awareness of dangers in the field needs to go beyond the individual researcher or research team and should be seen as an important issue in safety at work for social researchers in general. The ability to deal with risks during qualitative research are, at present, perceived as part and parcel of the informal socialisation of the researcher. However, professional associations are becoming more concerned with the dangers that their members may face in the field. For instance, the British Social Policy Association is currently developing a code of practice for safety in the field. This growing interest in researcher safety, led by researchers themselves, should, one would hope, lead to the development of formal procedures of safe research practice.

Basic measures, discussed in this chapter, such as keeping others informed of your whereabouts, carrying a mobile phone and undertaking research in daylight and office hours, can help safeguard personal safety in the field and are easy to put in place. Furthermore, the relative advantages and disadvantages of utilising gatekeepers, or the services of professional survey organisations, to identify and access potential respondents should also be seriously considered in the effort to reduce researcher risk. The provision of safe spaces in which to undertake interviews is also of prime importance, as travelling to and from, and interviewing inside respondents' homes can be a source of danger. There is also value in visiting research sites prior to undertaking fieldwork and discussing potential risks with colleagues and supervisors as a matter of course, both before and during the research. These are the types of issues that should be addressed in terms of researcher safety training and should be considered when planning interviewing or participant observation. However, training and planning can only ever minimise risk; alertness to threat and exercising caution when in the field remain of key importance to researcher safety.

## Bibliography

Biernacki, P. and Waldorf, D. (1981) 'Snowball sampling: problems and techniques of chain referral sampling', *Sociological Methods and Research* 10: 141–63.

Brewer, J. (1993) 'Sensitivity as a problem in field research: a study of routine policing in Northern Ireland' in C. M. Renzetti and R. M. Lee (eds) *Researching Sensitive Topics*, Newbury Park, CA: Sage.

Brown, R., Bute, S. and Ford, P. (1986) *Social Workers at Risk: The Prevention and Management of Violence*, London: Macmillan.

Farrington, D. P. (1996) *Understanding and Preventing Youth Crime*, York: Joseph Rowntree Foundation.

Farrington, D. P. and West, D. J. (1981) 'The Cambridge study in delinquency development' in S. A. Mednick and A. E. Baert (eds) *Prospective Longitudinal Research*, Oxford: Oxford University Press.

Graeff, R. (1993) *Living Dangerously: Young Offenders in Their Own Words*, London: Harper Collins.

Graham, J. and Bowling, B. (1995) *Young People and Crime, Home Office Research Study 145*, London: The Stationery Office.

Hagell, A. and Newburn, T. (1994) *Persistent Young Offenders*, London: Policy Studies Institute.

Howell, N. (1990) *Surviving Fieldwork: A Report of the Advisory Panel on Health and Safety in Fieldwork*, Washington, DC: American Sociological Association.

Jamieson, J., McIvor, G. and Murray, C. (1999) *Understanding Offending among Young People*, Edinburgh: The Stationery Office.

Lawrinson, S. and Harris, J. (1994) 'Violence in research settings – experiences from the front line', *Applied Community Studies* 2, 1: 52–68.

Lee, R. M. (1995) *Dangerous Fieldwork*, Qualitative Research Methods Series 34, London: Sage.

Maruna, S. (1997) 'Desistance and development: the psychosocial process of going straight', paper presented at the British Criminology Conference, Queen's University, Belfast.

—— (1998) 'Deconstructing deviant adaptations: when the "inner-logic" of deviance breaks down', paper presented at the Annual Meeting of the American Society of Criminology, Washington, DC.

Mason, J. (1996) *Qualitative Researching*, London: Sage.

Muncie, J. (1999) *Youth and Crime: A Critical Introduction*, London: Sage.

Pearson, G. (1994) 'Youth, crime and society' in M. Maguire, R. Morgan and R. Reiner (eds) *The Oxford Handbook of Criminology*, Oxford: Clarendon Press.

Renzetti, C. M. and Lee, R. M. (eds) (1993) *Researching Sensitive Topics*, Newbury Park, CA: Sage.

Rex, S. (1997) 'Desistence from offending: experiences of probation', paper presented at the British Criminology Conference, Queen's University, Belfast.

Shover, N. (1985) *Ageing Criminals*, Beverly Hills, CA: Sage.

Sluka, J. A. (1990) 'Participant observation in violent social settings', *Human Organization* 49: 114–26.

Social Work Services Group (1991) *National Standards for Social Work Services in the Criminal Justice System*, Edinburgh: The Scottish Office.

West, D. J. and Farrington, D. P. (1973) *Who Becomes Delinquent?*, London: Heinemann Educational.

—— (1977) *The Delinquent Way of Life*, London: Heinemann Educational.

# 5

# BACTERIA AND BABIES

## A personal reflection on researcher risk in a hospital

*Gloria Lankshear*

## Introduction

Academic research into organisational issues and new technology would seem to provide a safe and, some might even say, boring environment. The purpose of this chapter is to dispel the myth of the sanitised and safe construction of such research by discussing the physical and emotional dangers it can involve. I work in this field as a research fellow on fixed-term contracts. My previous and current contract, both three-year terms, have involved work in hospital settings. This chapter illustrates the dangers which lurk even in the most unexpected settings and uses a reflexive approach to consider notions of safety and danger. Similar to Jamieson in Chapter 4 I argue that planning for research often fails to address some of the dangers experienced in the field and these are often only acknowledged after the project is finished or not until it is well under way.

Lee (1995) brings to the fore the idea that fieldwork can be dangerous, but there are omissions. Lee (1995: 6) says, 'The hazards faced by researchers in Western urban environments are perhaps less striking than those that confront anthropologists. At least the former are spared the problems of disease … ' In fact, this may not be so, especially if conducting research in, for example, hospitals and laboratories, which are increasingly chosen as organisational research sites. Such sites seem to present a safe environment, but this is not always the case. Additionally, Lee (1995) deals in particular with physically dangerous settings. An important point to be highlighted is that there are settings which in themselves are not dangerous, but which may pose an emotional danger to a researcher because of their individual life experience.

I discuss two settings in this chapter, the first is a laboratory involved in testing specimens that presented a physical danger and the second a maternity delivery suite which, for the writer, involved an emotional danger which proved to be more difficult to deal with than anticipated. I would suggest that most researchers, whilst possibly being reflexive, do not publish reflections on their own everyday exposure to danger. It is often 'safer' to leave some issues unspoken, because reporting on such things can expose us to yet other dangers. For instance, it may lead to having to confront painful feelings or leave one open to criticism from colleagues for being subjective.

An illustration of this point is Durkheim's (1897) *Suicide: A Study in Sociology*. This thesis might be more open to criticism if we take into account the fact that the work was undertaken after a close friend of Durkheim's had committed suicide. I have always found it fascinating that the vast majority of those who write about Durkheim and *Suicide* give no background information to show that he had a personal interest in suicide. A rare exception is the work by Lukes (1973) who reports that Victor Hommay, one of Durkheim's closest friends whilst he was a student at the Ecole Normale Supérieure in France, committed suicide in 1886. Durkheim wrote of Hommay after his death:

> ... for I cannot recall any particular circumstance giving birth to a friendship which soon became for me the sweetest intimacy. Throughout our three years at the Ecole, we truly lived the same life; we worked in the same room, we pursued the same studies, we even spent together almost all our days of freedom. In the course of those long conversations, what plans did we not make for each other! I can now no longer recall them without sadness and bitterness.
>
> (Lukes 1973: 49)

Durkheim publishes no foreword on his personal interest in suicide. A critic might argue that as suicide at that time was against the law, a crime in the eyes of the church and considered a cause for moral outrage, then he might have had a more than good reason to attempt to prove that suicide was not the fault of the individual, but of society.

If sociologists such as Durkheim did not declare 'interest' or potential areas of bias, it is unsurprising that we, as researchers, protect ourselves by not publicly acknowledging similar interests. Where personal biography interweaves with research topics there is indeed potential for conflict. Such aspects of danger, however, if publicised and discussed, can promote awareness of the possible pitfalls to be negotiated by those involved in field research. Publication of actual experiences, rather than 'corridor talk', can be a valuable resource for researchers who might be considering entry to potentially 'dangerous' environments. There needs to be a greater recognition that emotions are present in the public world of work and that although they can present difficulties they can also help our understanding of social settings.

The definition of danger used in this chapter is, 'exposure to chance of evil, injury or loss; peril; risk' (*Webster's English Dictionary* 1996). The chapter describes and discusses two research settings which on first examination did not appear to present any potential dangers. The laboratory initially appeared safe because of ignorance of the finer detail of the work processes carried out within the setting. The maternity suite presented problems related to the interweaving of biography and the subject of research, which, although known to me, presented more difficulty than had been envisaged. In both cases the way that my experience of danger contributed to understanding the settings is emphasised.

## The laboratory setting – an experience of physical danger

The first study was of a laboratory information system which had been implemented in the laboratory of a large hospital in the two months prior to the beginning of the research. In order to put into perspective the place of the system in the daily work of the laboratory an ethnographic study was commenced. This involved observing the setting as a non-participant observer, shadowing the laboratory technicians, asking questions and trying to understand the implicit rules they used to order their work. The laboratory was organised into 'benches', each of which dealt with a different type or group of specimens. Examples of the types of specimens that arrived in the laboratory and had to be tested were: bloods, wound swabs, faecal samples, urine, genital swabs. The more infectious specimens such as tuberculosis (TB), diphtheria, H.I.V. and E Coli 0157 were dealt with in separate rooms into which I did not go. I spent five days on a number of benches 'shadowing' workers and learning what they did. I made a process flow diagram of the work and checked this with the staff, together with diagrams of the parts of the laboratory I had examined, showing the siting of computers.

I was told that I must don a white coat every time I entered the laboratory and on leaving the laboratory I must remove the coat and wash my hands thoroughly. There were numerous danger signs around the laboratory, skull and crossbones signs, and detailed instructions above the sinks on how to wash one's hands. However, no one had mentioned the subject of Health and Safety until the following throw-away remark by the Director of the unit. When this incident occurred I was only a few days into the research. At the time of the interaction I was busy carrying samples of bodily substances to a bench for testing:

Director:    You have done Health and Safety I assume.
G.L.:        Oh, yes of course.

This was not exactly true but my immediate reaction to the question was my concern to protect my access to the unit. Negotiations for access had been carried out with a senior member of the laboratory. Explanations were provided to management and other staff about the process of ethnographic research and the type of questions the researcher would be asking the technicians. Once approval was given the research began. In what I thought was a 'good' approach to ethnography, I tried to fit into the laboratory and lend a hand where possible. Actually, as the work is highly skilled, such shows of willingness were confined to fetching and carrying. But I remained unaware of the Health and Safety training which should have been completed. On beginning the study I had not seriously considered the health risk aspect of the fieldwork and none of the people I had discussed the research with in advance – office manager, consultant, laboratory manager, etc. – had mentioned it either. In retrospect, I was perhaps rather naive and too accepting of the hospital as a 'safe' environment.

After the director's remark I went back to the bench and asked one of the laboratory staff what he meant. I was told that before they started work in the laboratory all staff had to have had injections for Hepatitis B; other injections were voluntary, diphtheria, tuberculosis and typhoid being among them. On further enquiry I found that most of the laboratory staff had had all the recommended injections. In fact I was given contrary information from different staff and was then informed that there had been two diphtheria cases in the last two months in other similar laboratories (not this one).

### Now eat your sandwiches!

One distinctive aspect of the experience of work in the laboratory was the number of different smells vying for supremacy. Most of them were very unpleasant, many of them positively disgusting, to the point of making one feel physically sick. When I mentioned this to a technician he replied:

'Oh yes, we don't notice most smells now, or they don't worry us, you get used to it. But when we have parties of people being shown around some do faint, actually pass out. You can see them going, you try to catch them before they fall.'

The revolting smells were a constant reminder of the presence, however well contained, of dangerous bacteria on the site. During the first three or four days (even before the Director's remark) I was worried about eating my sandwiches at lunchtime. Although I carefully took off the laboratory coat and washed my hands as instructed, the thought of touching food when I had been in the laboratory was unpleasant. Even though I was not handling specimens I felt that bacteria could fall on to the bench and I might have inadvertently picked them up. At each bench bacteria are taken from the specimen bottles in which they arrive and transferred to uniformly-sized dishes where they are cultured. In some instances, later in the process they were lifted off one medium on to another. Being invisible you were never certain where they were. Also the smells were so repellent at first that I was quite put off my food.

The faecal bench was particularly interesting. There was a special hooded chimney which was used when the specimens were 'plated'. The objective of using the chimney was to draw the bad smells out of the laboratory. This chimney was fairly new. The laboratory assistant working on the bench said that on one occasion in the past, a technician had to keep leaving the laboratory for five-minute spells or he would have been sick because of the 'bad' smell. This indicates the way staff never really become immune to the repugnant aspects of the setting, and neither did I.

Staff spent one month on each bench in turn, thus maintaining their skill levels on different benches. Staff said that this meant that the benches perceived as dealing with more monotonous work were 'shared out'. Although no one actually mentioned this aspect, it also meant that the more 'unpleasant' benches were shared out. When speaking to different staff they all said that at some point they had been ill when working on the faecal bench. An excerpt from one of the tape transcriptions shows a typical experience:

Technician:   I caught a viral infection from the faeces bench, that's why we have the hood there. It was a viral infection that goes round hospitals. It has been on the news again because they have to shut wards down occasionally. It is a very vicious little virus and can make you violently sick … I think most of us in here have caught it from that bench. I was ill for three days … I am really fit but it really pulled me down. But on these benches we know what we are handling and therefore we are very careful and that is why you see everyone washing their hands. So long as you're aware of the risks.

G.L.:   But being aware didn't stop you getting that did it?

Technician:   No, but since they brought in the hood that has eliminated a lot of it. With bugs on a plate it is quite safe so long as you don't touch it and put your fingers in your mouth. Right, this is another lady on Wallace Ward …

The technician soon changed the subject from illness caught in the laboratory and back to his work. It almost seemed as if he did not want to acknowledge that there was a danger of catching any of the diseases or other 'bugs' they dealt with on a daily basis. In line with what I found to be the informal rules understood by the laboratory workers, he diverted attention away from the threat of danger and brought the conversation politely, but firmly, back to the 'routine' work. When researching workers in the nuclear industry Zonabend (1993: 3) found that workers reported that they saw the risk to themselves as nil, 'Consequently any questions about danger incurred or risks run will be rejected, denied, or parried in some way.' I seemed to be meeting a similar reaction. Zonabend (1993: 4) also argued, 'it is reasonable to suppose that what is involved here is a way of the speaker not saying, or not hearing himself say, something he wishes to conceal.' Therefore, a level of self-deceit is involved, with the result that danger becomes an unmentionable topic.

After being on the faecal bench for the first time, the next morning I woke up and thought I had stomach pains! I think this was related to a fear of catching something because I was perfectly well when I got up. However, these feelings of constant threat made me aware that the staff must be perpetually vigilant and physically self-aware. For example, there could be no sucking or chewing of pens, no biting of finger nails or touching of one's face or mouth. Also, strict adherence to the rules about hand washing was necessary and I found that I became meticulous about this, washing my hands before going to the lavatory as well as after! However, staff did break the rules sometimes. For instance, I eventually found out that the staff were recommended to wear rubber gloves, but few did, except on the faecal bench. This absence of gloves whilst undertaking most of the bench work was another indication of a denial of danger.

Contradiction in reported levels of safety in the laboratory was common between laboratory workers and, indeed, within individual accounts. For instance, on one occasion when I was observing the blood bench, a technician was going to test whether one of the samples contained something which he argued could be 'quite dangerous, quite pathogenic or a more harmless type of stuff'. I used this as an opportunity to ask him whether he had been ill working on that bench. He said:

'No, people very rarely get laboratory acquired infections. They do happen. A couple of years back somebody was dealing with Neisseria Meningitidis, a meningococcus, and they got meningitis from it because they were making a heavy suspension on a plate and they created a lot of aerosols and breathed it all in. So whenever we have one of those now, we deal with it in a safety cabinet. The same goes for E Coli 0157, because somebody in the laboratory actually got that disease.'

Thus the technician in one breath told me that people rarely caught laboratory infections and, in the next, mentioned two instances where they had. However, he also, in line with his peers, quickly changed the subject away from disease and back to work.

Looking through my field notes I found it interesting that none of the staff, even when I was spending days in the laboratory shadowing them, suggested that I should have injections against disease. As an illustration here is an excerpt from the transcript of a conversation with one of the more senior staff who had worked in the laboratory for eleven years:

*G.L.:* I am surprised people do not get even more diseases than they do.

*Senior Technician:* We are immunised against a lot of stuff: TB, typhoid, diphtheria, rubella.

*G.L.:* I am not immunised against those!

*Senior Technician:* You don't work in a lab though.

*G.L.:* I am very close though.

*Senior Technician:* I am just going to take some of this growth …

Once again the subject of disease and level of risk was avoided and the job in hand continued.

Clerical staff also came into contact with the specimens, but only in the reception area. This was another 'white coat and washing' area that is considered a 'dirty area'. Here the specimens were received either from the hospital through the 'pod' system (a shute system with pods that carry specimens around the hospital) or from outside sources, such as general practitioners. The specimens arrived in different kinds of containers such as glass bottles, phials and tubes and although they were usually contained in a plastic envelope together with an identifying card, sometimes the envelope had disappeared. Clerical staff had to ensure that the sample was matched with the correct accompanying card and some samples had to be removed from their plastic outer envelope. This meant they had to handle potentially 'dirty' containers. As clerical staff were only on duty in reception for one hour periods, they did not have designated half-hour breaks for tea. However, they were still in contact with potentially dangerous substances and there were certain procedures to follow if they should drop anything in reception. The following was reported to me by a clerk:

'I took something out of a pod and you know the bags are supposed to be sealed. Well as I took it out, it wasn't sealed. The blood went. There was no way I could stop it so I just jumped back … . Splat! Blood. You are not allowed to touch it, that's what I am getting at. You go to the blood bench and tell somebody round there. That's your responsibility over. They will come round and put crystals on it. Which solidifies it. Then I believe it has to be a senior who comes round and moves it.

Sometimes you drop a wee. That's not so crucial and you've got this here. [She showed a bottle, unlabelled.] But you are supposed to let the benches know. Spillages are out of our area really.'

Although the clerical staff told me that spillages were 'out of their area', and although they did not have to deal with them after they had happened, they were still a potential area of risk and danger to the clerical staff. However, these staff did not appear to take much notice of this dangerous aspect of their work. One of the clerks told me in a very matter-of-fact way about the procedures to be followed if a TB specimen came out of its protective wrapping. It is important to remember that tuberculosis is a highly contagious disease which can be contracted through inhaling or touching the bacillus.

Clerk:     If you get a TB that arrives through the courier system that's come out of the bag, you must tell James [Head Laboratory Officer] because James is very hot on that. Anything that's got danger of infection must be secured, if it's not you let him know and he sorts it out.

G.L.:       What will James do?

Clerk:     James is keeping a record of it and James would contact the sender and give them what for. Because basically you could be endangering a lot of people, the porter bringing it, and it could contaminate the system. A few weeks ago we had one of these [blood]. It shattered. We put it down and blood was leaking and we did not know if it happened here or in the system. They had to shut down the whole system and clean it.

This clerk, however, did not mention the danger to the clerical staff, or make any personal remarks about danger.

The majority of clerical staff seemed to play down the presence of danger in relation to their work in the laboratory. This was illustrated when a clerk was showing me how urines were put in the trays. She told me that rubber gloves – . which she was wearing at the time – should be worn when doing this type of work. I saw her the next day and asked if she usually wore gloves and she said, 'I should wear gloves, as I was saying, but they make my hands swell, so unless I have got really bad cuts on my hands, then yes I would, but in this instance I'm not.' At various times I asked the clerical staff whether they wore gloves and most did not. Only one consistently wore gloves and said, 'I don't know how they can't wear gloves. They think it's funny that I wear gloves, but at the end of the day if anything happens at least I am protected.' When I did observe staff wearing gloves, I was quite aghast at the amount of dirt observable on the gloves at the end of their one-hour shift in reception. In general the clerical staff did not appear to recognise the dangers they encountered during their work, although they were handling specimens which sometimes escaped from their containers and wrappings; because these staff members ignored risk I did not initially recognise it or perceive it to be important in their workplace procedures.

### Invisible danger

Contemplation of the possibility of danger when embarking on social research in laboratories or in hospitals is probably not common. Initially I assumed the hospital to be a place of cleanliness and safety, a research site free from threat. Although the potential threat of malaria or similar tropical diseases is mentioned in the anthropological literature, the study of technology in one's own culture would seem innocuous in comparison. Even a remote possibility of catching diseases such as diphtheria, which have mainly been eradicated in modern industrial nations, had not been anticipated prior to entering the field. However, danger defined as 'exposure to chance of evil, injury or loss; peril; risk' was certainly present in the laboratory setting. Serious threats were faced with little protection and this was the case not only for me as researcher but also, interestingly, for the workers who were often put at risk by their work.

The only person in this research setting who contemplated any risk to me was the Director of the unit. Others had not even mentioned the possibility of risk. When I went back and asked senior hospital staff (other than the Director) whether I should have the 'compulsory' Hepatitis B injection and the other recommended injections the opinion was that it probably 'was not worth it'. They seemed to disregard the risk to me. I was then in a dilemma. Should I have the potentially 'nasty' injections or not? Should I remain in the setting but refrain from carrying out what I considered 'real ethnography'? This would involve confining myself to observation and questions only and concentrating on the office side of the laboratory rather than exploring the dirty, smelly, potentially risky bench work. It is possible that these kinds of threat were part of the reason why I could find relatively little recorded ethnographic work related to similar laboratories.

In the event I did not have the injections. I carried on with the ethnographic study but did not touch anything unless wearing rubber gloves. In a way, similar to the laboratory workers themselves, by not having the injections I was also denying the potential dangers present in the setting. However, some risks are not worth taking in the name of social research. I decided that I would minimise threat to myself by not going into the 'dangerous area' where the most infectious disease samples were dealt with. Provision for my own safety was left for me alone to consider and decide upon, whereas the risk to the research participants, both from their work itself and arising from taking part in the study, was assessed and planned for in a variety of ways. This illustrates the way that social research-ers can often find themselves operating outwith formal health and safety frameworks in the field.

## The hidden dangers of the delivery suite

The second site I wish to discuss involved a different kind of danger: emotional rather than physical. The emotional danger present in any setting, differently from physical danger, will vary according to the researcher's personality and life experience. As researchers we do not always have the luxury of choosing our research sites; we might be geographically constrained because of time and money; our topic might mean we act within narrow confines; we might join a project where the site is already a *fait accompli*. This site was an example of this, having been already negotiated. The focus of my work here was new technology and the work process related to professionals and semi-professionals. Of particular interest was the design and introduction of a 'decision support system'. This is a computer monitoring system on which medical staff in the delivery suite record details of the birth as it is in progress, with the intention that the system will make suggestions for management of the patient's care. The site was the central delivery suite of a large hospital, which delivered the majority of babies (over four thousand a year) for a large city and surrounding area. Although the site had moved, it was the same hospital at which my babies had delivered. There were long-serving staff in the maternity suite who had been present when my babies were born, one sixteen and the other twenty-one years ago.

Once again an ethnographic approach was being taken. Although ethical considerations meant that the midwives were not actually followed into the rooms where they attended delivering women, I observed the rest of their work. The research involved asking the midwives questions, sitting in their work areas, listening to conversations, absorbing the atmosphere and asking them about the technology they used and how decisions were made during labour. The midwives were friendly, fairly welcoming (if initially worried that I was undertaking time-and-motion studies), and easy company. This appeared on the surface a 'plum' research site: comfortable, warm, tea and toast and company always available. Of course even in such 'easy' sites, as a researcher one never 'relaxes', there is a tension, an awareness of the importance of 'fitting in', of being liked, or at least not disliked. But no apparent danger here; no physical danger.

However, on this occasion for me there was danger, and its nature was emotional. The danger related to my biography and some painful personal experiences. I will try to give an account here of how my biography and research work overlapped and caused a threat to my sense of self. This account is very personal and contains what may appear superfluous details, but they are deliberately included to give a glimpse of the kind of painful memories and emotions which were experienced during the research. Far too often, research findings appear to be sanitised, as if emotions that a specific environment engenders are somehow invalid and should be hidden. In fact researchers' emotional responses can aid the understanding of the phenomena under examination and may raise important unanticipated insights into the research topic.

I am typing up my field notes, which on this day refer to a woman with high blood pressure. I have become aware that this condition is viewed very seriously by clinical staff and I have the blood pressure readings for the woman concerned in front of me. I myself had high blood pressure when pregnant and I decide to look for my own notes, to see how my blood pressure during my second pregnancy compared with the woman in my study. These are filed away at home in an 'official' brown envelope that all expectant mothers are given to take with them to the different clinics they attend. I find my notes and see that my blood pressure readings were quite high. However, I subsequently had a 'normal' delivery of a healthy baby girl. I find tucked into the notes a hand-written page torn out of a notebook, on which I had written a few details about the birth. They were about the progress of labour and other details, and ended with, 'baby delivered at 5.20 am by Midwife Brown, nice midwives.' By coincidence, the chief collaborator in the delivery suite is currently named Brown and I take my notes into the suite and mention the coincidence. She laughs and says, 'Well, I was working here then and as far as I know there was no-one else named Brown. Let's check the Birth Register.' This is done and yes, she is the midwife who delivered my baby sixteen years ago. But no danger yet, I had actually noted 'nice midwives'.

What did return was my memory of attending a registrar appointment two days before the birth, and my saying to him that I did not want to be induced (have any medical interference aimed at starting the labour). I had even gone so far as to take my husband with me into the consultation for 'protection'. However, once in the consulting room the registrar had asked me to get on the couch so he could examine me. He then did an internal examination which was not comfortable and said, 'Well that should get you going. It won't be long before we see you.' He was correct, I started labour thirty hours later. However, he did not say what he had done and I certainly was not sure.

In the event I produced a healthy baby. However, I remained resentful of what I considered a blatant disregard for my wishes. I really 'hated' that registrar for his interference – real or imaginary. This procedure is very unlikely to be used now. Artificial rupture of the membranes (which I had suspected) is even less common. Waiting until the cervix is 'ripe' (the technical term), which means waiting until the birth process starts naturally, when it is more likely to result in a normal birth, seems to have become the orthodox way to proceed. I thought at the time, and the research situation brought this back to me, that the internal examination, undertaken with no explanation, was a blatant disregard of my wishes. It is difficult to describe the feelings of resentment I still feel towards that registrar, his arrogance and disregard for my feelings and even my safety. However, it is not something I have ever talked about. All the feelings of powerlessness and anger engendered by the experience came back to me whilst in the research site. On occasion during the study, midwives made comments about the high-handed attitude of some of the registrars, which, without my previous experience, I might have taken as just 'personal animosity'.

The more difficult pain I had to face, again relived during the study, was related to the birth of my first child (now twenty-one) who was born in the same hospital. I was aged thirty, with high blood pressure. Therefore I was induced at term, given syntocinon to speed up labour, and an epidural (a spinal anaesthetic) to bring down the blood pressure. However, at that time cardiotocographs (CTGs) were uncommon so there was no electronic monitoring of the baby's heartbeat to discern foetal distress. The birth appeared to go well, epidurals certainly make childbirth pain free, and a six-and-a-half pound baby boy was the result. My son was whisked away for a few hours because he was jaundiced, but I was told it was nothing to worry about. He was returned (I assumed) in perfect health. I breastfed for nine months, did all the 'good' mothering I could, but was not sure how he was progressing. He did not seem to smile as other babies did. I was told by the health visitors that babies did not smile when really young, and that he was fine. I had no experience of small babies or children; I did not know what 'normal' was and most of the childcare books I read said that babies and small children develop at their own pace. When he was three and not speaking as I thought he should, I asked for him to be tested for deafness, but he was not deaf. He had no ability to concentrate and was constantly 'on the move', but he was physically extremely fit and never ill.

I felt there was something wrong with my son but, after a few visits, the medical attitude of 'fussy mother' kept me away from general practitioners. I thought that perhaps I was just not very good at coping. I could not have paid more attention to my child but a health visitor remarked about his lack of speech, 'Well, if you put his toys or sweets out of reach and only give them to him when he asks, he will soon speak.' And, 'if every time you go for a walk you tell him colours and say things like "look at the green grass" he will soon learn colours'. Needless to say, these things, which I was already doing, did not work. My child went to school at five and I was told he was fine.

My son had been at school a year when the headmistress, on noticing his lack of progress with reading, asked to see me. She said that she would teach him personally and gave her assurances that she would 'have him reading by the end of term'. Her confidence was comforting and another year passed. However, at the end of the year she very sadly told me that she had not succeeded. She thought there must be a problem and I should see a paediatrician. My heart sank. The headmistress, who had been so confident, had given up. It was at last acknowledged by 'somebody' – the first person other than myself – that something was wrong. I will never forget that meeting and that day. I can picture it now and writing about it makes me cry. (In a train to a conference with colleagues – rather surreptitiously I wipe the tears away.) Of course I already knew the truth about my son but because I had been continuously fobbed off and because the reality of not having a perfect child is so hard to face, I had buried my head in the sand and hoped. Even now I am not sure what else I could have done. Later, I paid for private reading lessons (having tried hard myself) and this resulted in some progress. Eventually I went privately to an educational psychologist who labelled dyslexia and spatial inability, although I knew my son's problems were more serious. Later he attended a 'special' school for slow learners.

What has all this to do with the delivery suite? Have you not guessed? I had long suspected that whatever damage had been done to my child's brain might have been due to events around the time of his birth. I had gone over and over in my mind what I might have done wrong, what had happened during his birth. Now, undertaking research in the delivery suite, I was privy to clinical knowledge about childbirth, to the difficulty of medical decision making, to the unscientific nature of knowledge now – let alone twenty-one years ago. Being in the research setting brought back painful memories that I did not want to confront. It made me aware of dangers I had not known of during my pregnancy.

Now, in the unit I was studying, women could not have epidurals without also having a CTG, which monitors the foetal heartbeat and the maternal contractions. Thus the baby is constantly checked for signs of distress and if there are problems remedial action can be taken. Having access to this information through my research made me recognise the possible effect of my epidural and wonder whether different decisions could have been taken about my baby's birth. However, I also recognised that knowledge had moved on from my experience of twenty-one years ago. Perhaps the best had been done under the circumstances, but although I acknowledged this, I still felt sad that such technology had not been in common use, in time for my birth experience.

I also began to reflect on my lack of knowledge about high blood pressure and wished that I had known more about the dangers of having this condition. I felt that one of the staff who provided my antenatal care might have made more clear to me the dangers, not only to myself but to the unborn baby. Or perhaps I should have pursued the subject myself and read more about high blood pressure and its effects. I suffered feelings of self-blame and uncertainty; perhaps I should have rested more when heavily pregnant and it was all my fault? All of these thoughts and emotions were revisited, now backed by knowledge I was gaining on the research project. Tears were privately shed, but I told no one of my self-reflection.

Another disturbing aspect of the research that made me feel uncomfortable was the tendency of some of the staff to make comments on the test results of the technology I was studying. Remarks which to them were just 'throw away' comments made me once again reflect on the place of new technology. One of the pieces of equipment being used in the delivery suite was a blood-gas testing machine. Immediately after the baby was born a piece of the umbilical cord was placed in a dish and blood from the vein and the artery were tested. The level of gas found in these blood samples could indicate whether the foetus had been starved of oxygen and hence whether the baby required special attention. (The test cannot tell if the baby has been permanently damaged by any lack of oxygen.) Nothing was said by midwives about how, if there was lack of oxygen, this might affect the baby. Comments were made at times, however, by auxiliary nurses, if the results were higher or lower than average. For instance, on one occasion, when a result was higher than normal an auxiliary nurse remarked that baby might grow up to be 'super intelligent'. Conversely, after a low result another auxiliary made the comment, 'But will he ever be a brain surgeon, that's what I'd like to know.' I am not aware of the results of research on the correlation between high blood-gas level and intelligence in children, but it could be significant. If that test had been available and had been done on my baby, I might have been able to find out whether there was any likelihood that damage could have occurred during his birth. Not for blame purposes, or litigation, but just to know. Perhaps then the professionals might have believed me when I said all was not well with my baby.

## Reflections on my experience of emotional danger

So how did this personal background affect the research process? First, it meant that at times the process was painful for me. It made me confront and remember things I preferred to block from my mind. Also, it generated questions but could not give me answers. My view of and feelings about my life and past were threatened. The research was without doubt dangerous emotionally for me. Second, it meant that I felt a personal connection to the research and was more committed to it as an important area of investigation. Looking at technology and how it influenced decisions was not an abstract concept for me because I knew that if a wrong decision was made lives could be affected. Statistics appear scientific and objective, but being one of the statistics brings a broader under-standing of what those numbers mean in human terms. Third, it meant that I had to be careful how I analysed and interpreted data and how I reported the literature. I became more aware of my personal beliefs about birth. For instance, I had always thought that natural childbirth was best and that clinicians should err on the side of caution when making the decision to do a caesarean. Now I began to question these beliefs and sometimes wondered why caesarean procedures were not carried out sooner. The thought of any mother having to face what I had faced perhaps clouded my view. Therefore I had to work hard to prevent my personal experience from affecting my work, and I was particularly careful to remain reflexive and to discuss the data with my research colleagues.

Finally, I am sure my insight strengthened my understanding of the feelings of the professionals. Actually being present when decisions were being made about how to proceed with difficult births, witnessing the impossible nature of some of these decisions, experiencing the professional worry about the outcome and seeing the emotions of staff, revealed much to me about decision making. It provided an understanding of why, even though 'decision support systems' are thought to be flawed in areas of complicated decision making, professionals might still welcome them. I do not think I would have understood their interest in expert systems if I had not had my own experience of a difficult birth process. I could understand that the use of such a system might not be so much about protecting staff from litigation, but provided another tool that could help avoid the relatively low, but highly important, incidence of damage to babies during birth. I was therefore able to see what the literature presents as conflicting views by both re-experiencing the feelings of the disempowered patient but also seeing from the 'other side' the powerful logic and rationale driving the 'medical model' of patient care.

A different kind of danger, but once again a personal danger in this second research site, was the danger of appearing a loser. How would I cope if staff in the unit knew I had a child labelled a 'slow learner' and if they knew of my first birth experience? There were two possible ramifications of this: first they might feel sorry for me which would damage both my self-image and my professional image. Second, they might feel uncomfortable that I was studying the fine decisions made during birth, which can result in damaged babies. They might feel I was not suitable to study this topic or that I would have a one-sided view on the subject of birth technology.

Consequently, I did not reveal to anyone at the site that my first child had any problems. I could not face the loss of self-image that I suspected would result. I did not regret my decision because at times during the study, nursing auxiliaries made illuminating comments which I am sure would not have been made had they known my personal details. There were remarks made about the safety of babies during birth and the role of technology, and judgemental comments about some of the women who were being delivered in the suite and their families. In some instances there were comments about patients being 'thick' or stupid. In other instances the auxiliaries made negative remarks about the personal hygiene of patients and their families and this was often related to the idea that they must be 'thick'. These revealed a lot about auxiliary attitudes to some of their patients. Perhaps if I had labelled myself in their eyes, I might have missed much illuminating data.

## Discussion and conclusions

The research settings discussed above each presented potential hazards for the qualitative social researcher. The first site involved physical danger which, although initially unrecognised, was comparatively easy to confront once identified. My position was as an outsider and visitor and as the laboratory workers did not see me as a colleague, they did not consider me to be at risk. In retrospect this is not surprising because they did not openly acknowledge that there was any real threat to themselves. If asked a direct question on this point they changed the subject. Perhaps their way of coping with potential daily danger was denial of the importance of the risks.

Reflecting further on this, how did I resolve the threats to myself? In a way, I denied and avoided the issue by not having the injections and by subsequently avoiding the more 'dangerous' areas of the laboratory. This did not compromise my work in this setting because I had already completed the study of the laboratory benches when I discovered my lack of medical precautions. If I had to enter this part of the laboratory in the future I would have the necessary and recommended injections. So, should researcher safety be more thoroughly investigated prior to fieldwork by grant holders and research leaders? Although the answer to the question must be yes, the apparently innocuous nature of a hospital research site, although illusory, led to the failure by both the grant holders and myself to carry out any such prior investigation. In retrospect, it is difficult to know how one would have dealt with this issue, because to draw too much attention to it might have jeopardised entry to the research site. This would then have possibly necessitated protracted negotiations for access to a new site, difficult to accommodate once research is under way and time deadlines must be met.

The second site involved emotional hazard, which I found far more difficult to deal with. My experience highlights the problems created by research settings which link with our own biographies. Should the rape victim study rape; should the woman whose baby has possibly been damaged during birth study a delivery suite; should a person whose friend committed suicide study suicide? There is danger for these individuals both on an emotional level and because they may be open to professional criticism about the objectivity of the research. Conversely, there is also an argument that the very fact that the subject is so important to them may improve perceptions and understanding. Also increased might be the level of enthusiasm, endeavour and commitment both within the research site and to the topic in general. Kleinman (1991: 184) points out the positive aspect that:

> Fieldworkers do not think of feelings as disturbances that impede objectivity and thus should be overridden. Rather, feelings become resources for understanding the phenomena under study.

If the research is undertaken with a colleague or in a team the over-subjectivity 'danger' can be more easily overcome. The personal emotional danger is more problematic. Those undertaking fieldwork, funding bodies and committees providing ethical clearance for research, customarily guard against damage to the participants in the research, but how the researcher may be affected is usually forgotten. Research can be a lonely business, even on the few occasions when we have the 'luxury' of a research team; meetings may be few and far between and practical matters take precedence. This is not social work where team members can seek mutual help and there is little thought of emotional support. The research culture tends to be more individualistic. Kleinman (1991: 192), in explaining why she did not look to colleagues for support during her research, argues:

> Academia is supposed to constitute a community of scholars. Yet this is undermined by individuation (doing something others have never done) and individualism (working on one's own), which are taken seriously and put into practice. Hence I assumed that admitting self-doubt was unacceptable.

I am a very private person, by which I mean that I do not easily share my personal problems with others. So how did I cope with the emotional aspect of this research? I have not 'shared' the emotional difficulty I confronted either with co-workers on the project or with research participants. It is still too painful and speaking about it would make me feel vulnerable. I do not want pity and I do not want to be seen as different. Only one person in my department knows about my personal biography and was perceptive enough to realise how it might present difficulties in the research process. Early on in the study she asked how I was coping. I found this short discussion helpful and supportive. However, I would not instigate such a discussion myself. My way of dealing with the emotion was to confront it alone, when I could not avoid it. I too used the strategy of avoidance. So why am I writing this? I think there is a dearth of literature on the emotional aspects of research. Whilst we are students we are often encouraged to be reflexive, but once we embark upon paid research careers the reflexive aspect of our work is more guarded and private. For those such as myself who are contract researchers, it is important to be seen as professional and 'objective' as we know the image we present is crucial to gaining our next contract. This aspect of the risk of gaining the next contract, therefore, conflicts with open reflexivity.

Emotion work used to be an under-researched area of occupations. However, since Hochschild's (1983) study there has been a gradual increase in its recognition. I originally thought of it, in relation to social work and nursing, as an undervalued and under-discussed part of the work process. Then Fineman's (1993) text drew my attention to the validity of acknowledging emotions in all kinds of organisations. Young and Lee (1996) further acknowledged the emotion work undertaken during and after fieldwork. They argued that ' ... the first person fieldwork accounts capture the dissonance between what fieldworkers feel they ought to feel and what they admit to feeling.' They continue, 'the difficulties or the stress portrayed in these accounts reflect the emotion work undertaken in attempting to manage the tensions between involvement, comfort and identification. We suspect that tensions of this kind are inherent in fieldwork' (Young and Lee 1966: 11).

It could be argued that there is not enough acknowledgement of the solitary nature of research and the need to support those carrying it out, but who can safely bring this out into the open? Those applying for funding are often so busy and involved in survival that they cannot build in either the time or the funding required for such support. Those carrying out research are usually funded on short-term contracts, in which I include any finite term contract – those working on a three-year contract feel just as vulnerable as those on shorter-term contracts – and as such are going to resist opening a 'can of worms'. By this I mean that they are not going to bring up issues which might result in future employers questioning their ability to carry out the work. They may be considered personally inadequate, either for requiring support during the research, or for declaring some personal interest which might be construed as giving them a predisposition to show bias in a research project. In spite of these hazards, recognition of how personal biography can present danger to the researcher needs to be more widely recognised and widespread publication of reflexive writings may help with this recognition. Such accounts should be seen as contributions to a shared learning process rather than criticised as unscientific and unprofessional.

There is no definitive answer to the personal difficulties that might confront individual researchers because of their personal biographies. Each individual has to find his or her own answer. Differing attitudes towards privacy and how to handle emotions might mean that for some researchers denial is the only way of coping; others might find support from their family or friends, from peers or their research team. Some may be able to gain support at a distance from peers at other institutions, for instance via e-mail. I have found this type of networking very useful. However, recognition from colleagues and co-researchers that the research site is not always easily or comfortably negotiated is important. For this reason, some prior discussion of the possible pitfalls would be a valuable item of discussion between all management and research staff at the beginning of a new project. Himmelweit (1998: 552) said that:

> Following from Hochschild's pioneering study a whole literature on 'emotional work' has developed to characterise paid work in which workers have to regulate their own emotions to perform the job properly.

Perhaps in the future fieldwork will begin to be considered more seriously as emotionally challenging work.

## Bibliography

Durkheim, E. (1952) *Suicide: a Study in Sociology*, trans. John A. Spalding and George Simpson, edited with an introduction by George Simpson, London: Routledge & Kegan Paul.

Fineman, S. (ed.) (1993) *Emotion in Organisations*, London: Sage.

Himmelweit, S. (1998) 'Gender, care and emotions', extended review, *Work, Employment and Society*, Vol. 12, No. 3, pp. 551–53.

Hochschild, A. R. (1983) *The Managed Heart: Commercialisation of Human Feeling*, Berkeley: University of California Press.

James, V. and Gabe, J. (eds) (1996) *Health and the Sociology of Emotions*, Oxford: Blackwell.

Kleinman, S. (1991) 'Fieldworkers' feelings: what we feel, who we are, how we analyse' in W. B. Shaffir and R. A. Stebbins (eds) *Experiencing Fieldwork*, Newbury Park, CA: Sage.

Lee, R. M. (1995) *Dangerous Fieldwork*, Thousand Oaks, CA: Sage.

Lukes, S. (1973) *Emile Durkheim. His Life and Work: A Historical and Critical Study*, London: Penguin.

Young, E. H. and Lee, M. R. (1996) 'Fieldworker feelings as data: "emotion work" and "feeling rules" in first person accounts of sociological fieldwork' in V. James and J. Gabe (eds) *Health and the Sociology of Emotions*, Oxford: Blackwell.

Zonabend, F. (1993) *The Nuclear Peninsula*, Cambridge: Cambridge University Press.

# 6

# DANGEROUS LIAISONS

## Auto/biography in research and research writing

*Gayle Letherby*

## Introduction

In this chapter I explore some of the emotional and professional dangers of autobiographical research writing. I also consider how the dangers involved can contribute to greater academic insight (both substantive and methodological) rather than just being obstacles to avoid and overcome. The chapter discusses my research on involuntary childlessness and the autobiographical nature of my approach to this topic. Unlike Lankshear (Chapter 5), who is a contract researcher and thus constrained by the projects she is employed to undertake, my field is a research area I chose because of my own life experiences. Thus I am concerned here with highlighting the risk and threats a researcher may experience when they make choices about studying their own situation, along with that of their participants. The chapter also develops Lankshear's discussion of the problems of 'writing in' one's emotions and personal experience for the consumption of others.

The chapter begins by explaining my research area and personal motivations towards it and outlines the use of autobiography in social science research. I then discuss the nature of my research relationships with participants and the personal dangers involved in studying a topic which is close to one's personal experience. In particular, I develop the idea of research as emotional work for both the researched and the researcher and discuss the personal costs of this labour. Finally, I examine the issue of the autobiographical research product and the dangers that publication and public consumption can incur. I argue that there are positive and negative aspects of using the self as a resource in research. Issues of gender, specifically in terms of me as researcher and me as writer, are addressed throughout the chapter.

## Personal and academic influences

In 1984, after several months of 'trying' I became pregnant. At sixteen weeks I miscarried. I have never (to my knowledge) been pregnant since. Three years later I began a single honour Sociology degree and from the very beginning I knew that in my final-year research project I wanted to focus on the experience of miscarriage. I felt this was an experience that was often misunderstood and negated. The small-scale qualitative study that I undertook confirmed this (Letherby 1993).

Whilst studying New Reproductive Technologies (NRTs) on my undergraduate degree course, I became particularly interested in the politics and experience of 'infertility' treatment. I felt that the way the feminist and social science literature focused on the medicalisation of this aspect of women's and men's experience ignored much of the social and emotional experience of 'infertility' and/or 'involuntary childlessness'. My doctoral research was concerned with these issues. My study group comprised self-selecting individuals who defined themselves as 'involuntarily childless' and/or 'infertile' at that time or at some time in the past. I interviewed twenty-four women (up to five times) and eight men (seven of whom were partners of women I interviewed) who defined themselves this way. I corresponded with another forty-one women and several men wrote their own comments at the bottom of letters from these women. From inception to writing up, each of my projects were informed by my feminist identity and by my academic background as a sociologist. In this chapter I focus on my postgraduate experience and so, unless otherwise stated, reference is to my experience of researching 'infertility' and 'involuntary childlessness'.[1]

Early in my undergraduate career I became interested in methodology. Like Payne et al. (1989: 267) I felt that:

> Methodology is not a specialist topic: it is simply the practice of sociology itself.

Throughout my first degree I was fascinated by all things methodological and read everything I could about ethics, values and politics in research. This interest developed early in my postgraduate career into an interest in autobiography and its relationship to the biographies of research respondents and the research process itself. Like Ribbens (1993: 88) I believe that:

> A critical and reflexive form of autobiography has the sociological potential for considering the extent to which our subjectivity is not something that gets in the way of our social analysis but is itself social ... I would suggest that the key point is that 'society' can be seen to be, not

'out there', but precisely *located 'inside our heads'*, that is, in our socially located and structured understandings of 'my-self', 'my-life', 'me-as-a-person', and so forth [original emphasis].

Thus, our identities are situated in structures and discourses which are themselves social and it is necessary to locate the individual in the social, and vice versa. In this chapter I explore some of the implications of doing this as researcher.

## Approaching auto/biographical research: involvement and subjectivity

In order to frame some of the dangers which researchers who use autobiographical material face, in this section I outline what taking such an approach entails and the ways that this approach has been perceived by the academic mainstream. Within the normative model of research there is no place for the self or for researcher emotions. The typical format of social research until quite recently has been to exclude such information and certainly not to place it as central to one's understanding of a research area. In the preface of his book *Deviance, Reality and Society*, Box (1986: v) wrote about the lack of personal inclusion in academic writings:

> In the initial moments of contact with a new book most readers turn to the preface ... I think that the preface is searched hopefully for some personal glimpse of the author.

With reference to the research process it has now become more common for researchers to locate themselves within the research process by employing the sociological concept of reflexivity to produce 'first person' accounts. This involves a recognition that as researchers we need to:

> ... understand and become aware of our own research activities as *telling ourselves a story about ourselves*.
>
> (Steier 1991: 3, original emphasis)

Weber (1949) was among the first to write about personal involvement in research. He was aware that the selection of research was value laden, based on the problems of a society – which will change from place to place and over time. He argued that social scientists need to be clear about their own values and ideals and how these will affect their work. In the same spirit, Wright Mills (1959: 204) argues that:

The social scientist is not some autonomous being standing outside society. No-one is outside society, the question is where he (sic) stands within it.

And further Becker (1971: 123) argues that:

... the question is not whether we should take sides, since we inevitably will, but rather whose side are we on.

Despite this, until recently the 'self' has been hidden in mainstream social research. Metatheorising – analysing and theorising theory – has historically been the central concern of social scientists. It was felt that in order to do this properly it was necessary for the researcher to remain 'detached' and 'objective' (Oakley 1981). In support of this tradition many students in the social sciences were (and sometimes still are) instructed as part of their academic training not to write in the first person (Ribbens 1993). Yet as the writers above point out the self is always present affecting every aspect of the research process from choice of project through to presentation of 'findings' whether acknowledged or not (Cotterill and Letherby 1993; Ribbens 1993; Stanley and Wise 1993).

Feminist writers in particular have exposed the hollowness of claims to objectivity. They go further than Weber, Wright Mills and Becker in making a much more explicit recognition of the researcher's self. Stanley and Wise (1993) argue that to ignore this personal involvement is to downgrade the personal. As Okely (1992: 9) notes:

... the Women's Liberation Movement argued that the 'personal is political'; I contend that in an academic context 'the personal is also theoretical'. This stands against an entrenched tradition which relegates the personal to the periphery and to the 'merely anecdotal' ...

Stanley (1991: 209) argues that all feminist work should be fundamentally concerned with how people come to understand what they do. Thus in producing feminist theory it is important that we recognise the importance of our 'intellectual biography' by providing 'accountable knowledge' in which the reader has access to details of the contextually located reasoning process which gives rise to the 'findings', the 'outcomes'.

When beginning my research I felt that my personal involvement with the issue I was researching would have an impact on what I did. Several feminist researchers have noted that women researchers often choose topics which mean something to them and argue that drawing and theorising on one's own personal experience is valuable (Oakley 1981; Cotterill and Letherby 1993, 1994; Stanley and Wise 1993; Ribbens and Edwards 1998). There is also a large amount of writing which recognises the impact of difference within the research relationship (Ramazanoglu 1989; Ribbens 1989; Cotterill 1992). Others have argued that difference in terms of representing the other needs further theoretical considera-tion (Berger et al. 1991; Bola 1995; Wilkinson and Kitzinger 1996). Some writers have been critical of the inclusion of personal experience. For example, Kelly et al. (1994: 29–30) argue:

> Whilst personal experience undoubtedly influences one's perspective and understanding, many current references to it are determinist and es-sentialist. Experience/identity is substituted for, or deemed to be equivalent to, politics, as if critical awareness and understanding are in-scribed on a person through forms of oppression, with an implicit or ex-plicit presumption that such awareness is inaccessible to those who have not 'lived' through the experience.

I would argue that this is a simplistic reading of the feminist scholarship in this area. In relation to my own work I do not see my own experiences as an essential ingredient of my approach, but they do make a difference. This difference is important to consider practically, theoretically and politically, not least because sameness may distance 'participants (researcher and researched) from a critical reflexive research process' and may privilege 'one point of view over another' (Hurd and McIntyre 1996: 78). With this in mind, as I wrote my thesis, I was concerned to detail my intellectual and personal biography as well as the biographies of my respondents in an attempt to demonstrate the relationship between the process and the product. Even in research writing that is not explicitly auto/biographical the 'weaving of stories' is not unusual:

> As feminist researchers studying women's lives, we take their autobiog-raphies and become their biographers, whilst recognising that the auto-biographies we are given are influenced by the research relationship. In other words respondents have their own view of what the researcher might like to hear. Moreover, we draw on our own experiences to help us understand those of our respondents. Thus, their lives are filtered through us and filtered stories of our lives are present (whether we ad-mit it or not) in our written accounts.
>
> (Cotterill and Letherby 1993: 74)

The attention given to these epistemological issues has also been criticised. Kelly et al. (1994: 32) refer to what they call the current 'romance with epistemology' which they argue:

seems more concerned with attempting to convince the predominantly male academy that a privileged status should be accorded to 'women's ways of knowing' than with enabling us to better discover and understand what is happening in women's lives, and how we might change it.

Again, I see this as a simplistic description of much feminist work. Like Okely and Callaway (1992: 2) I would argue that reflexivity and/or autobiography is neither 'mere navel gazing' nor a form of 'self-adoration'. As Okely (1992) adds, 'self adoration' is quite different from self-awareness and a critical scrutiny of the self. Indeed, those who protect the self from scrutiny could well be labelled self-satisfied and arrogant in presuming their presence and relations with others to be unproblematic. Thus, like Stanley (1993: 49–50) I see the 'autobiographical I' as 'inquiring and analytical' and:

> The use of 'I' explicitly recognises that such knowledge is contextual, situational and specific, and that it will differ systematically according to the social location (as a gendered, raced, classed, sexualised person) of the particular knowledge-producer.

I hope that my work reads as an expression of my own autobiographical I.

There are, of course, problems in writing that is so closely linked to one's own personal biography. bell hooks (1989: 158) argues that autobiography 'is a way to find again that aspect of self and experience that may no longer be an actual part of one's life but is a living memory shaping and informing the present'. However, it is important to be aware of the fine balance between 'uncovering the past in as many layers as possible' and reconstructing the past to fit the present (McMahon 1991: 29).

A further problem is the issue of power. As a researcher interested in the biographies of others (and the relevance of my own biography to the research) I obviously have the power of editorship. As Iles (1992) argues, it is the researcher who decides who to research and determines what is included, what is left out and how details are presented. Also, it is not easy to present oneself in a critical light. This was brought home to me when a colleague asked whether it was easy for me to include myself as an 'innocent' party. She suggested that I might feel differently researching an issue about which I may feel guilty in some way. She cited the examples of a woman who had given up her children for adoption doing research on adoption and a child abuser researching abusive relationships. I am sure she was right in saying that it would feel much more dangerous to include the self in such research; I know that my motivation and enthusiasm towards the project related in part to my feelings about my own experience. Added to this I am also aware that 'coming out' (a term which as Kosofsky Sedgwick (1994: 71) argues is now verging on an all-purpose phrase for 'admitting' to almost any politically charged identity and experience) is much riskier when an aspect of one's identity is likely to make one vulnerable to legal, medical and social stigma and penalty.

Thus the use of autobiography is a contentious and difficult area for social research as it involves working at the margins of established research paradigms and academic writing protocols. If used in research, an autobiographical approach involves the researcher in self-examination and scrutiny. One potential effect of this is exposure to emotional threat. It is to this issue that I now turn.

## Doing auto/biographical research

### Making and maintaining relationships

I did believe that my personal experience would make it easier, rather than harder, to do research in the area of involuntary childlessness. Oakley (1981) suggests that by appealing to sisterhood researchers can equalise their relationships with their respondents. Factors other than gender can facilitate good research relationships. For instance during her research on clergymen's wives Finch (1984: 79) found that revealing her own identity as a clergyman's wife greatly improved her interviews. Once respondents had placed her as 'one of them' they were happy to talk. Similarly, in my research the following was typical:

*Moira:*  It's nice to talk to someone who understands.
*Gloria:*  Had I known of your own personal involvement in the issue I would have got in touch sooner.

After initial shyness, which I experienced in meeting all the respondents for the first time (especially those who were much older than me and/or those who appeared to be more knowledgeable about the issue), I generally felt very comfortable. All the people I interviewed and wrote to told me highly personal details about themselves and others close to them. In terms of the power balance and risk to respondents, there are serious problems with the trust that this implies. As Finch (1984) argues, research about private and personal issues, particularly those concerned with taboo topics, may make people vulnerable and verbal guarantees carry very little weight. It is also possible to argue here that my personal involvement encouraged respondents to tell me intimate details of their lives that they may otherwise not have done. Indeed, although I do not agree with Oakley (1981) that research relationships often lead to friendship, I did find that after two or three hours in a woman's house talking about painful and distressing 'infertility' treatment, miscarriage and child death and/or marital breakdown, there was an 'intimacy' between us not normally associated with first meetings. This 'intimacy' has the potential to be either positive or negative for researcher and respondent as I explore further below.

To balance the vulnerability and risk that respondents may have felt in terms of disclosure, and in an attempt to 'equalise our relationship', I was concerned that each interview should contain as much of my experience as my respondents asked for. I referred to my own experience to varying degrees in different interviews, and I realised that my desire to invest myself within the fieldwork stage of the research was at least in part structured by the wishes of respondents. They all asked me why I was interested in this particular topic. Once told, most appeared to accept this as sufficient justification for my interest and it was rarely mentioned again. This accords with Ribbens's (1989) view that research provides an opportunity for respondents to talk about themselves at length and that if the researcher volunteers information unasked, this may be seen as an unwelcome contribution and not part of the research contract. Although I told myself that my concern here was for respondents, an experience early in my fieldwork made me think again.

Sarah was one of the first people I 'recruited' into Primary Study Group One. After the second interview with her I wrote in my field diary:

> There is not a lot of space for me. I say bits and pieces and she agrees and follows up with an example. She mentioned a friend [in a similar situation] that she 'helps' and describes this as not a two-way relation- ship. I don't think ours is a two-way relationship.

Soon after writing this I realised that this diary entry not only expresses the role Sarah allotted to me but also suggests that I expected her to be more than a respondent. It is possible to argue that this is an example of how a researcher can become so involved with a research issue (particularly likely perhaps if it is an issue already of personal importance to the researcher) that they become concerned only with their own emotional response and interpretation to the detriment of the researched. However, this experience did lead me to explore with Sarah, and other respondents, the significance of support and the differences between that offered formally and informally. Thus, a personally negative experience led to academic insight. Also, although I cringed as I read this diary entry, and I do not believe that the interview should be a counselling session for respondent or researcher, it did make me think further about research relation- ships. Like Collins (1998) I believe that the interview is a complex social construction within which roles and selves are jointly negotiated.

This was confirmed for me by the fact that many of the interviews did involve a lot of two-way discussion, and respondents often adopted a role other than that of interviewee, evident in the concern they showed for me. Several women wrote or said they were worried that what they were saying might upset me. For example, in the middle of answering a question on her experiences of mother-hood, Fiona said that it must be very difficult listening to women's positive views of an experience I had hoped for myself. Anne wrote that she felt worried about describing non-motherhood as positive to me. Others actually said that they felt positive about the experience of talking/writing to me and asked if they could 'do anything for me'. This suggests that many people in this situation who have felt supported by others go on to offer support themselves (Letherby 1997).

During the research I talked and wrote to many people whom I felt I shared something with in terms of experience. I also communicated with people who had experienced what I felt to be worst-case scenarios. However, on reflection I do not feel like Katz Rothman (1986: 50) that 'I could not have understood it (the respondent's experience) intellectually I don't think, if I had not experienced it emotionally' or like Wilkins (1993) that I would not have attempted the research without my personal experience to draw on. Despite the inspiration it has given me, I do not credit the work I have done to my biologically childless state, I feel sure that I would have been equally interested if I had had children. Also, it is worth considering further the 'self-other' equation (Wilkinson and Kitzinger 1996: 16) and recognising that:

> Self and Other are knottily entangled ... Despite denials, qualitative re-searchers are always implicated at the hyphen ... . By *working the hyphen*, I mean to suggest that researchers probe how we are in relation with the contexts we study and with our informants, understanding that we are multiple in all those relations.
> (Fine 1994, cited by Wilkinson and Kitzinger 1996: 16, original emphasis)

Zdrodowski and I considered this in relation to my work and hers, hers being concerned with examining women's experience of body image with a primary focus on the experience of being overweight in a society that values thinness:

> Our own experiences are both similar and different to those of our re-spondents. At times we feel empathy with our respondents, whereas at other times, we find that we cannot identify with the experience and/or feelings of those we research. We identify with the general theme of our projects, but each study has indicated that experience is much more com-plex than the definitions of infertility, childlessness, overweight, and eat-ing disorder imply. When reading letters and in undertaking interviews,

we have found that we feel a strong sense of identification with some of our respondents, whereas at other times we have found it difficult, if not impossible, to relate to their own personal definitions.

This was not, in our case, with respect to differences of class, race, sexuality and age, but to our different experiences of the research issue.

(Letherby and Zdrodowski 1995: 586)

In my case I interviewed and wrote to women who had pursued 'infertility' treatment or adoption for years in order to achieve motherhood, women whose children had died and women who were distressed when previous partners went on to have children in another relationship. None of this had happened to me. Overall, I agree with Temple (1997: 5.2) that:

It is by listening and learning from other people's experiences that the researcher can learn that the 'truth' is not the same for everyone.

Further to this, as Woollett (1996) notes, researchers' identities shift and change just as respondents' do. Certainly the fact that towards the end of the fieldwork period I moved in with my partner and his two teenage sons placed me as 'other' to many of my respondents who had no such daily contact with children. Yet I was (and remain) emotionally involved with the issue, as were my respondents. Although I did not/do not see myself as 'obsessed' with this issue I have sometimes felt that others did see me in that way. A close family member once described my academic interest in miscarriage as morbid; colleagues at work and my general practitioner have told me that 'given the world's population problems there are more important things to be concerned with'.

### Risks and emotions

Any discussion of emotional involvement involves a consideration of emotional management and emotional work for the researcher (and the researched). As Shaffir et al. (1980: 4) note:

The intensity of the fieldwork process is typically accompanied by a psychological anxiety resulting in a continuous presentation and management of self when in the presence of those studied.

Meerabeau (1989), interviewing sub-fertile couples, found the advice of Owens (1986) – to avoid eye-contact when discussing potentially embarrassing subjects – helpful. This approach was inappropriate for my research in several ways. First, I felt that such a denial of emotion and personal involvement went against the principles of feminist research. Second, I was interested in respondents' emotional experience and increasingly it became clear that emotional management and work was an issue for the 'infertile' and 'involuntary childless' so it was inappropriate to 'avoid' the emotion generated by the research process. Also, many respondents made it clear that they wanted to talk about how they felt and were interested in how I felt too. Some of the emotions generated during interviews (and evident in letters) were dramatic, but embarrassment was extremely rare. Respondents spoke and wrote about sorrow, guilt, anger and joy and tears were common, as was laughter. Obviously, displays of emotion can be difficult, even dangerous, for both the researcher and the researched. I never cried during interviews although I sometimes had to work hard not to. When women cried I always offered to turn off the tape but only once did an interview end early because a respondent was distressed. In fact we were not talking about her 'infertility' but about a problem she had at work. As McRobbie (1982: 55) notes, at times the researcher may feel like she is 'holidaying on people's misery' but others have argued that being able to reflect on and re-evaluate experiences as part of the process of research can be therapeutic (e.g. Cotterill 1992; Opie 1992).

My experience of research leads me to support this contention. At the beginning of our first interview Sarah said, 'I'll just use it as therapy'. May said, 'It's good to talk about it [pause] it's therapeutic' and G. Rogers wrote, 'I feel I could go on and on … I actually feel it's been quite therapeutic to put all this on paper as I've not done it before'. Conversely, I was often worried that I had left people distressed. Indeed, sometimes respondents informed me that they did find the process upsetting. Angela wrote, 'Sorry about all the mistakes but I'm very upset' and Kate said, 'I was very upset when you'd gone and for a while I didn't know whether I wanted to go through it again'. All those who referred to being distressed opted to continue their involvement, but I did wonder sometimes if I had encouraged respondents to re-live difficult experiences and then abandoned them to come to terms with their distress alone. (For further discussion of this issue see Maynard 1994.) I still feel uncomfortable about this aspect of the research.

The display of emotions is gendered. It is less acceptable for women to display stereotypically masculine emotions such as anger and for men to display stereotypically feminine emotions such as grief and distress (Hochschild 1990). James (1989) argues that the results of the gender division of labour is that men are held responsible for bringing in the income and women for the routine running of the home and the care of children. Within this allotted role, women are primarily responsible for working with emotions. Thus, women are held responsible for others' emotional needs while men are not. My respondents' experience supported these views. Women and men both felt that it was easier for women to be 'upset' and women would refer to the work they engaged in to protect partners, family and friends from distress and/or embarrassment when the topic of children came up. James (112: 496) observes that:

> The skills of emotional regulation are learned at home, ... and trans-
> ferred to workplace carework where they have to fit in with workplace
> priorities.

This is relevant to women fieldworkers who, as Warren (1988: 45) notes, have traditionally been portrayed as 'more accessible and less threatening than men' which 'coupled with their "superior" communicative abilities' makes the interactions of fieldwork generally easier. Scott and Porter (1983) argue that as a feminised activity interviewing has become devalued academically. Clearly, this is not only sexist but denies the work involved in managing research relationships. I shall illustrate these with some examples from my own research experience.

I interviewed Tracey and Mike five times. On all of those occasions I felt like a facilitator of a row and I also felt that Mike placed me in the 'irrational woman' category in which he put Tracey. I found some of their views on parenthood frightening, and consequently developed some very judgemental views on their ability to parent. I also found it particularly difficult when asked by one of them to disagree with the other. Throughout the interviews with them I often had to work hard not to display my own very different views and ensure that I did not 'take sides'.

I interviewed Jean three times but I felt very ambivalent about my relationship with her. Field diary entries include: 'this is a wonderful, brave and powerful woman' and 'I'm so exhausted she wants so much of me'. The latter was after the second interview. We talked for six hours (three of which I have on tape) during which time Jean became very distressed and pulled me towards her in an embrace. Normally a tactile, demonstrative person I felt extremely uncomfortable with this. I felt 'used' by Jean and thought her behaviour was inappropriate. I tried to be empathic towards her but went away feeling that she wanted more from me.

I recognise that Tracey, Mike and Jean may have had a different view of our relationship to me, especially as there are no laid-down prescriptions of behaviour for the researched. There were other occasions when, because of our similarities, respondents expected me to agree with their choices and views yet because of the differences between us I did not. At these times responding to direct questions in a way that was honest yet did not negate respondents' experience was not easy.

As well as having to 'manage' my own emotions in relation to the experience of respondents there were also times when I found respondents' views of my experience difficult to cope with. In many letters and interviews respondents asked questions about me and about what treatments I had undergone. Many expressed surprise that since my miscarriage I had not had fertility treatment of any sort. Several who lived locally suggested that I go to visit this or that doctor and/or clinic. May went as far as to say, 'I can see you with a baby in your arms yet'. I felt ambivalent about this. I thought it ironic that May should say just the kind of thing that she and other respondents felt was inappropriate for others to say to them, yet at the same time I realised that she was showing concern for me. In comparison I felt only anger when both Bob and Neil (both partners of women I interviewed) suggested that it was my own fault that I had no children if I was not prepared to have treatment and, as Neil put it, 'Get sorted out'. I did not display this anger but shrugged and said 'Maybe'.

Halfway through the fieldwork I felt very low. The travelling, interviewing and transcribing alongside the preparation and marking for the teaching I was doing meant that I felt physically and mentally worn out most of the time. The emotional involvement and emotional work involved in the fieldwork also led to emotional exhaustion. May talked about a period when she was unsuccessfully trying to conceive a child as her 'time in the wilderness'. I felt that this was mine. During this period when respondents asked me how I felt and thought in relation to the moral, emotional and factual aspects of 'infertility' and/or 'involuntary childlessness' I often said that I no longer felt able to make a judgement as my mind felt so full of everybody else's accounts that I was both lost for words and thoughts. At this time it felt like the research represented a real threat to my sense of self.

The difficulties I had were compounded by the fact that there were no formal support systems for me. As Brannen (1988: 562) points out:

> Even professional confidants − counsellors and psychotherapists − have their own confessors. On most research projects these issues are rarely considered and researchers are left to find their own individual solutions outside their formally prescribed roles.

I did find my own solutions. Supervisors and friends never pressed me for details, instead they allowed me lots of time just to be upset. I did talk a lot to the other women postgraduates with whom I shared an office, and found these informal support and friendship networks more important at that particular time than the formal supervisory support offered by the institution (see Holliday et al. 1993). However, as I had promised anonymity and confidentiality to my respondents I was not able to talk in depth about them and their impact on me. I often used my research diary to grapple with these issues instead.

I was also able to gain support from my family. Throughout most of the fieldwork period I shared a home with my mother and was supported by her both practically and emotionally. In terms of my own quest for a child the period of 'trying to get pregnant', the miscarriage and the following eighteen months were intensely difficult for me. My mother had lived through this with me and the distress I felt during fieldwork involved her too in some reflection on the past. It was not until about six months after the fieldwork was over that I began to feel less confused emotionally and able to 'place myself' within the whole experience.

In terms of data analysis, though, these difficult experiences were to prove positive. When working with the data and reading fieldnotes I was sensitive to gender differences and similarities and the gendered nature of my own emotional work in the field when answering such questions as, 'Why don't you have any children?' I began to consider in greater detail the choices and emotions associated with the experience of 'infertility' treatment, the pursuit of social parenthood (e.g. adoption) and the decision to remain childless. Also, in order to 'feel better' I rethought my personal position and realised that each of my respondents were engaged in similar reflexivity. Indeed, change and adaptation became important themes in my work.

Several writers have argued that emotional work is an inevitable part of fieldwork (e.g. Ramsay 1993; Young and Lee 1996). Like Ramsay (1993: 19) I think that:

> attending to *emotional responses* to experiences in the field is a method of finding out where the researcher stands in relation to those being studied ... an exploration of the level of *emotional management* required in the relationship between researcher and respondent places the researcher clearly within the research process. This also allows a discussion of how the process affects the researcher ... viewing qualitative research, and the PhD experience in general, as *emotional labour* locates the process clearly within a discussion of the academic mode of production (original emphasis).

With specific reference to auto/biography I think it is relevant to refer to Stanley (1995: 185) who argues that, by 'becoming academics' as women and as feminists, we position ourselves both as insiders and outsiders. She argues that we are 'perpetual strangers but strangers within' (1995: 185). In this instance I was not only a native when interviewing and corresponding with women due to my womanhood but also when interviewing and corresponding with women and men due to my 'infertility'/ 'involuntary childlessness'. Like Stanley I believe that this involvement does not disempower me intellectually; I can still be critical and analytical about this issue just as my respondents often were. Indeed, I feel that being critical and analytical about my involvement as well as about the issue results in a 'fuller' picture.

My position as a 'native' or a 'stranger within' is obviously relevant to research relationships. In some instances it appeared to me that the shared identification between the respondents and myself affected the data that I obtained. However, for some respondents it was my status as 'stranger' that made them feel comfortable writing or talking to me. Several of those who wrote (including the three who wrote anonymously) stressed the fact that they would not have been able to talk about these issues face-to-face. Similarly, when I asked Clare if it was different talking to me than to friends and family, she said:

> 'Yes it's different. Preferable really. It's something to do with emotions. It doesn't matter very much if I express emotions in this context. Somehow it's preferable than talking with friends. Yes.'

This returns us both to a consideration of the danger of exploitation in research and to the management of emotions. As previously noted, giving people a chance to talk and write about an experience which is often 'taboo' can bring forward vulnerable people who may 'give away' more (both substantively and emotionally) than they later feel comfortable with. After all, why trust a stranger? Maybe respondents balance any risk they feel against the fact that they are never likely to see the researcher again. On the other hand, as some of my respondents stated, involvement in research can be a way of anonymously 'putting the record straight' and as previously noted some felt positive about the expression of emotion in this context. Simmel (cited in Wolff 1950: 404) describes the stranger as a potential wanderer, the 'person who comes today and goes tomorrow', a person who is perceived as being unlikely to censure confidences and unlikely to gossip to other members of the group. Thus:

> The stranger also often meets with the most surprising openness: confidences characteristic of a confessional which would be carefully withheld from a more closely related person. This is chiefly, but not exclusively, true of the stranger who moves on.

Clearly though it is not just my status as stranger that is relevant here, but my position as a 'stranger within'. A status which, as I have indicated, is likely to involve the researcher in their own feelings of risk and vulnerability.

# Presenting auto/biographical research: audiences and responses

Early in my postgraduate career I began to look for writing that was concerned with presentation and found Goffman's (1981: 137–38) observations on audiences interesting:

> Audiences hear [and read] in a way special to them ... Indeed, and fundamentally, the role of the audience is to appreciate remarks made, not to reply in a direct way. They are to conjure up what a reply might be, but not utter it ... They give the floor but (except during the question period) rarely get it.

I think that academic audiences, to written and verbally presented work, have more power than this implies. Postgraduates are in a particularly vulnerable position. As undergraduates it is necessary to be able to discuss concepts and ideas. However, most postgraduates are likely to be talking about their *own* concepts and ideas for the first time and not just in the relatively safe environment of their own institution but in the wider academic community. Postgraduates, like other researchers, write for many audiences which in this instance includes examiners and potential employers. Challenging established paradigms or working within marginalised methodologies can have a serious impact upon how your scholarship is received. However, it could be argued that it is easier to write something controversial once one is established.

Writing auto/biographically brings the danger that you will be accused of being non-academic and producing what Katz Rothman (1986: 53) calls 'sensational journalism' in order to deal with your own personal problems. I also felt extremely apprehensive about the world at large seeing me wear my heart on my sleeve. This is a problem that traditional researchers do not face because they reveal less about themselves. I expected to leave some things out and, whilst aware that we all 'manage appearances', I could not help but feel that somehow this was cheating. Yet at the same time I was aware of the necessity of protecting myself. Several things happened which led me to reflect on issues of inclusion and exclusion further.

During my first year as a postgraduate I wrote a piece on non-motherhood into which I wove my personal experience with my epistemological and theoretical position. I sent the piece to a feminist journal and felt very insecure when the rejection letter stated that the editors were not at all sure that I knew what feminism was. Later I sent the piece elsewhere and received a much more positive response. However, this time, one of the referees expressed concern on my behalf over the inclusion of personal details, as she had known similar material to be used against colleagues.

During the second year of my doctorate I watched with interest a programme concerned with non-motherhood on Channel 4, 'A Different Kind of Love', *Female Parts*, June 1992. I was disappointed with it as I felt the programme supported, rather than challenged, existing stereotypes. Specifically, I felt that it supported the dominant and simplistic image of childless women as 'desperate'. I wrote a letter to the producer outlining this, including nothing of my own personal experience. I received a reply that included the following:

> You are as you say 'undertaking research on the experience of involuntary childlessness and infertility' ... and that is reflected in the tone and content of your letter.
>
> I am interested in your own age and fertility status ... I feel your approach is clinical and objective. In a sense it is a justification for making the programme as I did.

Ironically, a review by a non-sociologist (Day 1993), published in the *Times Higher Education Supplement*, of an article I wrote with Pamela Cotterill (Cotterill and Letherby 1993) on the links between auto/biography and feminist research, accused us of the opposite. Day asserted that our approach was 'grossly self-indulgent' and 'sickly self-advertisement'. This illustrates the way in which, once the research becomes a product, the writer is vulnerable. When doing research on an issue with which one has a personal involvement and when writing in part about 'oneself', it is easy to feel that criticism is directed not only at your academic work but at you personally. More recently I have been advised by a commissioning editor to leave out the autobiography if I want to publish my thesis as a book and have been told by more than one academic colleague that auto/biography is 'sloppy sociology'. All of this clearly has implications in terms of professional identity and in terms of publishing one's work and getting on in academia.

Many feminist writers have written of how and why women's work is devalued and the ways in which women have been excluded from the making of knowledge and culture (Smith 1988; Stanley and Wise 1993). Historically, objectivity, rationality and value-freedom, rather than involvement, subjectivity and emotion, have been given academic status. Clearly there are legacies from this today. However, although the approach is historically gendered, the fact that it is historical and gendered means that as a social construction it is subject to choice and change. Indeed, it is not only women who are reflexively and theoretically concerned with issues of self and other (e.g. Hearn 1993;

Mykhalovskiy 1996; Morgan 1998). These male writers face similar issues, for as Eric Mykhalovskiy (1996: 139) notes:

> ... the criteria of sociological orthodoxy as expressed by a masculine academic discourse or voice, itself propped up by forms of thinking, writing, doing research and so on. As sociologists, this is a voice with which many of us are familiar; which we listen to and often reproduce as part of our apprenticeship. Authoritative, at times arrogant, it is a voice that speaks unitarily and with confidence ...
>
> Autobiographical sociology gives offence to this voice. As sociology, it comes to 'not' speak in that it does not rely on standard ways of being sociologically meaningful to readers.

In relation to respondents the power relationship is somewhat different. After leaving the field and whilst writing the research 'findings', the researcher has ultimate control over the material and authoritative resources. At this stage of the research the researcher holds the balance of power in that he or she takes away the 'words' and has the power of editorship (Cotterill 1992; Iles 1992). The active role of the respondents is over but they do continue to exert an influence. I know what my respondents think I should write: they told me. I hope that my research will make a difference to the way that the experience of 'infertility'/'involuntary childlessness' is viewed. Yet, at the same time I am aware that my work is not representative of all people in this situation, indeed it is not representative of all of those I wrote about and spoke to. They did not all agree with each other, I did not agree with all of them, and it is likely that I have misunderstood what some of them were saying. It is I who have been the adjudicator and the interpreter of respondents' accounts and in research writings I have control over my autobiography in a way my respondents do not over theirs. With this in mind, and because of other issues of respondent involvement and emotion addressed above, Stacey (1991: 114) argues that 'elements of inequality, exploitation, and even betrayal are endemic to ethnography'. Even if respondents have total access to what the researcher has written about their experiences, and if they feel that the researcher has 'got it wrong' and this makes them angry, they still have an unequal role in terms of response. Yet a recognition of respondents as people, and not just research subjects/objects, highlights the fact that they are not completely passive. However wrong the researcher gets it in terms of meaning it is unlikely that respondents' sense of self-identity and self-assurance will be damaged (unless of course a researcher's inaccurate 'findings' are translated into policy statements). Researchers take away words, not experiences (Skeggs 1994).

# Conclusion

In this chapter I have examined some of the risks and dangers of using the self as a resource, through a consideration of approaching, doing and presenting research. As I have highlighted, the dangers are personal as well as academic. Emotional and political involvement in research can mean that one's sense of self and one's professional identity and future are put at risk. Recognition of the risks and dangers for respondents and attempts to 'equalise the research relationship' can lead to further vulnerability for the researcher. Furthermore, the chapter has illustrated some of the sources of support which one can mobilise to cope with emotional threat arising from the research process, such as family relationships and the support of colleagues or peers.

Increasingly it is becoming usual for researchers to include aspects of the self in their research and their writing, yet there still appears to be a tendency to keep this outside the main report of a study. For example, as McMahon (1996: 320) writes in the abstract of her article concerned with her own experience as a non-mother researching and writing about motherhood:

> This article looks at how research accounts can conceal stories about the experiences of those who do not appear to be present in the research project. Some of those who do not appear to be present may be called 'significantly absent' because their invisibility holds particular significance for the sorts of research stories researchers tell.

Thus, despite the increased support for auto/biographical approaches, I think that many people still feel uncomfortable with this way of writing. This is probably both for personal reasons, in terms of issues of privacy, and for academic reasons, in that they may be criticised for self-indulgence and intellectually sloppy work. This fear has some basis in reality, as to include such material can bring professional dangers, as noted in this chapter.

Yet notwithstanding the tensions associated with the auto/biographical approach, there is theoretical and methodological value in an analytical consideration of the self. I am interested in lots of things, and given the resources I would like to research and write about many of these. Many of these issues have some bearing on my own identity and experience, sometimes directly, sometimes tangentially. In the work that I do I am always concerned with how the relationship between myself and my respondents, and myself and the issue, affects what I 'find' and what I write. Likewise, many readers will want to base their research on topics which reflect their personal experiences of everyday life, work, family, sexuality, leisure, etc. As I have demonstrated, this approach can lead to substantive and methodological insight. Auto/biography is fascinating, but when considering this approach it is necessary to think seriously about the emotional and professional dangers that using the self in research may bring.

## Acknowledgements

Many thanks to Pamela Cotterill, Jennifer Marchbank, John Shiels, Geraldine Lee-Treweek and Stephanie Linkogle for constructive comments on an earlier draft.

## Note

1    I write 'infertility' and 'involuntary childlessness' in single quotation marks to highlight problems of definition (see Letherby 1997). All respondents' names have been changed to protect their identities.

## Bibliography

Attar, D. (1987) 'The controversial feminist' in G. Chester and S. Neilson (eds) *In Other Words: Writing as a Feminist*, London: Hutchinson.

Becker, H. (1971) *Sociological Work*, London: Allen Lane.

Berger, V., Gluck, S. and Patai, D. (eds) (1991) *Women's Words, Women's Words, Women's Words: the Feminist Practice of Oral History*, London: Routledge.

Bola, M. (1995) 'Questions of legitimacy?: the fit between researcher and researched', *Feminism and Psychology* 5, 2: 290–93.

Box, S. (1986) *Deviance, Reality and Society*, 2nd edition, London: Cassell.

Brannen, J. (1988) 'Research note: the study of sensitive subjects', *Sociological Review* 36, 6: 552–670.

Collins, P. (1998) 'Negotiating selves: reflections on "unstructured" interviewing', *Sociological Research Online* Vol. 3, No. 3, http://www/socresonline.org.uk/ socresonline/3/3/2.html

Cotterill, P. (1992) 'Interviewing women: issues of friendship, vulnerability and power', *Women's Studies International Forum* 15, 5/6: 593–606.

Cotterill, P. and Letherby, G. (1993) '"Weaving stories": personal auto/biographies in feminist research', *Sociology* 27, 1: 67–80.

—— (1994) 'The "person" in the researcher' in R. Burgess (ed.) *Studies in Qualitative Methodology*, Vol. 4, London: Jai.

Day, G. (1993) 'Review ... special issue biography and autobiography in sociology', *Times Higher Education Supplement*, 20 October, pp. 37.

Finch, J. (1984) '"It's great to have someone to talk to": the ethics and politics of interviewing women' in C. Bell and H. Roberts (eds) *Social Researching: Politics, Problems and Practice*, London: Routledge & Kegan Paul.

Goffman, E. (1981) *Forms of Talk*, Oxford: Basil Blackwell.

Hearn, J. (1993) 'Emotive subjects: organizational men, organization masculinities and the (de)construction of "emotions"' in S. Fineman (ed.) *Emotions in Organisations*, London: Sage.

Hochschild, A. R. (1990) *The Second Shift*, London: Piaktus.

hooks, b. (1989) *Talking Back*, Boston: South End Press.

Holliday, R., Letherby, G., Mann, L., Ramsay, K. and Reynolds, G. (1993) 'Room of our own: an alternative to academic isolation' in M. Kennedy, C. Lubelska and V. Walsh (eds) *Making Connections: Women's Studies, Women's Movements, Women's Lives*, London: Taylor & Francis.

Hurd, T. L. and McIntyre, A. (1996) 'The seduction of sameness: similarity and representing the other' in S. Wilkinson and C. Kitzinger (eds) *Representing the Other: a Feminism and Psychology Reader*, London: Sage.

Iles, T. (ed.) (1992) *All Sides of the Subject: Women and Biography*, New York and London: Teacher's College Press.

James, N. (1989) 'Emotional labour: skill and work in the social regulation of feelings', *The Sociological Review* 37, 1: 15–42.

—— (1992) 'Care = organisation + physical labour + emotional labour', *Sociology of Health and Illness* 14, 4: 488–509.

Katz Rothman, B. (1986) 'Reflections: on hard work', *Qualitative Sociology* 9: 48–53.

Kelly, L., Burton, S. and Regan, L. (1994) 'Researching women's lives or studying women's oppression? Reflections on what constitutes feminist research' in M. Maynard and J. Purvis (eds) *Researching Women's Lives from a Feminist Perspective*, London: Taylor & Francis.

Kosofsky Sedgwick, E. (1994) *Epistemology of the Closet*, Harmondsworth: Penguin.

Kramarae, C. and Treichler, P. A. (1985) *A Feminist Dictionary*, London: Pandora.

Letherby, G. (1993) 'The meanings of miscarriage', *Women's Studies International Forum* 16, 2: 165–80.

—— (1997) ' "Infertility" and "involuntary childlessness": definition and self-identity', unpublished PhD thesis, Staffordshire University.

Letherby, G. and Zdrodowski, D. (1995) ' "Dear Researcher": the use of correspondence as a method with feminist qualitative research', *Gender and Society* 9, 5: 576–93.

McMahon, M. (1991) 'Nursing histories: reviving life in abandoned selves', *Feminist Review* 37: 23–37.

—— (1996) 'Significant absences', *Qualitative Inquiry* 2, 3: 320–36.

McRobbie, A. (1982) 'The politics of feminist research: between talk, text and action' *Feminist Review* 12: 26–57.

Maynard, M. (1994) 'Methods, practice and epistemology: the debate about feminism and research' in M. Maynard and J. Purvis (eds) *Researching Women's Lives from a Feminist Perspective*, London: Taylor & Francis.

Maynard, M. and Purvis, J. (eds) (1994) *Researching Women's Lives from a Feminist Perspective*, London: Taylor & Francis.

Meerabeau, L. (1989) 'Parents in waiting: the experience of subfertile couples', unpublished PhD thesis, University of London.

Mills, C. Wright (1959) *The Sociological Imagination*, Harmondsworth: Penguin.

Morgan, D. (1998) 'Sociological imaginings and imagining sociology: bodies, auto/biographies and other mysteries', Presidential Address, British Sociological Association Annual Conference, Edinburgh University (April).

Mykhalovskiy, E. (1996) 'Reconsidering table talk: critical thoughts on the relationship between sociology, autobiography and self-indulgence', *Qualitative Sociology* 19, 1: 131–52.

Oakley, A. (1981) 'Interviewing women: a contradiction in terms' in H. Roberts (ed.) *Doing Feminist Research*, London: Routledge & Kegan Paul.

Okely, J. (1992) 'Anthropology and autobiography: participatory experience and embodied knowledge' in J. Okely and H. Callaway (eds) *Anthropology and Autobiography*, London: Routledge.

Okely, J. and Callaway, H. (eds) (1992) *Anthropology and Autobiography*, London: Routledge.

Opie, A. (1992) 'Qualitative research: appropriation of the other and empowerment', *Feminist Review* 40: 52–69.

Owens, D. (1986) 'The desire for children: a sociological study of involuntary childlessness', unpublished PhD thesis, University College Cardiff.

Payne, G., Lyon, E. S. and Anderson, R. (1989) 'Undergraduate sociology: research methods in the public sector curriculum', *Sociology* 23, 2: 261–73.

Ramazanoglu, C. (1989) 'Improving on sociology: the problems of taking a feminist standpoint', *Sociology* 13, 3: 429–42.

Ramsay, K. (1993) 'Emotional labour and qualitative research: how I learned not to laugh or cry in the field', paper presented at the BSA Annual Conference, Essex University.

Ribbens, J. (1989) 'Interviewing: an unnatural situation', *Women's Studies International Forum* 12, 6: 579–92.

—— (1993) 'Facts or Fiction? aspects of the use of autobiographical writing in undergraduate sociology', *Sociology* 27, 1: 81–92.

Ribbens, J. and Edwards, R. (1998) *Feminist Dilemmas in Qualitative Research: Public Knowledge and Private Lives*, London: Sage.

Scott, S. and Porter, M. (1983) 'On the bottom rung', *Women's Studies International Forum* 6, 2: 211–21.

Shaffir, W. B., Stebbins, R. A. and Turowetz, A. (1980) *Fieldwork Experience: Qualitative Approaches to Social Research*, New York: St Martin's Press.

Skeggs, B. (1994) 'Situating the production of feminist ethnography' in M. Maynard and J. Purvis (eds) *Researching Women's Lives from a Feminist Perspective*, London: Taylor & Francis.

Smith, D. (1988) *The Everyday World as Problematic: a Feminist Sociology*, Milton Keynes: The Open University.

Stacey, J. (1991) 'Can there be a feminist ethnography?' in V. Berger, S. Gluck and D. Patai (eds) *Women's Words, Women's Words, Women's Words: the Feminist Practice of Oral History*, London: Routledge.

Stanley, L. (1991) 'Feminist auto/biography and feminist epistemology' in J. Aaron and S. Walby (eds) *Out of the Margins: Women's Studies in the Nineties*, London: Falmer.

—— (1993) 'Auto/biography in sociology', *Sociology* 27, 1: 41–52.

—— (1995) 'My mother's voice?: on becoming a "native" in academia' in L. Morley and V. Walsh (eds) *Feminist Academics: Creative Agents for Change*, London: Taylor & Francis.

Stanley, L. and Wise, S. (1993) *Breaking Out Again: Feminist Ontology and Epistemology*, London: Routledge.

Steier, F. (1991) *Research and Reflexivity*, London: Sage.

Temple, B. (1997) '"Collegial accountability" and bias: the solution or the problem?', *Sociological Research Online*, Vol. 2, No. 4, http://www.socresonline.org.uk/ socresonline/2/4/8.html

Warren, C. A. B. (1988) *Gender Issues in Field Research*, London: Sage.

Weber, M. (1949) *The Methodology of the Social Sciences*, Glencoe: Illinois Free Press.

Wilkins, R. (993) 'Taking it personally: a note on emotions and autobiography', *Sociology* 27, 1: 93–100.

Wilkinson, S. and Kitzinger, C. (eds) (1996) *Representing the Other: a Feminism and Psychology Reader*, London: Sage.

Wolff, K. H. (1950) *The Sociology of Georg Simmel*, New York: The Free Press.

Woollett, A. (1996) 'Infertility – from "inside/out" to "outside/in"' in S. Wilkinson and C. Kitzinger (eds) *Representing the Other: a Feminism and Psychology Reader*, London: Sage.

Young, E. H. and Lee, R. (1996) 'Fieldworker feelings as data: "emotion work" and "feeling rules" in first person accounts of sociological fieldwork' in V. James and J. Gabe (eds) *Health and the Sociology of Emotions*, London: Blackwell.

# 7

# THE INSIGHT OF EMOTIONAL DANGER

## Research experiences in a home for older people

*Geraldine Lee-Treweek*

## Introduction

The practices involved in gaining access to and retaining one's place within research settings are often works of astonishing emotional magnitude: the role playing, the management of others, the presentation of ourselves. However, where they are mentioned, emotional issues are often objectified into the more easily identifiable and clearly defined reflexive bit in the 'methods section'. In order to be useful to other researchers, emotional accounts need to be discussed as data and in relation to the generally unspoken emotion rules of the setting under investigation. When we begin to question the reasons we felt welcomed, distanced or angry and how this response compared to the way we expected to feel, a greater degree of understanding of how others experience the setting often emerges. There is also insight to be gained in the comparison between participants' emotional responses and our own, as we encounter people with different emotional rules and reactions that challenge our taken-for-granted attitudes.

This chapter discusses ethnographic fieldwork in a residential and nursing home for older people (Lee-Treweek 1994). Such places often exist in proximity to private domestic homes but function as separate interactional arenas to general society. They have particular tacit emotion rules and learning about these involved substantial emotional labour on my part. It is my belief that the final accounts (a PhD and research papers) were created, at least partially, out of a lived experience of the emotions at work in the home. This experience enabled me to present a cogent interpretation of care work with older people. The chapter discusses research in a nursing home I have given the name of Bracken Court. It considers the way emotional danger and insight were interwoven in the research and reflects upon the negative effects the fieldwork had upon my sense of self. (It should be noted that Bracken Court is a pseudonym and that the names of all individuals mentioned in this chapter have been changed to protect their anonymity.)

I assert that the emotional experience of research is a double-edged sword. From one viewpoint experiencing emotional threat during research can be positive; such experiences are usually shared with our participants and can provide insight into their understanding of risk. However, from another perspective, the emotional experience of research can turn out to be highly threatening to the self and therefore we need to think about the ways in which researchers can develop strategies to cope with this. In this chapter I use the definition of emotional danger proposed in Chapter 1, that is, serious threat to a researcher's psychological stability and sense of self derived from negative feeling states induced by the research process. However, rather than just discussing such threats as a problem, I contend that the negative emotions of the researcher often mirror those experienced by the researched (or particular sections of the researched group). When viewed in this way, feelings can be seen as important data in themselves. I concur with Letherby (Chapter 6) that social research should be seen as 'emotional labour' (Hochschild 1983; James 1989) and this should be taken seriously as part of the research process. Part of taking this seriously is to make adequate provision that all researchers, whether undergraduate or postgraduate students, full-time researchers or individuals fitting research around teaching commitments, have thought through the support they might need in the field. This issue is addressed later in the chapter when discussing the forms of support I used during my research.

## Dangerous fieldwork, a new agenda

Experiences of risk during fieldwork have always existed. For instance, one might argue that Chicago School sociology was built upon the elevation of the endurance of physical danger. Fieldworkers studied aspects of everyday life in the city, often focusing upon street life, male work cultures and gangs (for instance, see Anderson 1923; Wirth 1928; Whyte 1955; Becker 1963, 1970). Thus from the beginnings of the sociological use of qualitative research, the notion of threat to the researcher was firmly linked to physical threat. At this time the issue of emotional threat to researchers was perceived merely as a threat to the validity of one's data. Mirroring the natural science debates about the importance of objectivity, emotions within qualitative research were seen as potentially contaminating to one's findings.

These early ethnographies created the expectation that ethnographic research should be a tough experience of 'gritty' reality. This influenced contemporary attitudes within the research community towards danger in the field. The primacy of physical danger to the modern research agenda is visible in Lee's *Dangerous Fieldwork* (1995) in which psychological or emotional distress is only mentioned on a few occasions, the bulk of the book focusing upon a research world of gangs, thugs, drugs and physical threat. I am not arguing that this focus is not useful or that there is no place for discussion of physical danger; however, it does appear that there are wider issues being repressed in favour of an agenda which presents physical danger as the primary and most commonly experienced form of danger in ethnographic research. According to a research agenda focused around physical risk, most fieldwork goes on in danger-free situations. This argument is on two counts. First, the nature and focus of research work is changing and more researchers are being employed to carry out studies on areas such as health, the body, sexuality, and social-welfare-related work. These subject areas are not danger-free; instead they demand a heightened awareness of non-physical danger. During interaction between researcher and participant, there tends to be a greater focus upon the participants' feelings and protection of their well-being. This concern for those we research necessarily invites the researcher into a different relationship with risk, in which the emotions of participants are of prime importance. In the case of studying care work, the area I focus upon in this chapter, one is in the business of studying other people's emotions as a matter of course. I will argue that to understand settings fully the ethnographic researcher should also take heed of his or her own emotions as data.

### Emotion and caring work

My doctoral research focused on the work of auxiliary carers in two private homes for older people in Britain (Lee-Treweek 1994). While it contains the traditional 'reflexive bit' in the methodology section, my final thesis does not include much of what I discuss in this chapter about emotions and research. I recall being afraid that I would be interpreted as 'over-emotional' and would somehow invalidate my account by mentioning my emotions. However, in retrospect I feel that Bracken Court nursing home would have raised emotional and ethical issues for most people. The study of ageing provides a clear example of the problematic nature of an embodied, reflexive research agenda. It is not difficult to relate to a participant when she presents to you an image of yourself in later life. Fairhurst's (1990: 110) field notes in a rehabilitation unit for older people illustrate this point particularly well:

> In my research I know people who are of the same age as the people in my study. I think it could happen to them or my parents or even me. There is no way one can get away from this set up as it is my society.

These are issues which are not easy to discuss within academic circles. It is hard to go into supervision and say, 'I feel guilty' or, 'I feel anxious about ageing'; one's feelings are often not on the agenda and yet they are pivotal to the successful completion of one's work. The presentation of feelings in academic life is subject to as many disclosure rules as everyday life and not all emotions are acceptable.

Furthermore, as Kleinman and Copp (1993: 13) note, including material on one's emotions is dangerous in terms of how others will judge the validity of the final account. This is especially the case with particular emotions, for instance, disgust or dislike are probably less acceptable than empathy and joy. However, I would argue that you do not have to admire or like a social group to understand them. Indeed the basis of group interaction, as I found in Bracken Court, may be distance from one another and lack of close ties. I think it would be fair to say that dislike was the predominant feeling I had towards the auxiliary care staff when I was studying Bracken Court. Experiencing dislike was perhaps more discomforting here than in other settings because of what I expected of the work, i.e. that it was care work and because caring *for* is so closely associated with caring *about* in British society (Dalley 1983). One way of dealing with discomforting emotion in the research process, as Kleinman and Copp (1993: 33) note, is to ignore or repress it. I would add that we can also try and intellectualise it away; focus upon other aspects of data and make our emotional experiences less central to our final accounts. But using and analysing our emotion gives us access to how different our participants' emotion rules are from those used in other settings. For instance, although Bracken Court, like many nursing homes, was situated within a residential area of a major town, it functioned entirely separately to the community around it. Emotion rules developed in the home outwith those used in general society and were justified and maintained in particular ways. An analysis of these emotion rules, including my inculcation into these as a newcomer and my responses to this process, was essential to understand how emotion was managed in the home.

Residential settings for older people are, even in the best of cases, emotionally fraught places. When older people arrive they often exhibit distress and fear about leaving home and the changes they are experiencing. The period of adjustment to the new life may last some time and be punctuated with negative emotions, in some cases residents may exhibit chronic emotional distress. The researcher, unlike others formally at work in the setting, operates without a firm role in which to organise his or her emotional responses to the environment. My research concerned the labour of untrained auxiliaries (all of whom but one were women in Bracken Court) working in homes for older people in the South-West of England. Non-participant observation, in-depth interviews with care staff and the qualitative analysis of documentation were used to explore the world of the workers. In this chapter only my experiences within Bracken Court nursing home are considered. The clientele of this home were mainly older women who had substantial physical care needs.

Bracken Court nursing home had a hierarchical social structure with a trained nurse as matron at the head, trained nurses and then auxiliary staff. Lowest in the hierarchy, and outwith the nursing staff, were the cleaners, laundry women and cooks. They did not carry out 'hands on' care of patients. It was the auxiliaries, however, and their 'backstage' labour in the bedrooms, corridors, bathrooms and lavatories, who were the focus of my research. The auxiliaries' work produced clean and orderly patients who could be presented to visiting kin. These workers had no real space of their own, carried out the dirty tasks, had little contact with relatives or outsiders and were the 'hands on' carers of the patients. My research revolved around their work and their world. My peers undertaking doctoral research and other staff in my department did not consider this research to be personally threatening or problematic. The emotional implications of undertaking this study were never discussed or planned for. Consequently my emotions in the field came as quite a shock. This is not a criticism of the other people around me at the time, but is indicative of the way emotional aspects of research are rarely considered or thought through. The results of this lack of planning are discussed below in terms of my sense of self and need for support whilst in the field.

## Initial emotional responses to Bracken Court

My first response to Bracken Court was of complete despair. Day one, line one of my field notes reads, '7am, wanted to go home'. The ground floor corridor of the home was captured in my field notes:

> The place smells of acrid urine mixed with detergent, somewhere along here someone is repeatedly shouting 'nurse', someone else is making a banging noise and there is a buzzer going off.

The home was a completely alien and unsettling environment with an immutable routine that seemed unaffected by staff changes. Even the introduction of a new matron halfway through the research did not affect the day-to-day routine. Although I tried hard, I could not feel comfortable in Bracken Court. Previously I had been researching a residential home in which I had been able to punctuate the work with short periods of friendly banter. I had enjoyed my discussions with the residents and became close to some of them. In Bracken Court I felt I was alone with the staff because the majority of patients could not communicate without great difficulty and I was rushed off my feet following the auxiliary staff about. My research diary shows a first week of intensely depressed comments and then a theme of fatalistic despondency developing that permeates the whole fieldwork experience.

After my first day in the field I began to approach the study as a chore, something I had to force myself to do and really work at. I found the auxiliaries gruff and distant and felt I had no idea whether I was accepted or not. I turned to a strategy of meticulous note taking, almost to the point of obsessiveness, as a way of judging on some level that I was doing OK. A good batch of notes for the day allowed me to leave with a sense of progress. My overriding response to studying the home was to create, where possible, a physical and symbolic distance between the field, its contents and myself. Ironically, on entering the field I had been very concerned about the idea of 'going native' and getting too close to my research participants. However, the problem I experienced at Bracken Court was quite the opposite, I wanted to desert the place and my study.

Time keeping became a fixation as I struggled to contain my urge to walk out. I always left on the dot and arrived just before the time I was supposed to begin observation. I stayed around only as long as I had to and, at least initially, had little sense of empathy with the staff around me. I felt angry with the auxiliary workers, with whom I spent all my time, because of the way they interacted with patients. It was true that patients' physical needs were fulfilled and I did not witness any physical violence. However, I rarely saw any positive spontaneous physical contact such as hugging; and the auxiliaries did not talk about the patients with affection. When patients would not do what was asked of them, a variety of threats, coercion and punishment of the sort used on children were used to get them to eat, move, go to the toilet or whatever the auxiliaries felt they should be doing. Patients were talked about as if they were physical tasks, subsumed under the name given to the area of the home in which their room was situated. The feelings I had about examples of poor treatment of patients were not issues I felt able to take into my PhD supervision. When I did, sometime after fieldwork had finished, I was told by one member of the supervision team that my feelings were negatively affecting my analysis of the home and therefore were best left hidden.

### Membership issues

My route into the home was seen as very suspicious by the care staff. I had gained access through the proprietor of the home and then been introduced to the auxiliaries by the matron. The auxiliaries indicated their mistrust of me in my initial visits and first weeks of observation by falling silent when I entered a room. When I asked what was going on I was provided with the official line on the events of the day or, alternatively, they would gloss over occurrences with comments like, 'You know how older people are' (Lily). As I did not know, and was interested to find out, I found this intensely irritating and assumed it to be a personal response to me, intended to hinder my information-gathering. But from the auxiliaries' perspective my role must have appeared decidedly ambiguous; I was in and around the home on a regular basis watching what went on, I interacted with workers but I did not appear to do anything and had no firm role. I must have seemed shadow-like, transparent and perhaps even lazy as I followed people about whilst they worked. Physical work was of central importance to the auxiliaries as they defined themselves in relation to 'non-workers' like 'lady muck' (Mrs Morecombe, the home's owner) and the residential home staff, who worked in a home across the road from Bracken Court and were seen as 'soft cows', not used to real hard work. This too made me feel very uncomfortable; was I doing the research wrong? Surely, I was supposed to have good rapport with my participants. What would be the effect on my research and data if I did not?

Later on I began to get the sense that I was being tested by the auxiliaries, I was invited to sell information about the home owner or matron to buy credibility. For example,

'You been in Mrs Morecombe's house then, what's it like?'

(Maddie)

'What did Matron say about us? She doesn't like me does she?'

(Polly)

At other times the auxiliaries tested me with 'dares'. When there were particularly dirty or unpleasant tasks to be done they would dare me to go in and observe. For instance, the male auxiliary suggested:

'You ought to go into the bathroom down there, the smell's unbearable. Go on and observe that if you want.'

(Frank)

Another time when a worker was sacked I was quizzed over whether I thought it was fair. Through this I gained some sense of being part of the home, but still the pervasive feeling was of isolation. Although my presence through long shifts courted some admiration from the auxiliaries, my lack of work excluded me from being a 'worker proper'. By the end of the fieldwork I was gathering good and rich data, despite my feelings of being an outsider. I seemed to have been granted the role of trusted outsider, which made interaction with the auxiliaries slightly easier, but at the same time I was thoroughly unhappy. I lived mechanically through each shift with meticulous note keeping taking the place of real mental processing.

## Distance and denial

As the fieldwork progressed I found the division in my mind between Bracken Court and my domestic life became marked. At the end of shifts I took on the air of an escapee, returning with relief to my flat to write up my field notes. I often felt that I did not want to go back. There were a number of ways I explained my feelings of distance in my research diary. First, Bracken Court was a horrible place to be, physically cut off from the outside world and not pleasant inside. But second, I felt a need to distance myself from its grinding routine and the mistreatment of patients by the auxiliaries. For instance, the auxiliaries had a generalised view of the older person as having a narrow range of behaviour. Older people were perceived as wilfully childish, always 'trying it on' and attempting to emotionally manipulate staff through crying and exhibitions of distress. The auxiliary response was to resist the emotional needs of their patients and focus upon basic bodily care. They also used threat and fear to control behaviour. For example, because all the patients were frail and/or unable to walk, it was possible for even the smallest auxiliary to use her physical size to indicate threat or emphasise her power:

> Rosie began to cry. Vera, an auxiliary, looked over and said, 'Stop that, we treat you well, don't we?' (This was said as a statement.)
> 'Well you do but at other times ... '
> Vera stopped what she was doing and walked over, hands on hips. She leant over Rosie's wheelchair, very close to her face.
> 'Now what do you mean by that?'
> Rosie stammered, 'I mean you're lovely girls to me a lot, you're very good.'

Unsurprisingly, Rosie completely backed down and did not feel able to say what had made her cry.

There were good reasons for patients to keep themselves in the auxiliaries' good books. It was the auxiliaries who washed them, got them up, took them to the toilet. Patients needed them for all their basic needs. When staff were really annoyed they implemented small punishments which caused distress and discomfort to patients. For example, ignoring the buzzer or removing it from the patient's reach, shutting doors (so their calling went unheard) or leaving people until last for the toilet, etc., were common auxiliary punishment strategies. The impact of such treatments on the feelings and well-being of patients only becomes clear when one considers that they were virtually all unable to move under their own steam. Also, due to the high level of communication problems and the general disbelief of patients' accounts, they had problems complaining about their treatment. In such circumstances these types of behaviour on the part of auxiliaries served as an effective form of social control. In one case, Dotty, a patient in a group bedroom, had her buzzer removed for pressing it 'too much' in the night. In response she got another patient, in the same room, to press hers. This resulted in Dotty being wheeled downstairs and sat in a corner of the lounge until she 'seemed quiet'.

Studying the auxiliaries at Bracken Court made me feel intensely guilty. I was unable to come to the rescue of patients and felt ambiguous about myself and the role I should play. Furthermore, patients identified me with the negative activities of staff. For instance, one woman accused me of working with the staff. She wanted to go home and asked me to take her. When I said I could not she replied, 'A big strong girl like you could, you're just like them, no better, a collaborator.' Unsurprisingly, I found this very hurtful. The last thing I wanted was to be associated with the uncaring behaviour I witnessed in the home.

Given my growing concern with maintaining a boundary between me and the home environment, it is perhaps unsurprising that I developed rituals to reinforce this division. On arrival at Bracken Court I would wash my hands, and put on moisturiser and lipstick. Throughout the day I would return to the toilet to 'remake' myself, often after writing up field notes. I deduced this to be an individual response to the stress I was under, but it also served the purpose of providing a sense of separation from Bracken Court and the auxiliary work. Again, I interpreted this creation of difference and division as a sign of personal inadequacy. After all, I had not read many accounts where complete dislike and attempts to create distance were key components of a researcher's response to their participants. Such feelings seemed to breach the taken-for-granted notions of how we are supposed to experience relationships with those we study.

I became convinced that these feelings were my problem, an indication of a bad attitude to the field. Getting some kind of emotional feedback became absolutely essential. I used a personal counsellor as a sounding board for my data and ideas about home life. She was particularly helpful in supporting my process of disengagement from the distress of the home. This is a process which I now believe to have been essential to my gaining my PhD. It was also crucial to my decision to work hard in order to finish as soon as possible and publish, with the (somewhat naive) aim of engaging with the debates about abuse and care of older people. Soon after I finished the research I was able to publish material about the home, but my greatest regret lies in the fact that I did not directly help those patients who were in the home at the time of the research. I felt untrained to intervene and to prevent patients from being depersonalised and treated in negative ways by the auxiliary staff. In essence my general sense was one of powerlessness that was, at least in part, due to my lack of anticipation of the emergence of issues around mistreatment arising in the field. On the other hand, given the negative attitudes to patients that were deeply encoded within the auxiliaries' working culture, the possibilities of change through my intervention in the setting were limited. Later on, the publication of the research findings and my involvement with training agencies did positively impact upon training programmes for formal carers of older people. However, this 'deferred' help still seems difficult to justify in relation to those patients who were resident at Bracken Court during my observation period.

## Making sense of emotions as data

These events and feelings make uncomfortable reading, but presented without a discussion of their inter-relationship with the data, they provide little more than an account of my own distress in this setting. At the outset I felt that my account of my emotions whilst studying Bracken Court contributed nothing to the research. Like most social researchers I viewed my research diary as useful but ultimately separate from the analysis proper. As the diary made such depressing reading it also felt like pure masochism to look at it again. I had to put the field notes and the diary away for two weeks after finishing observing before I could return to them and begin analysis. I then realised that the record of my emotional responses had something to contribute to my understanding of Bracken Court and the emotional threat experienced by people who worked there. Many of the auxiliaries who I found the most tough and threatening had been at the home for some time. In the case of newer workers I recognised similar responses to the environment to my own.

Bracken Court was a depressing and frightening place to be. Whether researcher or new auxiliary, people are not generally presented with that level of distress on a day-to-day basis. Furthermore, the patients were those whom others (relatives, residential homes, hospitals, home-help services) could no longer cope with. Yet somehow a sparsely-trained group of auxiliary staff were expected to carry out the bulk of the care with minimal support, low wages, no job security and no space of their own within the home. The predominant experience of caring in this setting appeared to be a constant confrontation with distress and feelings of being out of control, especially as distress could often be neither predicted nor prevented. When it occurred little action was open to auxiliaries other than to patch it up or try any strategy which would allow them to get on with their work without cracking up. The testing of individuals was often on the basis of their emotional mettle. By exhibiting non-compliance to patients' needs and not showing fear or upset the auxiliaries were judged by their peers as being made of 'the right stuff'. In this setting it was little wonder that new workers were regarded with some suspicion; after all, new people entering this kind of emotional context and exhibiting the incorrect emotional composure would rock the boat.

The auxiliaries dealt with emotions by repression: any analysis was dangerous, the work had to be done and no thinking was required. My situation as researcher was in many ways similar to the auxiliaries'. I had no space, little support and as a new person I was as much of a threat as a new worker. Like them – like anyone – I was fairly powerless to change things. For instance, I could not take a patient home when she begged me and I could not help another when she asked to be 'put to sleep'. These experiences and my response of distancing myself were not unique; all the workers at Bracken Court were trying to wrestle with such events all the time. One found oneself torn between the normal desire to help and yet overwhelmed by the size and relentlessness of the task. By the end of the research, my caring emotions had turned into a need to cope and look after number one, rather like the auxiliaries. Similar to them, I had little recourse to support and dealt with what I saw in a contingent manner. This is mainly because support during lone research work is difficult to find. Also, established courses of action to seek support do not exist within ethnographic fieldwork. Some social science disciplines provide guidelines on how to tackle ethical and procedural difficulties, but they do not (and probably could not) provide frameworks for every eventuality.

My feelings of being an outsider I took to be about my status as 'researcher' rather than as worker. In my diary I interpreted the resilience of the culture to my attempts to be, and feel, accepted, as a sign that I was being a bad researcher. After all, good researchers always liked and got on with their participants; they did not want to be distant but close, I thought. However, my analysis of what it meant to be a new auxiliary revealed a long process of being kept outside the accepted group and only very gradually let in. The terms used for new workers were 'rats', 'moles' and 'sneaks'. They were regarded with suspicion by the other auxiliaries for some months before full staff membership was awarded. Although many women working in the home came from the local area, all were recruited either by the home's owners or the matron. Therefore, there was always the possibility of a plant, and as a university-educated young woman floating about and not appearing to do any hard work, I fitted the bill. More generally, I was part of the 'outside' placed within a usually airtight, small organisation. My feelings of isolation were part of the general socialisation of auxiliaries, the customary testing out of all newcomers. Potentially they had a good deal to lose if I had turned out to have other allegiances, such as to the home management. In order to carry out their work in the time they were given, the auxiliaries rarely followed rules and tended to cut corners. The shortcuts were mainly applied to the psychological care of the patients, which, if discovered, could have led to sackings. Circumstances had forced the auxiliaries into this situation and, faced with little capacity to change or challenge things, they got on with the work as best they could. It also transpired that someone who had visited the home previously had magnified their fears about being watched. An auxiliary, Vera, said to me,

> 'This bloke came around, friend of Mr Morecombe, from industry. I kept walking into him by accident and saw he had a watch, timing us he was, timing us in the loo and everything. Some kind of pervert if you ask me.'

This supposedly covert attempt to evaluate the auxiliaries' jobs had clearly done little to boost their confidence in outsiders.

Also, I feel there was a particular fear of my 'misunderstanding' the dirtier parts of the job. Trust was compromised initially because the workers feared that I may see their work, and therefore them, as low status. It was made clear to me that I had to understand the work and the way the auxiliaries saw the nature of the patients. They wanted me to recognise, in a way they perceived the home's owners, the matron, trained staff and even their own families did not, that the work was stressful and challenging. The auxiliaries spoke of going home to husbands who would ask, for instance, 'How was your day with the old dears?' The innocuous image of the kindly granny was inconsistent with the reality of the individuals with which the auxiliaries worked. The older people in the home needed total care and much of the work involved lifting and washing soiled patients. There was also a high incidence of verbal and sometimes physical assault by patients upon staff. This ranged from being called a bitch, to being spat at and hit with a walking stick. I too found my research was labelled by friends and family as helping out at an old people's home, as if I went down and folded a few sheets or sat around chatting. It was partly this social misconception of my work as easy and stress-free which led me to seek out the support of a professional counsellor. However, for the care staff this strategy was probably, for financial and cultural reasons, not available.

One way for the auxiliaries to discover if I valued their work, or if I was 'too good for it', was by testing me in various ways. The questioning I was subjected to about Bracken Court's management and the invitations to watch dirty chores being undertaken can be seen in this light as 'tests'. Central to their ideas about testing was the notion of being tough. Toughness could be proved or disproved in a number of ways. In a partial way I was able to be seen as such through observing long shifts. It was known for instance that I did not nod off on nights, I was always alert. This was an oddity to the auxiliaries and was interpreted as a form of toughness. However, there were other measures of toughness I did not meet. I was not a worker, I was not involved in clearing up mess, taking patients to the toilet or restraining the violent. I was the shadowy figure behind the 'real' workers. Therefore, I could never truly belong but could at best hold accepted visitor status.

The benefits of thinking through my emotions are I hope becoming clear. Although my predominant feeling during fieldwork was of isolation and difference, I shared many of my emotional responses to the work with new auxiliary staff. Like them, I had to learn the emotion rules of Bracken Court and how to respond in a context-appropriate manner. One of the home's tacit aims was the creation and maintenance of an orderly care home environment. This included the containment of disorderly emotions in the patients by the workers. Likewise, the auxiliary staff had to learn to get on with the constraints of the job without questioning how they felt. As I was not involved in the work I had more time to reflect upon what was happening and my responses to it. Therefore, my feelings of being an outsider indicated a reality about my role within the home, as an observer my full integration was never really possible.

## Contamination and escape

Given the nature of events within Bracken Court it is not surprising that within a week of intensive observation, I began to feel anxious about being around the place. I presumed these wishes to escape were just my own, and interpreted them as an indication of lack of experience of research or personal weakness. However, it transpired that escape was of deep significance to the auxiliaries, watching the clock was common, absence was high and moving on to other employment a daily and serious topic of conversation. There was a strong division between work and home life, with little socialising occurring between the auxiliaries outside. Many also indicated that they did not talk about work at home and felt that no one would be interested in the goings on at Bracken Court. I felt I could not mention my experiences to other people for just the same reason.

By the end of the research I felt extremely disillusioned about what care work was about. Before I entered Bracken Court I had a personal view of care work as something positive, nurturing, facilitating, usually based on a one-to-one relationship in which the needs of the cared-for were the central concern. Recognising my own disillusionment was one way of engaging with similar feelings that new auxiliaries underwent. After all, life in Bracken Court did not resemble the social images of care or the depiction of nursing-home life available in the home's brochure and thousands like it across Britain.

My response to such disillusionment was denial and such self-styled rituals of detachment as the makeup routine. However, it turned out that I was not the only one engaging in such rituals. On one occasion I observed Zara, a nineteen-year-old auxiliary, getting ready to leave after her shift. She had taken off her overalls and was busy spraying herself all over with a perfume body spray, when she said to me:

> 'Tell me, do I stink? I feel like I stink of shit and of this place. You must notice because you're not working with it … I often think if I get the bus or something that people are looking at me, smelling this [the home].'

Separating oneself from the home was an issue for everyone who worked there. It was a threatening environment and distance was created in different ways by individuals in order to cope with the stress. This understanding of auxiliary work only developed after the fieldwork was over, when I was able to recognise the similarities in our predicaments.

There was also the experience of patients continually asking for help, to which the only resolution seemed to be to walk away. Even with my belief that patients had a right to know the truth and that they should be comforted when they were distressed, by the end of four weeks of daily observation I found that I too was avoiding difficult subjects, trying to distract patients from their negative feelings and, on occasion, having to walk away. I realise now that I was privileged in my ability to do this. This strategy was not available in the same way for the nursing auxiliaries. For them, there was a lack of any realistic chance of escape, barring gaining employment elsewhere. However, although the younger staff were sometimes able to find retraining opportunities and move on to other types of work, for most the reality of changing jobs involved moving from one home to another. Thus, a number of workers found themselves trapped in low-status care posts. It was this group who were most resistant to patient needs but, ironically, as the longest serving and most experienced, it was they who were paired up with new staff to help them 'learn the ropes' and informally pass on the emotional rules.

## Discussion: learning from emotional danger and practical implications

In this chapter I have used the example of carrying out ethnographic research in a nursing home, to illustrate the way that emotional danger can help us understand the social world of participants. I have argued that the inclusion of our own emotions in accounts of the field are often downgraded as 'personal' and the emotional account gets hidden completely, or disengaged from the whole in separate, 'experience-based' texts (Bell and Encel 1978; Bell and Roberts 1984). However, our emotional responses are formed in relation to particular settings and have much to contribute to our understanding of participants' emotions in the field. A careful consideration of our own role and participation is needed to understand the parallels between our experience as researchers and that of those we study.

It seems that a new role is needed for the qualitative researcher, one which takes account of the way qualitative inquiry impacts upon those expected to do it. Arlie Hochschild's (1983) and Nicky James's (1989) work on emotional labour had a radical impact upon the study of work and occupations. Qualitative social research is 'people work' and is also emotional work. Indeed, it expects more of the individual researcher as an emotional worker than many occupations, as a role for the researcher is not usually prescribed. As social researchers are so exposed to emotional dangers it is pertinent to think about ways in which they can develop strategies to cope with such threats.

The recognition of the importance of emotional skills in research and the importance of 'dealing' with emotional difficulties has implications for practice and the way research is organised and supported. Some qualitative researchers may resist the discussion of research as emotional labour because of time constraints and a fear that thinking about this area will lead to researchers becoming too entangled in their emotions. However, it is the possibility of such entanglement that makes good supervision and discussion of emotions crucial between co-researchers and especially between supervisory and field staff. As Kleinman and Copp note (1993: 33), the emotions of research are important to both the researcher's ability to cope and the quality of the account they produce. Ignoring or repressing feelings about research is more likely to produce distortion of data, rather than clarity. However, those who manage or fund research may well argue that there is not the time or the money to schedule-in support or even de-briefing sessions.

In terms of undergraduate research projects, the best advice I can provide is that emotionally disturbing subjects or settings are probably not the best sites for research projects. Although topics of personal significance often appear interesting and inviting, it is important to think ahead to the possible conse- quences of focusing intensively on a distressing area. In postgraduate research, where the student will have to engage with a topic for some time, there may be a need for supervisors to accommodate processing work or for the student to seek alternative forms of support, such as counselling, when difficult issues arise. Ultimately students themselves have to decide whether a topic is likely to be threatening to them given their life experiences and attitudes.

Unfortunately, gaining support at work, or in your studies, may be difficult. As researchers we are not trained to deal with emotionally dangerous situations or even to support others who are researching them. Occupational groups who undertake 'people work' on a regular basis, such as social workers, tend to have a well-defined role through which to understand and organise their responses to the distress of those they meet. They may also receive training or supervisory guidance which focuses upon the emotional nature of the tasks they are expected to do. Social scientists (including, ironically, researchers in the field of social work) generally do not have such support structures or training. Because of this, gaining feedback on emotional issues in research is often best sought from friends rather than colleagues or supervisors. Joining a study group or student society in your discipline or your particular study topic may also provide invaluable informal support.

One of the main sources of my distress in this piece of fieldwork was observing events I felt to be unacceptable and ethically unsound but not really knowing what to do about them. This was both an emotional danger and an ethical dilemma: should I tell and who should I tell? Here I feel my planning of the research was definitely lacking. I had spent little time considering the possible ethical issues I might experience in the field. My reading of the literature about institutions and ethnography in general should have alerted me to the possibility of ethical problems, but I failed to predict the nature of the dilemmas I might face. Reconsidering my negligent attitude to this aspect of planning, I cannot emphasise enough the need for all researchers, whether they be undergraduate students or experienced researchers, to consider thoroughly, *before* the work begins, how ethical issues will be handled in the field. This is not to say that unforeseen ethical issues cannot and do not arise, but careful planning is essential. The emergent nature of ethics and risk in the field does not obviate the necessity of early consideration of these issues by the researcher.

## Conclusion: prioritising emotions

This chapter draws attention to two key issues. First of all, emotional danger needs to be recognised as a common but important experience for the researcher that may have serious consequences. There are personal costs to experiencing this form of threat and we need to treat it seriously when organising and planning qualitative research. Second, we need to think about the risks the setting naturally holds for participants and the way that the researcher's experience of emotional threats, while personally problematic and unpleasant, can provide insight into the social life of that setting. The discussion of Bracken Court presented in this chapter serves to illustrate that we are not separate entities wandering around research settings, we often share feelings of personal threat with participants and this is useful information that needs to be considered important to the research process.

Whilst acknowledging the insight provided by negative emotions in the field, we should remain mindful of our own limitations and the times when our own needs should come to the fore. Qualitative research may need to take a few lessons from the support structures provided by other occupations in this respect. For instance, in particularly stressful types of work, directors of research or supervisors could make clear provision for staff or students needing extra help. Individual researchers may find it useful to think through how they would deal with personally problematic issues, should they arise. The answer would seem to be planning, forethought and peer and/or collegial support when necessary. These strategies sound straightforward but in reality one has to work at creating a support network and asking for extra support is often not easy. As Jamieson notes in Chapter 4, even working within a research team does not always mean that informal support will be available when needed. The scheduling of tasks, the frantic push to get the research project finished on time and within budget, and the nature of the relationships between co-researchers, are factors which affect the level of support one might receive. However, a minimal amount of support and supervision that recognises the emotional dimension of studying social life, may allow emotionally-challenging situations to change from obstacles to understanding into insightful data. We may be defined as the outsider, a newcomer, a learner, an expert, a woman, a parent (often in a number of ways at different points) by participants. From our emotional responses and observations to these allotted roles, we may detect important aspects of a group's world view or a social setting, reflected by our very presence.

# Bibliography

Anderson, N. (1923) *The Hobo: the Sociology of the Homeless Man*, Chicago: University of Chicago Press.

Becker, H. (1963) *The Outsiders*, New York: The Free Press.

—— (1970) 'Practitioners of vice and crime' in R. W. Habenstein (ed.) *Pathways to Data*, Chicago: Aldine.

Bell, C. and Encel, S. (eds) (1978) *Inside the Whale: Ten Personal Accounts of Social Research*, Oxford: Pergamon Press.

Bell, C. and Roberts, H. (eds) (1984) *Social Researching: Politics, Problems, Practice*, London: Routledge & Kegan Paul.

Dalley, G. (1983) 'Ideologies of care: a feminist contribution to the debate', *Critical Social Policy*, No. 3, Autumn.

Fairhurst, E. (1990) 'Doing ethnographic research in a geriatric unit' in S. M. Peace (ed.) *Researching Social Gerontology*, London: Sage.

Hochschild, A. R. (1983) *The Managed Heart: Commercialization of Human Feeling*, Berkeley: University of California Press.

James, N. (1989) 'Emotional labour, skill and work in the social regulation of feelings', *Sociological Review* No. 37.

Kleinman, S. and Copp, M. A. (1993) *Emotions and Fieldwork*, London: Sage.

Lee, R. (1995) *Dangerous Fieldwork*, London: Sage.

Lee-Treweek, G. (1994) *Discourse, Care and Control: An Ethnography of Residential and Nursing Home Elder Care Work*, unpublished PhD thesis, University of Plymouth.

Whyte, W. F. (1955) *Street Corner Society*, Chicago: University of Chicago Press.

Wirth, L. (1928) *The Ghetto*, London: University of Chicago Press.

Young, E. and Lee, R. (1997) 'Fieldworker feelings as data: emotion work in first person accounts of sociological fieldwork' in V. James and J. Gabe (eds) *Health and the Sociology of Emotions*, Oxford: Blackwell.

# 8

## *RELAJO*

### Danger in a crowd

*Stephanie Linkogle*

## Introduction

This chapter focuses on a range of dangers encountered in the field whilst conducting research on the religious dimensions of social change in Nicaragua. It considers three types of danger: physical, ethical and emotional, which are examined with particular reference to my own research experience and more broadly in terms of the challenges and dilemmas presented by cross-cultural research. Risk taking is often inevitable but deciding what risks are necessary and how worthwhile it is to take them is one of the key challenges of negotiating the field. The idea that the researcher 'shares' the danger experienced by participants in order to understand their social world can negate very real differences between researcher and participant. In some circumstances the researcher may be more protected from physical danger by virtue of his or her status and relative prosperity. However, in other situations, researchers may be more vulnerable because they lack the culturally specific skills to recognize and defuse potentially hazardous situations. This chapter also examines the ethical dangers presented by cross-cultural research, highlighting the fraught nature of claiming knowledge or access to the meaning of diverse discourses and practices. This is further complicated by the power of the researcher to represent or misrepresent such diversity to the world at large. Finally this chapter explores the emotional dangers I encountered and argues that probing such experiences can make the researcher more attuned and able to recognize honestly their own limitations and that of their work.

I had come to Nicaragua to look at women's involvement in radical Catholic activism and the role of religious faith in the process of political change more generally. Although the focus of my research was 'organized' forms of religious activism in which relatively few people were involved, around me popular religious festivals provided a counterpoint of 'disorganized' religious expression in which relatively large numbers of people engaged. Of these festivals Santo Domingo was the most unconfined and spontaneous. Here it seemed an abrupt rupture of the *status quo* was being symbolically rehearsed. In the course of conducting research on the festival of Santo Domingo in Managua, danger was a recurring theme both in popular understandings of the festival and in my own subjective experience of the festivities.

Santo Domingo is described as a *relajo*, or an overturning of the existing order. It is a week-long festival held every summer, framed by two boisterous parades in which a small statue of the patron saint of Managua, Santo Domingo, is transported between two Catholic churches. As a researcher, my experience of the festival included both the generalized sense of danger that permeated the Santo Domingo experience – the threat of violence in the form of 'riot', robbery, assault or accidental injury from celebratory gun fire – and the experience of being an outsider in the midst of a highly culturally specific activity. Further, as I moved clumsily between the roles of participant and observer, maintaining the academic thread in what was in many respects a sensuous experience called into question my role as a sociologist.

This chapter will examine danger as a fluid condition which envelops both researcher and researched. I will examine how my encounter with physical danger generated greater insight into the meanings of Santo Domingo for participants. Due to the chaotic and uncontrolled character of the festival, multiple dangers were experienced by those taking part. Although my experience was not 'the same' as the Nicaraguan actors, I too shared in the sense of physical and emotional destabilization that was part of the festival environment. Whilst Santo Domingo was a chance for normal social relations to be set aside, there were constant attempts by religious and governmental authorities to contain, regulate and redefine it. Competing constructions of the essence of the festival and the scope of legitimate devotional activity were advanced.

Danger is an integral part of the celebrations and as a researcher it was neces-sary to partake in this in order to understand the content of the experience. Physically dangerous aspects of the research will be considered, as will the way in which the fear of violence opened up potentially destabilizing ethical and emotional dangers. My own sense of danger heightened my awareness of my position as an 'outsider', raising questions about the purpose of my research and my right or ability to conduct it. At the same time all participants including myself negotiated their exposure to danger.

Roger Lancaster (1988) describes Santo Domingo as a 'turning upside down' of normal social relations. This view of popular religious festivals is echoed by Christián Parker who maintains that they constitute 'the introduction of an extraordinary time-space' that introduces 'a means of expressing freely the contradiction of discontinuity, the grotesque and the spontaneous' (Parker 1993: 190). The Nicaraguan term *relajo* conveys the sense of breaking free from everyday moral and political conventions. It also implies a group context: a lone individual engages in a transgression; a group has a *relajo*. In this chapter I explore the multiple levels of danger experienced by research participants and myself in the contested and mutable space of the festival of Santo Domingo.

## The festival

One needs to grasp the charged symbolism which runs through the festival, and its changing manifestations, in order to understand the dangers which pervade the celebrations for both participants and researcher. The Santo Domingo festival is unique to Managua, the capital city of Nicaragua. It begins on the evening of 31 July when crowds gather at Las Sierritas church in the foothills of Managua where a small statue of Santo Domingo resides. After a night of revelry including copious drinking and dancing both inside and outside the church, the statue is carried down through the city to the church of Santo Domingo where it remains for the next nine days. It is transported in a festooned vessel known as 'the boat'. Those that carry the statue are known as 'carriers' and the crowd that surrounds the statue in the procession is referred to as 'the vigil' or *la vela*. Although it is forbidden to carry arms during the ten days of the festival, the firing of live ammunition into the air is a Santo Domingo tradition that continues unabated. The detonation of fireworks that sound ominously like gun shots also fill the sky and add to the clamor.

The festivities continue once Santo Domingo reaches his eponymous temporary home. For the nine days that Santo Domingo is in residence, there is a fairground atmosphere both inside and outside the church. A number of masses and special religious services are performed in the Santo Domingo church during this time. On 10 August the statue is returned to Las Sierritas where it rests until the following year. The procession that accompanies the statue on its journey between the two churches is a loud, boisterous and colorful celebration on the move. It is not uncommon for more than 50,000 people to accompany the statue on its nine kilometer journey between the two churches (Trejos Ubau 1992).

That the Santo Domingo festival is centered around a small statue and its physical journey from one end of Managua to the other is significant to understanding the manner in which Santo Domingo, the man, the statue, and the festival, is popularly perceived. Writing about Latin American popular religion, Christián Parker asserts that an icon itself can serve as a 'concrete symbol of a transcendent reality' and can be 'catalyst of emotions and desires in a precise time-space [the patronal festival]' (Parker 1993: 196). In my observations, the

Santo Domingo statue seemed to be invested with a sacredness that went beyond the notion of a 'concrete symbol'. In effect, the statue not only represented Santo Domingo but also embodied him, in both a 'sacred' and a 'profane' sense.

In terms of the statue's status as a sacred incarnation, it was clear from the fact that participants were keen to be as close as possible to it that it was considered sacrosanct. During the days when the statue was temporarily at rest in Santo Domingo church, religious services held in the patron's honor were largely ignored. The center of attraction was the statue itself, which sat in the corner of the church. Here there were long queues of parents and children waiting to touch the glass casing around the statue. This popular emphasis on the statue itself reflected not only its accorded sanctity, but also the fact that actual control over the statue and its movement was ambiguous and contested.

Although nominally a Catholic festival, Santo Domingo has never been fully under the control of the Church which has sought to curb the festival's excesses. Thus, the devotion to the statue in its journey through Managua arguably reflects not only a genuine sanctification of the statue itself but also demonstrates a repudiation of the official Church's attempts to exercise greater dominance over the festival, in particular to curtail the drinking, dancing and general 'party' atmosphere. It is this notion of the 'sacred in aid of the profane' that characterizes the Santo Domingo festivities. In terms of the statue's profane embodiment, there is an intimacy and familiarity between the statue and the faithful that manifests itself in the popular perception of Santo Domingo as 'one of us' and a 'man of the people' (Lancaster 1988: 39). In conversation and newspaper stories alike, the statue is referred to by the diminutive nickname 'Minguito'.

This investiture of sacredness in an icon is a feature of popular religion that is not restricted to Nicaragua or to Latin America. Throughout the world, popular Catholic festivals and rituals have often centered around a particular image of a saint that has taken on a sacred character for its devotees (Behar 1990; Badone 1990; Parker 1993). In this sense I argue that popular religious festivals can be dangerous to established religious hierarchies in that they are a space for spontaneous and highly emotional expression which is often outside the control of religious and secular authorities. In analyzing contemporary popular religious practices and beliefs in rural Spain, Ruth Behar notes the resistance of villagers to post-Vatican II attempts to 'desanctify' images and icons and to 'supplant the pantheon of saints'. Despite its rational and modernizing thrust, the Church's attempts to demystify concrete representations of saints and to downplay patronal devotion is continuous with a centuries-long battle waged by the Church against 'idolatry' (Behar 1990).

While the struggle over the meaning of icons is not unique to the Santo Domingo festival, Nicaragua's particular history of colonization is significant in the sanctity accorded to 'Minguito'. The Spanish set out to conquer the Americas under the slogan 'With the Sword and the Cross'. In other words through military conquest and religious conversion the Spanish sought to establish control over the peoples and the natural resources of the Americas. Yet the result of this evangelization was rarely the total replacement of indigenous religious systems with Catholicism. Much more frequently a synchronization of indigenous religious systems and Catholicism occurred through which indigenous peoples were able to preserve aspects of their culture and traditions within the heart of the spiritual cosmos of the colonizers. Early evangelists in Meso-America used the Nahuatl word *ixitla* to mean 'saint', perhaps unaware of its full meaning. In Nahuatl *ixitla* indicates 'effective presence and immanence' (Rowe and Schelling 1991: 69) rather than merely intercessor or mediator as the term is defined in Catholic dogma. It is against this historical backdrop that we can understand the Santo Domingo icon not only as an example of the syncretism between indigenous religion and Catholicism but also more explicitly as a manifestation of indigenous adaptation and resistance to colonialism.

Thus, in the traditions of the festival a syncretism of elements of indigenous culture and European Catholicism can be seen. Moreover, mass cultural images were also prevalent, demonstrating the fluidity and permeability of cultural expression. There was a notable commercial dimension to the festival with a number of small groups in the procession dancing around cars with loud speakers blaring out music interspersed with advertisements for different products and services. The 'cows' which danced in the parade often had advertisements emblazoned across the contraptions which supported their horns. In this way, the popular religious festival is 'faithful only to itself' (Lancaster 1988: 203).

Most of the participants in the procession wore some type of costume; the most prevalent being devils/'Hollywood Indians', women in embroidered dresses with flowers in their hair and pantomime cows. The devil/Indian is symbolically one of the richest characters in the cast of Santo Domingo characters. This figure simultaneously portrays the devil as an indigenous Indian prior to the conquest. The costume usually consists of a feathered head-dress, a stick/spear and a complete body coating of thick, black motor oil. The origins and meanings of this costume are somewhat obscure and the equation of the indigenous person and the devil is a complicated one. Although the conflation initially seems retrograde, the character is usually presented as more mischievous than evil. At times it seemed that the devil/Indian was both a confirmation of Spanish prejudice as well as the embodiment of their worst nightmare: a proud and bold opponent with access to magical powers. In the Santo Domingo procession, the devil/Indian, not the Spanish conquistador, has the power. Further, one Managuan told me that the oil also symbolized the African slaves who were brought to Nicaragua. From this costume emerged the practice of 'greasing', i.e. smearing motor oil on bystanders or other participants.

'Greasing' someone in the 'audience', particularly someone perceived as 'privileged', was a way of taking them down a few pegs. 'Tarring' them, as it were, with the brush of slavery. The tradition of 'greasing' grew out of the copious quantities of oil that were used in creating the devil/Indian costume and usually consisted of a quick swipe across the arm or back.

## Physical danger

Standing at the sidelines of the procession, I experienced this 'greasing' first hand. A group of four or five young men, a couple of whom were completely covered with grease, spotted me and my companion and cried: '*cheles!*' (in this instance, white foreigners). They laughed and smeared our heads, face, and clothing with 'grease', in fact motor oil. This was done in 'fun', one of the young men even urged us to dance with him. Many people laughed, pointed and smiled, more in sympathy than in mockery. Other people in the crowd and on the sidelines repeatedly assured me that there was no need to worry because the grease would wash out. My 'greasing', neither the total body painting of those in full costume nor the smudges that were more the norm for those on the sidelines, was quite noticeable.

Despite the lack of malice in the interaction I felt intimidated and destabilized by the encounter. This sense of vulnerability was underlined by the fact that I am a short woman lacking in physical strength. Furthermore, if indeed the festival was a *relajo* – a turning over of the world as it is – what better way to concretize this metaphor than to attack someone from the US? Was my fear 'genuine' or 'legitimate' and to what extent did it draw on a repository of colonial discourse? As unnerving was the sharp reversal of roles. Whilst I had been the observer, I was suddenly the 'observed' under the scrutiny of curious spectators in the crowd. Strangely, after experiencing relief when the youths ran back into the crowd, I was also exhilarated by having been drawn much more fully into the spectacle. The atmosphere was heady with danger and risk-taking bound up with the pleasure of the experience.

### *Levels of participation*

My own participant observation, within the context of the Santo Domingo festival, was marked by a shifting relationship between participant and observer roles. This shift was effected at different times by both myself and my 'research subjects'. Here I functioned primarily as an observer. However, as I have noted, a large proportion of those present stood on the sidelines rather than fully participating in the revelry. In this way I 'participated' as a fellow spectator. Yet I was observing not only the 'participants' but also the spectators. In a sense, part of my observations involved looking at those who looked. For both observers and participants my obvious status as a foreigner marked me as an outsider. However, in the midst of the general confusion and boisterous activity, my prominence as an outsider varied in significance.

James Clifford (1988) defines participant observation as an 'amalgam' of 'intense personal experience and scientific analysis'. In his conception, the participant observer is constantly moving between the 'inside' and the 'outside' of events (Clifford 1988: 34). As I learned, the process of entering into another environment with the intention of belonging yet remaining apart is a fraught and challenging endeavor. This dialectic of experience and analysis is a part of both the actual fieldwork and the later documentation and theorizing, and it is this tension which is often so theoretically productive. My participant observation allowed me access to the lived experience of popular religious practices. Yet my status as an outsider helped me to retain at key moments some critical distance from the thinking of my research subjects.

Much of the literature detailing popular religious festivals tends to concentrate on the attitudes and experiences of active participants (Badone 1990; Lancaster 1988, 1992; Parker 1993). In my observations, there were many more people on the sidelines and partial participants than those who had surrendered themselves completely to the *relajo*. In a sense this partial participation could be described as 'audience participation'. Clearly, observing can be a form of participation and the lines between the two, particularly in the popular celebrations, are often fluid and blurred. Many of those on the sidelines were smeared with grease and thus were drawn into more active participation. Sometimes those on the periphery had brought small children in costume but held them back to prevent them being jostled or lost in the crowd. They generally entered the fray with a sense of guardedness whilst they danced and clapped on the sidelines.

Class and gender identities structured the context for participation. Many well off Managuans, for example, did not participate in the 'popular' festival activities, preferring the safer equestrian parades which will be discussed in greater detail later in the chapter. At the other end of the class spectrum, for poorer and unemployed Managuans, the festival was an income-generating opportunity. There were a plethora of vendors selling fireworks, straw hats, t-shirts with images of Santo Domingo on them, crucifixes and other religious mementos. In addition, a variety of food and drink was on offer, from a plastic bag filled with water to an elaborate meal wrapped in banana leaves.

A disproportionate share of vendors were female, not surprising given the more limited income-generating opportunities open to women in Nicaraguan society. In fact in my observations of the Santo Domingo festival, it was through their economic activities that women were most effective. Although women were responsible for 'dressing' the saint and 'perfuming' his special pedestal, they were largely excluded from positions of power in the organization and administration of the festival. The office of 'pretty Indian', in effect a beauty queen, was the most senior position held by a woman in the organizational structure of the festival. Given the 'free for all' that the festival usually becomes, this lack of integration into the festival's organizational structure would not necessarily indicate or limit female participation. However, women clearly did not participate to the same degree as men in some of the defining (profane) activities of the festival.

There are a number of factors that underlie this difference. First, given the highly gendered division of labor, women are significantly less 'free' to engage in all-night drinking and dancing. Second, traditional constructions of femininity limit both women's ability to participate or engage in behavior which contravenes these conventions (i.e. physical aggression, public drunkenness, etc.). Third, and related to the above two factors, many women festival-goers perceived some of the more profane aspects of the festivities as physically risky and spiritually dubious. Most of the women I spoke to expressed reservations about the festival – generally that it was 'out of control', potentially dangerous and not indicative of genuine religious devotion. As one woman I spoke to maintained: 'It is better to celebrate it inside the church rather than outside. In the streets there is too much violence. There is more devotion [inside the church]. It is more Christian inside the church.'

Thus in broad strokes it could be argued that Santo Domingo is a 'masculine' celebration. This distinction would also follow Ekern's development of the male/street–female/home dichotomy whereby the 'street' is the male sphere of authority while the home is the female domain (Ekern 1987). Yet this distinction appears somewhat simplistic. It was evident from my observations and informal interviews that the 'male' elements of the Santo Domingo festivities alienated not only women but also men, many of whom voiced the same objections as women. It was clear that most people, both male and female, were primarily observers rather than participants in the Santo Domingo festivities. A number of the men with whom I spoke dismissed the activities around the processions and simply chose to stay away. One supporter of the revolutionary government in the 1980s said that he did not attend the popular celebration at all for fear of violent reprisals from emboldened right-wingers. Indeed, the large jostling crowd that comprised the *vela* had a markedly different feel than that of other crowded public events that I attended – there was more threat of violence and more actual violence.

The male/female distinction is further complicated by the fact that a number of women did participate actively in the festival, albeit usually in a more relaxed fashion. A good example of this distinction was the difference between the cows portrayed by men and by women. The costume consisted of a circular rigging

139

held up by a strap around the neck. Attached to the apparatus were bull horns resting at the level of the genitals. The cow role was played by both men and women who danced on their own and with other revelers. One male cow I observed 'charged' those around him, encouraging them to play the role of the matador. He even playfully pinned a police officer to the side of his vehicle. The female cow did not engage in this mock fighting, preferring to dance on her own or with willing partners.

## The equestrian parades: a different Santo Domingo

In speaking of the revolution, many Nicaraguans say that the Sandinistas, the group that headed the revolutionary government of the 1980s, had a 'big *relajo*'. Sometimes the speaker uses the term critically, other times approvingly. The Santo Domingo festival was considered a *relajo* because of its transgression of accepted notions of propriety; here anything could happen. People ate, drank and danced continuously throughout the all-night vigils and processions which marked the beginning and the end of the festival.

While the Santo Domingo festival was 'opened' and 'closed' by large and lively processions through Managua, it was also framed by more middle- and upper-class equestrian parades. The parades themselves, besides a show of horses and equestrian skill, featured a number of commercially-sponsored bands playing in large lorries while people danced. There were also a number of pick-up trucks with groups in the back waving to the crowd. Most of the people on the lorries and pick-up trucks appeared relatively young (late teens to early twenties) and seemed to have better quality clothes and lighter skin than the participants in the processions. There were none of the extremes of the procession: no outlandish costumes, no exceptional acts of religious devotion, and certainly no grease. Instead of the *relajo* that characterized the processions, the parades were relatively tranquil, the participants observed traffic signals and there was a negligible police presence – a total contrast to the popular processions.

Unlike the processions accompanying the statue, the equestrian parades felt safe – both symbolically and physically. In the equestrian parade there was a marked distinction between the performers (those with access to horses, pick-up trucks and connections to the companies sponsoring the floats) and those who watched in a very passive way. Here, the middle and upper middle classes rode horses and danced on the floats in contrast to their conspicuous absence from the popular celebrations either as participants or observers. The upper and middle classes were the participants by virtue of their social status – everyone else watched. There was little of the fluidity between participant and observer that characterized the processions. Fittingly, given the social class of the participants the most common costume in the equestrian parade was the 'cowboy' rather than the 'Indian'.

## Physical and emotional danger: am I an internationalist or am I an imperialist?

The 1979 revolution which overthrew the dictator Somoza initiated a process of radical socio-economic transformation in Nicaragua. Like many North Americans opposed to the United States government's subsequent attempts to overthrow the Sandinistas, I participated in solidarity groups committed to the revolutionary project for social change. My first visit to Nicaragua was in the 1980s when I picked coffee in the Matagalpa region of Nicaragua as a member of a solidarity brigade. Despite the hardship of the contra war, revolutionary Nicaragua was an exciting and inspirational place to be. This *relajo* was intoxicating and the three weeks I spent in Nicaragua were one of the most profoundly moving periods of my life. Above and beyond the experience of witnessing dramatic improvements in people's lives, I was taken up by the 'force of myth' to which Mariátegui refers (Mariátegui 1958).

In the 1990s, the period in which I conducted my fieldwork, Nicaragua was starkly different. The Sandinista's 1990 electoral defeat saw a retreat from the redistributive ethos of the revolutionary years with the implementation of stringent structural adjustment policies. I, too, was different, returning as a postgraduate student to conduct research on changing forms of political activism. Although during my visit in the 1980s I had been based in what was technically a war zone, 1990s Managua in peacetime seemed a far less safe place to be. One experience brought this sharply into focus for me. Walking down one of the main streets of central Managua, Avineda Bolivar, I passed a pile of burning tires blocking the traffic. This form of protest against the government had been a common sight over the past few days. I quickly walked down the street, more concerned with the intensity of the sun and the prospect of a long queue at the central post office, than the scene before me. Along the roadside demobilized soldiers were protesting the government's failure to fulfil its commitment to provide them with financial assistance. Walking along the same street on my way home, the atmosphere had become palpably more tense and I was warned by the soldiers that there was going to be trouble and I should leave immediately. I did not ask too many questions and hurried up the road. A short while later, there was an exchange of gunfire across the boulevard between the police and the former soldiers. This experience of literally almost being caught in the crossfire heightened my sense of physical insecurity. In addition to political violence, street crime and gang activity were increasingly common as high levels of unemployment and underemployment increased social and economic polarization. As a relatively affluent foreigner I felt particularly vulnerable and on occasion took extreme precautions such as taking a taxi one block rather than walking down a street that felt unsafe.

At the same time, I experienced a range of physical maladies linked to the change in diet and the anti-malaria prophylactics I was taking. Just as I was fearful of violence on the street, I was filled with apprehension in my room as the night air filled with mosquitoes and the large insects and arachnids seemed yet another source of risk. Clearly, in a politically unstable country where the diseases of poverty are far more common than in the West, caution was warranted. However, my sense of physical danger in my calculation of both safety and health risks began to border on if not slide into paranoia. Moreover the feelings of dislocation and isolation that often accompany entering 'the field' added to this distress. I had not anticipated this emotional danger and was quite surprised when I realized just how restricted I had become in my activities. In contrast to the boundless optimism I had felt as a result of my visit to Nicaragua in the 1980s, pessimism began to color my sense not only of post-1990 Nicaragua but also of myself as a researcher and as a person. Yet this personal and political 'loss of faith' was never total. I eventually began to achieve a more balanced sense of the 'field' as I saw how Nicaraguans were coping with the dramatic changes which they had experienced in the past decades.

## Ethical dangers : looking at and speaking about others

In acknowledging the impact that physical and emotional danger had on my research, a set of ethical considerations come into play. These center primarily on how the research impacts on participants. In the informal interviews that I conducted with festival-goers, I was able to give respondents some idea of what my research entailed and to gain their consent to be interviewed. These interviews were conducted primarily during the events themselves and so the scope for extensive discussion of my research and indeed the desire on the part of respondents to know more was limited. Still, for this dimension of the research, informed consent was obtained.

However, for the participant observation dimension of the research, no such consent was obtained nor would it have been possible to do so. At the same time this research does not fit into the covert paradigm for a number of reasons. Key amongst these is that festival activities were public events where everyone was potentially on show. In the context of the festival, honoring Santo Domingo was a public performance rather than an act of private devotion. Many participants, for example, were fulfilling 'promises' made to Santo Domingo in thanks for a blessing believed to be the result of his intervention. These promises took a number of different forms, some based on seeming indulgence and some on sacrifice or deprivation. Amongst these, for example, 'promise fulfillers' or *pagadores de promesas* walked a part of Santo Domingo's journey on their knees whilst others kept a promise to dance through the night.

In addition to watching each other, festival participants, sliding in and out of 'watched' and 'watching' roles, were also under the scrutiny of the police and the Church. The former was concerned to preserve civil authority whilst the latter sought to maintain control over the meaning and scope of devotional activities. Both aimed to contain the *relajo*. Another set of observers were the media, who extensively covered all aspects of the festival. As a researcher, I was differently placed to these other observers and bound by a responsibility to behave in an ethical manner towards participants. Although gaining informed consent in these circumstances was impracticable, clearly I was not absolved from ethical accountability. A significant ethical issue was also how participants would be represented in the research and the wider implications of such representations. The conundrum of how justly to represent others has been an important theme in the literature on research methodology. However, this issue has often been considered through disputes on which methodological strategies are able to produce the most accurate data and on more abstract debates on the possibility of producing research which is able to make 'objective' claims about social groups.

This reflexive account of research has stressed the ways in which danger I encountered in the field impacted on my research. Hence I accept that my research does not present an objective picture of the Santo Domingo festival as understood by participants. As physicists working in the field of quantum mechanics demonstrated so elegantly, the very act of observing a phenomenon alters it (March 1978: 230). This is also true in the social sciences where the presence of the researcher and the methods that s/he employs similarly impact on the research environment. If epistemologies emerge from ontologies (Stanley and Wise 1993) – and it is difficult to see how these can be fully disengaged – then my research on Santo Domingo emerged from a combination of the lived experiences of the people who were the focus of this research in combination with my own background and perceptions as a researcher. Whilst there are a number of reasons for questioning the possibility or desirability of 'objective' research, my research on the Santo Domingo festival provided me with a clear sense of the productivity of a subjective engagement in the research process.

Looking at the culture of others is not a neutral act. The researcher carries with her/him not only a personal history shaped by gender, class, race and a myriad of other factors, but also an institutional location marked by the weight of academic and disciplinary tradition and, not incidentally, her/his own career and professional concerns. As a privileged outsider, my role as a researcher could be construed as a form of cultural or 'academic' imperialism. Fieldwork carries with it a set of assumptions regarding the 'other' and the researcher's relationship to the subject/object of research. As an outsider with a relatively comfortable lifestyle in England, I lived and worked in Nicaragua with the knowledge that whatever difficulties I encountered were temporary. Outside the context of the fieldwork, I had the power to determine not only how participants were represented to the outside world but if they were represented at all. In effect, in common with almost all forms that utilize ethnography: 'The predominant mode of modern fieldwork authority is signaled: "You are there ... because I was there" ' (Clifford 1988: 22).

## Conclusion

In looking specifically at some of the dangers in my research, my aim in this chapter has been to make difficulties more explicit and to acknowledge the power imbalances and problems of representation. I also have striven to make myself explicitly present in the research process, rather than maintaining a strictly 'objective' or 'detached' stance. Yet it must be accepted that even with greater sensitivity to power differentials, the differences between the researcher and the subjects of research in cross-cultural research, and indeed in all research, are to some degree irresolvable.

This reflexive account has not been intended as a personal narrative parallel to and discrete from the research itself. It has also not been an attempt to 'overshadow' the experiences of participants and re-introduce in new garb the supremacy of the researcher's voice. Rather, I have explored the dangers which I experienced as a researcher, placing these alongside those encountered by participants. I have argued that for both myself and participants danger was negotiated in particular ways. For participants in the Santo Domingo festival, gender and class structured the extent to which participants engaged in the *relajo*. So access to the 'free for all' and the temporary overturning of the established order was not open equally to all participants. As a researcher my engagement with the *relajo* was also shaped by these factors and additionally with the specific character of my observer role.

Whilst I was deeply affected by the dangers experienced during my fieldwork in Nicaragua and I developed a range of coping strategies, it is hard to extrapolate from this a set of cautions which would be useful for other researchers working on similar or related projects. However, one overriding feature of my experience was the shock I felt when confronted with danger; I had not fully appreciated that the field would be dangerous nor the nature of the risks with which I might be faced. On this basis I would maintain that the researcher must not become so immersed in the machinations of research and the social identity of their profession that they lose sight of their own physical and emotional vulnerabilities.

144

Researchers may be driven by a commitment to their discipline and a quest to generate new knowledge but this does not provide any special protection in the field. In fact it can create a perilous sense of hubris.

The romance of the lone researcher contributing to a body of scholarship through individual acumen and hard work facilitates an ethos of self-reliance which can make it difficult for researchers to ask for help or envisage ways in which they could be supported by others. It is also hard for institutions to grasp how to provide such assistance given a research culture that elevates individual scholarship. Although I conducted my research on Santo Domingo as a postgraduate student registered at a university, I received no training which might have prepared me for the dangers which I encountered. Once in the field I was 'on my own' thousands of miles from my institution and communication with my supervisor was generally by mail. One way of providing additional support to researchers working away from their university or research unit is to provide more frequent communication with supervisors or project managers. This can be facilitated by access to e-mail which is now increasingly common in many parts of the world. Institutions must develop effective means of, as far as possible, preparing, advising and supporting researchers in the field.

Finally, although this chapter has highlighted the destabilizing and potentially harmful aspects of research danger, it has also indicated the potentially productive character of such risk. It is this contradiction which is contained in the notion of *relajo*.

# Bibliography

Badone, Ellen (ed.) (1990) *Religious Orthodoxy and Popular Faith in European Society*, Princeton, NJ: Princeton University Press.

Behar, R. (1990) 'The Struggle for Church: Popular Anticlericalism and Religiosity in Post-Franco Spain' in E. Badone (ed.) *Religious Orthodoxy and Popular Faith in European Society*, Princeton, NJ: Princeton University Press.

Clifford, J. (1988) *The Predicament of Culture: Twentieth-Century Ethnography, Literature and Art*, Cambridge, MA: Harvard University Press.

Ekern, Stener (1987) *Street Power: Culture and Politics in a Nicaraguan Neighbourhood*, Department of Anthropology, University of Bergen, Norway.

Lancaster, R. (1988) *Thanks to God and the Revolution: Popular Religion and Class Consciousness in the New Nicaragua*, New York: Columbia University Press.

—— (1992) *Life is Hard: Machismo, Danger and the Intimacy of Power in Nicaragua*, Berkeley: University of California Press.

Léon-Portilla, Miguel (ed.) (1980) *Native Mesoamerican Spirituality, Ancient Myths, Discourses, Stories, Doctrines, Hymns, Poems from the Aztec, Yucatec, Quiche-Maya and Other Sacred Traditions*, London: SPCK.

March, R. (1978) *Physics for Poets*, Chicago: Contemporary Books.

Mariátegui, José Carlos (1958) 7 *Ensayos de Interpretacion de la Realidad Peruana, Empresa*, Lima, Peru: Editora Amauta.

Parker, Christián (1993) *Otra Lógica en América Latina: Religión Popular y Modernización Capitalista*, Santiago: Fundo de Cultura Económica.

Rosaldo, Renato (1993) *Culture and Truth: The Remaking of Social Analysis*, London: Routledge.

Rowe, William and Schelling, Vivian (1991) *Memory and Modernity: Popular Culture in Latin America*, London: Verso.

Stanley, L. and Wise, S. (1993) *Breaking Out Again: Feminist Ontology and Epistemology*, London: Routledge.

Trejos Ubau, B. (1992) 'Todos a Traer a Minguio', *Barricada*, 1 August.

# 9

# BODY, CAREER AND COMMUNITY

## The implications of researching dangerous groups

*Arthur J. Jipson and Chad E. Litton*

## Introduction

Studying extremism from a sociological or social anthropological perspective raises certain dangers. This chapter discusses the issue of studying 'dangerous' groups by focusing upon our research experiences whilst studying extremist groups in the United States of America.[1] Some of the dangers we mention are associated with the process of fieldwork in general, such as negotiating access with participants, while others are specific to the study of extremism or dangerous groups. In particular ethical issues are raised when studying groups that hold threatening beliefs about other members of the community and which may be engaged in illegal activities.

We argue that there are three central categories of danger associated with academic work of this nature. The first is the direct physical dangers to the researcher, which manifest themselves in terms of real and threatened physical confrontation with extremists, groups protesting against extremist activities and law enforcement. The dangers to the researcher's academic career are the second theme we explore. Following a research agenda examining the so-called 'fringe' elements of society may push a social researcher to the edges of respected academic circles. The legal and ethical problems involved in qualitative research among separatist populations can mean overextended time commitments for the researcher. This can lead colleagues and administrators to question why an academic might study extremism as opposed to a more mainstream topic. The final theme we discuss is the issue of dangers involving the wider community. The explicit conflict and tension between extremist populations and their environment often leads to confrontations with conventional social organizations. The publicity generated by qualitative research projects on extremist thought and action is often mistakenly perceived within general society as support, some type of propaganda, or is simply dismissed. Research needs to be sensitive to the

147

ethical issues raised by studying groups who represent a threat to the wider community. In reconstructing the academic images of extremists and extremism as acceptable subjects of inquiry, we are able to recognize and deal with the dangers that frequently accompany research on extremism.

We maintain that the term extremism determines the boundaries of a social group, organization, or individual actor who is defined by the wider community as holding an ideological position that runs counter to the accepted legitimate ideas of the community. Moreover, extremists act upon these unconventional ideas through both individual and collective action. Given this definition it is quite possible for one to hold an extreme view and not be perceived as an extremist because there is some social support for the argument or action. For example, the Christian right in the United States uses conventional forms of social protest to achieve an unconventional result. We will consistently use the term to reflect a position that places the advocate in a high degree of tension in relation to their social environment such that beyond their immediate social contacts, there is little or no support for their position and agency.

In this chapter we shall use the general terms 'Racialism' and New Religious Movements (NRMs) because they are broader and more inclusive of the various forms of extremism we have studied in our research. We use the term 'Racialism' because the majority of members of the so-called white supremacist movement self-identify as 'Racialists'. They do so because they argue that they are not racist but instead are 'advocates for their race'.[2] The term New Religious Movements is used because it conveys the general category of unconventional religious organization.[3] There are clear moral and ethical difficulties with the activities and ideologies of such groups because many of them advocate non-tolerant positions to others. For instance, several extremist groups call for outright violence and forced social reorganization that would result in harm to other people. In the case of extremist groups in the United States, particular members of society, such as people of color, lesbians and gay men, Jewish people, and non-dominant nationalities and ethnic groups, are targets for 'Racialists'. It is worth noting that for 'Racialists', whites who do not share their beliefs are also frequent targets of violence. A particular problem is how we study such social groups without promoting or reinforcing the threat to other members of society. However, despite the difficulties, we would argue that it is important to study dangerous groups in order to understand their actions. Through an informed understanding of these social movements and individuals, social control agencies can review their response strategies and prevent violent actions in the future by better predicting disruptive and violent action.

# Methodology

Qualitative research has a long tradition in social research. However, debates about the validity and reliability of qualitative approaches to comprehend the complexity of social experience are still current (Shaffir and Stebbins 1991; Bernard 1995). Recent shifts in theoretical paradigms have challenged the entire basis of the ability of a qualitative researcher to make generalizing claims concerning subjects (Agar 1980, 1986; Clifford and Marcus 1986). In response to these critiques, we advocate a process of qualitative research where the research subjects are allowed to reflect on their internal understandings and meanings through dialogue with the researcher throughout the research process. The researcher's observations connect the macro-level influence of the structure of society and the process of culture on the micro-level experiences of individuals. All social experiences occur in a sociological tension between wider social forces and the individual's actual daily life. The strength of ethnographic research is in understanding cultural and social processes from the viewpoint of participants and the meaning they give to those processes. In response to the detractors of qualitative research paradigms, we would maintain that the best way to explore meaning construction is through a rigorous process of observation and ethnographic interview.

The data acquired during the collection process will direct the progress of the research and influence the types of theoretical analysis used to analyze the information (Whyte 1955; Lee 1970; Speier 1973). The ethnographic approach deals primarily with the use of observation (Glaser and Strauss 1967; Spradley 1980; Lofland and Lofland 1984; Miles and Huberman 1984) to help define a situation or problem and the use of ethnographic interviews (Spradley 1979; Bernard 1995) to help clarify the participants' understanding of that setting. It is important to access the individuals, organizations, and social networks in as open and non-judgmental a manner as is possible (Denizen 1989). This 'openness' is clearly differentiated from anti-movement organizations (e.g. Anti-Defamation League, KlanWatch, Cult Awareness Network) that focus their energies and activities on deconstructing and actively opposing extremist groups. We believe that an accurate and reliable accounting of extremists is dependent upon assembling the accounts and meanings used by members from within, rather than descriptions from other sources (Denizen 1989; King and Hunt 1990). An understanding of what action(s) extremists are capable of committing is tied to their world views. By examining and reviewing these ideas, social control agencies can better assess any immediate and distant threats such groups pose to society and formulate responses.

Analysis of ethnographic data is not divorced from the early stages of research. As Spradley (1980) aptly comments, as a researcher you 'cannot wait until you have collected a large amount of data ... Instead of coming into the field with specific questions, the ethnographer analyzes the field data compiled from participant observation to discover questions' (Spradley 1980: 33). It is crucial to be as reflective and open as possible to the nuances of belief and activity of extremists so as to approximate the meanings that they assign to particular actions. Jorgensen (1989) correctly notes that the process is a painstaking one: 'What is taken to be the problem for research by participant observation is the result of a flexible, open-ended, ongoing research process of identifying, clarifying, negotiating, refining, and elaborating precisely what will be studied' (Jorgensen 1989: 32). As we will demonstrate, the requirements of this particular research process create the greatest dangers involved in researching extremism. The process of intimate involvement with groups that are self and socially defined as anti-systemic and oppositional social movements, exposes the researcher and others to a variety of dangers.

## A conceptual approach toward 'dangerous subjects'

Building on detailed empirical, qualitative, archival, and Internet research on extremism (Blum 1977; Barker 1986; Katz 1986; Richardson 1991; Barkun 1994; MacLean 1994; George and Wilcox 1996), we address the nature, organization and activities of the major participants of the 'Racialist' and New Religious Movements from a qualitative and emergent perspective. We see extremist social movements as socially, politically and culturally constructed. This approach presents an alternative view to the popular deviance perspective, which contends that 'Racialists' and NRM actors and institutions should be understood simply as pathological deviants or intrinsically different from non-movement members (Becker 1963; Adler and Adler 1994). We argue that these movements should not be defined exclusively on the basis of the public perceptions of their actions. Instead, one must analyze the socio-economic, cultural and institutional links among self-designated extremists. These linkages require both a micro- and macro-level analysis of the conditions and processes of late modernity that gave rise to these extremist social and political ideologies. What similarities exist in the processes of recruitment and retention of individuals into these movements? Are there any institutionalized mainstream organizational policies that assisted in the creation and proliferation of these extremist social movements? We contend that membership in these movements is patterned and consistent. In our research on 'Racialists' and NRMs we have found that individuals begin a process of reflection on current social conditions and find the conventional answers to questions of social organization and inequality lacking. Extremism appears to provide the individual with plausible answers to these perplexing enigmas.

Most mainstream discussions of these topics neglect social structure since they assume that membership of these groups is a consequence of individual pathology (Zeskind 1986; Dees and Fiffer 1991; Stanton 1991; Dobie 1992; Christensen 1994; Zellner 1995) or individual motivation (Ezekiel 1995). Our own perspective maintains that individual and collective actions are tied to both group and individual identity, within cultural, historical and structural constraints (Richardson 1985; Staples and Mauss 1987; Kox et al. 1991). There is precedent for such an analysis in the work of some scholars (Aho 1990; Blee 1991; Barkun 1994). These constraints are better understood through the collective behavior and social movement literature, rather than deviant behavior perspective. The nexus of class, status and other conditions must be incorporated into analysis of the motivations of these social actors.

There is a well-established literature on social movement and collectivity formation that addresses the establishment of solidarity and coherence among movement actors (Le Bon [1895] 1960; Blumer [1934] 1969; Smelser 1962). The problem with these approaches is that it views all forms of collectivity as inherently spontaneous and non-rational. Turner and Killian (1987) move closer toward the perspective we advocate here. They suggest that what occurs in crowd formation is actually a process of transformation of normative behavior toward new standards of acceptability that emerge and develop out of the current situation in which the actors find themselves. It is this shift in normative behavior that places these groups in the 'exotic other' category. The importance of this approach is that the individuals and structures of these groups are not seen as existing within a vacuum. Extremist groups are culturally and socially defined in advance as outcasts and dangerous. This view can lead to an inability for social researchers (and policy makers) to consider the wider issues involved with the formation and action of extremist groups.

In our work we combine a 'structural' resource mobilization view of social movements (McCarthy and Zald 1973, 1977; Tilly 1978), frame and resonance analysis (Snow and Bedford 1988), and a 'cultural' new social movements approach (Castells 1976, 1983; Touraine 1981). This theoretical construct allows us to identify the specific opportunities available at particular points in time to social actors and groups within a historically specific constellation of social networks. However, organizational building and implementation cannot overlook a consideration of the movement members' perceptions and understanding of various pressures, lures and options in joining a movement organization. Researchers must understand the movement, the structural organization and the reality through which members understand their world. The combination of these explanations allows for a process of identity formation that acknowledges the boundaries of biology, society and culture and the freedom of individuals to move within these boundaries as they define themselves and the groups to which they belong.

It is the expression of this freedom and the concomitant choices of organizational building and membership that we believe characterize the only possible difference between 'normal' patterns of behavior and 'extreme' patterns. In other words, we argue that there is nothing inherently physiologically or psychologically wrong with these people and we reject the assertion that members of extremist groups necessarily suffer from mental defects as is often asserted in various media. They have, however, chosen a particular definitional path that allows them to accept proof and evidence that a majority of their fellow societal members would reject (Luhrmann 1989). It is these constructs of proof and evidence that lay the foundation for the development of extremist social organizations. We argue that examining the definitions and explanations that extremists construct for their actions does not equate with blind acceptance or neutrality. Rather, we suggest that before action can and should be taken to respond to extremists or to reintegrate them into the community, a full understanding must be formed of their perspective. We acknowledge that this view is controversial and difficult for some. However, any adequate response must appreciate the complexity of the constructed world view of these groups.

While the processes used by extremists in their construction of meaning are not dissimilar to non-extremists, some of the actions that arise from these belief systems stand in opposition to the accepted normative structure of society. However, if a researcher defines extremists as problematic from the onset of research, he or she is, in essence, refusing to understand how these beliefs order a participant's world view or can become part of mainstream culture. Based upon our research, we support the argument that extremist ideology, while marginalized at one juncture, can be absorbed by the larger culture over time (Gabriel 1998). The point of research into extremism is to discern how these individuals and groups construct social organizations around their understandings (Luhrmann 1989). Our conceptual approach leads then to a midrange study of the historical, societal and definitional foundations of extremism. Without a broader approach to the individuals within, and structures of, extremism, policy makers, targeted groups and society in general will be responding to an entirely superficial presentation of potentially dangerous groups. Jipson's research has demonstrated that 'Racialists' are engaged in what they contend is the creation of an intellectual counter-hegemony to the popular conception of racism. As part of this process contemporary 'Racialists' are involved in the pursuit of careers that will produce tangible benefits to their movement, such as degrees in education, law and medicine. We turn now from the academic and social debates about how extremist groups can be understood, to a discussion of the dangers which emerge when carrying out research in this field.

## Direct danger: potentials of confrontation

Engaging in research on 'Racialists' and NRMs is fraught with possible physical and emotional dangers for the researcher. These dangers are directly related to several stages of the qualitative research process: participating in covert or overt research, gaining access, negotiating roles, involvement, and presenting research. While these issues are a feature of all qualitative research, the structural and emotional nature of extremist groups heightens the difficulty and danger. In the past, researchers have undertaken covert research among extremist groups under the guise of law enforcement or mass media (Thompson 1988). However, being perceived as a member of either institution can limit a researcher's access to data in terms of observation of internal interactions or even demonstrations and protests (e.g. Klan rallies). Given the particulars of extremist organization and belief, the most effective and ethical approach is as an overt, known researcher. In this way organizations under study can verify the identity of the researcher as a genuine academic who is interested in the topic. It has been our experience that the known researcher builds a rapport with extremists over time. In Jipson's experience, 'Racialists' became less suspicious as research progresses because trust was established.

The covert researcher's risk of exposure is tied to the viability of their research project. Because the covert researcher cannot be open about their research project, significant problems arise. On learning of the deceit an extremist group may act on their sense of violation by threatening or even physically attacking the researcher (Richardson 1991; Shaffir and Stebbins 1991). A less tangible consequence is the possibility that by breaking the trust of an extremist group a researcher may accelerate or heighten the tension and isolation the group feels toward society and may inadvertently make the group hesitant to participate in further research. An additional concern for the covert researcher is losing information because of an inability to contemporaneously record data. Being able to record data correctly is a serious concern when one is hiding the enterprise. The problem is compounded when one is dealing with groups whose existence is at least partially defined by conspiracy, isolation and a potential for violence to outsiders or targeted others (i.e. people of color and lesbians and gay men for 'Racialists'). While engaging in informed consent the researcher has an opportunity to explain the research project to those most affected by the outcome and presentation of the research. This allows for a series of quality checks on the study as the researcher conducts interviews and continues with the research. Because subjects are able to regularly interact with the researcher, popular assumptions and misconceptions can be reviewed and dispelled.

However, carrying out overt research with potentially dangerous groups also has its own serious risks. Gaining access can be a particularly threatening experience. In Jipson's experience, gaining entry with 'Racialists' not only required the need to juxtapose components of his racial identity but also to submit to close physical and intellectual inspections. The 'Racialist' organizations that were studied asked him about his intellectual training, connection to law enforcement, ethnic and racial background, and spiritual beliefs prior to allowing significant access to the groups. All questions were answered honestly and directly, even if they were not responses that would engender support for the research project. Fortunately, having a doctorate, no immediate connection to law enforcement, and majority European ancestry assisted access. However, the lack of accepted spiritual beliefs and what was perceived as tainted ancestry proved a hindrance for access to some 'Racialist' groups. While no attempt was made to hide elements of identity that were perceived as problematic, Jipson did not openly demonstrate these components of his identity while conducting research. No duplicity was involved but the manner of self-presentation was changed. Physical as well as intellectual tests were also administered and during one inspection the members of a 'Racialist' group in charge of security were physically rough with Jipson while requiring him to perform endurance tests. These included lifting weights and self-defense exercises. Jipson was informed that it needed to be determined if he was 'tough enough to survive spending time' in the group's compound.

Participant observation with 'Racialists' required a change in clothing, vocabulary and gestures in order to facilitate acceptance and access. Wearing conventional working clothes rather than suits assisted acceptance with some groups. Non-judgmental word choice and vocabulary were also crucial to gathering data. 'Racialists' preferred to be called 'Racialist' rather than supremacist or nationalist. Members of NRMs consider themselves church members or religious practitioners rather than religious oddities. Even given the different research subjects, we both noted the need for heightened impression management in interaction with extremists. Unsolicited criticism of extremist philosophy and action was always detrimental to data collection. Avoiding criticism while collecting data can allow increased access, although this does not mean that researchers should lose their perspective on the subjects. A researcher can study an extremist movement without becoming a member or supporter. Extremists do share some of their cognitive landscape with non-extremists and in those moments of convergence, extremist behavior can be better explained.

Because these groups exist in high-tension environments, members are often quick to judge researchers as a possible threat. This leads to potential problems in data gathering, as researchers often have to establish themselves as non-threatening to the group or individual. A danger exists that a researcher may move from empathy to sympathy with extremist individuals and groups. The attempt to empathize with research subjects is not equivalent to sympathizing; to empathize means that the researcher understands the nature of the belief system, while to sympathize conveys acceptance of the ideology. During several research visits we have found that as one becomes a regular member of a group and is concerned with impressions, there is a pull toward acceptance of the belief system. Thus we believe it is important to recognize the difference between empathy and sympathy.

In general the process of gaining access during qualitative research involves the investment of emotional work and meaningful involvement. Without the proper gatekeeper or with poor role definition from the outset of research, the entire project could yield little or no useful information. Often during qualitative research the role of researcher becomes blurred, as it is common for the researcher to try to take a useful role within the group rather than create a new role. Few isolationist groups can afford to create a position for an individual who hangs around the fringes of the group and never really participates but is always taking notes and asking questions. However, performing a useful function raises serious ethical concerns in terms of assisting an organization that many perceive and experience as a direct physical threat. Any useful role provided to extremist organizations, regardless of how insignificant, may be construed as supportive.

The potential for secondary roles for a researcher among extremist groups is also quite limited. First, one must be able to gain and maintain trust. This trust is quite tenuous considering that the researcher has no legal protection from testifying against the members of the group. Social scientists cannot claim protection akin to a doctor/patient or attorney/client privilege. A researcher might be compelled to turn over notes and code books created during the project to the authorities. This is a very real problem for researchers studying social movements or research participants who may be involved with illegal activities. For instance, American sociologist Rik Scarce spent several months in jail in 1993 for refusing to give information to law enforcement officials about whether he had interviewed people involved in a raid on an animal laboratory. Fortunately, neither of us has experienced violent incidents or witnessed plans to create and co-ordinate violent incidents. We make it a point to discuss the plan for dissemination of research findings with the individuals and groups participating in the study and the potential ethical dilemmas of violent or criminal actions. During this discussion the real potential for notes and materials to be forcibly taken from the researcher is addressed. The coding and screening of materials for confidentiality and anonymity becomes crucial to engendering trust. On several occasions Jipson has been asked by members of white supremacist groups for a chance to review his notes. On one occasion, when copies of the notes were turned over to one group, the members made surprisingly few corrections or comments. One member noted to Jipson: 'I can't believe that you changed everyone's name without us asking you to do that. Now we know we can trust you!' Such episodes help create a degree of trust between the researcher and his or her subjects that can lead to further access to a group's activities and internal documents.

A natural part of the ethnographic research process involves long-term involvement with research subjects. This involvement becomes much more problematic when studying extremists. A researcher caught in a fire fight between federal authorities and an extremist group, for example, would face obvious ethical dilemmas. For instance, how could a researcher be expected to defend him/herself without breaking the law or injuring a law enforcement officer? We believe that a researcher's personal ethical code dictates their responses to potentially violent situations. Some criminologists have conducted research on criminal enterprises without reporting the totality of their experiences to legal authorities because it would compromise their data collection. While being present during illegal activities is dangerous (Adler and Adler 1991), a lack of participation may result in attracting the ire of extremists while failure to report crime(s) may constitute a breach of the law. There is always the possibility that the researcher may be labeled an active participant simply by being present among members of the group. Attending a 'Racialist' or NRM rally may be enough to make a researcher a target of counter-demonstrators, law enforcement activity or at risk of retaliation from other groups in society. A researcher may return home after an event alone, while the group being studied may remain together to reinforce the 'rightness' of their cause through social solidarity. Furthermore, given the requirements of confidentiality, a researcher cannot discuss an event or situation with others immediately following the event. Emotional distress and physical danger may result from this social isolation.

A serious ethical dilemma arises when the group threatens to engage in violence toward a particular social group or the larger community. Where does the researcher's responsibility lie? While we have not had to face such a situation in our research, we contend that a researcher's assurances of data confidentiality are meaningless if at any sign – real or perceived – of possible violence, the researcher contacts law enforcement. We assert that such determinations need to be made on the analysis of each case. In Jipson's research with a 'Racialist' organization in the American Midwest, 'Racialists' seemed to be preparing for a violent act. After much personal reflection, Jipson decided to question the participants about their plans rather than contacting law enforcement. The entire plan was a charade meant to test the researcher's assurances of confidentiality. While this conclusion was clearly preferable, it does not remove the social and emotional burden relating to potential violent acts.

Another danger is that law enforcement may target a researcher directly as a participant. As a member of the National Guard, Litton was trained in ways to pick out leaders in civil disturbance situations. According to the training, the real leaders are not the loud and confrontational individuals, instead the leaders are identified as the person(s) in the background who observe the action, interject orders and track the progress of the event. This view of leadership could cast suspicion on researchers observing an event among extremists.

Given the propensity for extremist groups to be rife with strong emotive symbols and highly-charged interactions, over time it is possible for a researcher to begin to feel a close association with the group. This affinity may even intensify into self-identification, often referred to in the anthropology literature as 'going native'. However, emotional attachment to groups who can be extremely violent, or who might be caught in violent situations with the authorities, may lead researchers down a perilous emotional path. Prior to the fire at Mount Carmel, Litton contemplated traveling to Waco to contact and interview some of the Branch Davidians. However, the emotional scarring on him from the deaths at Waco and the associated deaths in Oklahoma City reduced if not eliminated Litton's willingness to discuss the deaths with the survivors.

As the researcher performs role(s) within a group successfully, the actual members of the group may begin to see him or her as one of them. Extremists may interpret interest in the group as acceptance and/or sanctioning of the beliefs, goals and means of the group. On several occasions, a group has affirmed its identity as 'Racialists' and included Jipson in the identification. While there is some degree of anxiety produced by being called or perceived as a 'Racialist', it is important for the researcher to discuss the nature, purposes and organization of the research with subjects. A process of self-reflection must accompany this level of acceptance. Is the researcher becoming too intimate or personally connected to the members of the group? Researchers must repeatedly clarify their role(s) and purpose within an extremist organization or group. We believe, however, that the establishment of emotional ties to a group is inherent and inevitable in the process of study. Jipson's response to being referred to as a 'Racialist' has varied. Depending on the situation, he has either directly asked subjects what reason(s) would lead them to those conclusions or responded to the label at a later time.

Displeasure with the project findings on the part of participants can also increase potential problems for the researcher. While all qualitative researchers must cope with this quandary, when researching extremists these issues are intensified. Extremists might regard the researcher as a propaganda tool to be used to promulgate their objectified reality. When the finished project report is published in the objective language structure of social research, the group(s) may accurately consider the study a pretense to uncover information about them. The group(s) may even view the researcher as a confederate of the authorities and may respond by accentuating their isolation and conspiratorial beliefs. One of the consequences of this is that future research in the group may become impossible. It is also possible the group may seek retribution on the researcher in some fashion. At best, extremists may seek to encourage a re-evaluation of research findings and/or their presentation, at worst, they may try to coerce an alteration of findings to better suit their extremist positions, or they may even assault the researcher. Jipson has been approached repeatedly by past subjects of research and asked why he has not become an active 'Racialist'. By not supporting their internal logic structures, a researcher may be perceived as a detractor of that logic. Again, it is crucial for the researcher to respond thoroughly to the assumption that simply being present in the group or knowledgeable about the belief system automatically makes one a member of the group. When asked this question, Jipson reiterated the purpose of the project and used the question to ascertain why the subjects would expect someone to become transformed by exposure to the group's beliefs.

In order to deal with these issues of presentation we incorporate a reciprocal research model in which the researcher sends the researched the preliminary report. This allows the subjects to comment on the accuracy and veracity of the claims and descriptions in the research. However, given the need for objective description and analysis, it is quite possible that participants will disagree with the wording, organization and conclusions of the report. We have discovered in our work that it is still possible to dialogue with movement members about the context of the research even when there is disagreement over wording and conclusions. This process often leads to a greater understanding of the boundaries of the meaning systems constructed and applied by these groups to their experiences.

To sum up our arguments in this section, it is essential that the researcher makes clear to movement leaders and members that s/he does not share the goals, strategies and activities of the movement. Rather, the researcher is trying to describe the particular case, event or movement as accurately as possible. This attempt at detachment can cause the group to become 'distant' but it helps to avoid some of the problems associated with identification and the presentation of the research report. Even with these caveats it is still quite possible that resentment from movement members may escalate into potential harm to the researcher. Although neither author has suffered any serious physical harm, we cannot stress clearly enough that potential physical harm is a possible consequence of researching extremism.

## Professional danger: so why do you want to study these groups?

One of the most disconcerting dangers to researchers engaged in work on extremism is the lack of acceptance by academic colleagues. This danger manifests itself most dramatically in the possibility of a lack of tenure or promotion, as well as a general level of disrespect for one's work and opinion.

Colleagues have repeatedly questioned us about the academic rigor of qualitative research on extremists. Questions about such work generally fall under two broad categories: first, that the researcher must either become an extremist or sympathize with extremism in order to conduct research in this area and second, that any research conducted in the area of extremism must be done with a view toward debunking extremist ideology.

The issue of sympathizing with, or becoming like, one's participants has long been identified as a difficulty within social anthropological and sociological research. This situation is particularly true in social anthropology where the image of the researcher being adopted by, and adopting, 'the natives' has been one of the most deserving targets of postmodern critiques (Brightman 1995). However, the general patterns of ethnographic affiliation should not be confused with actually 'going native'. For example, when Litton was conducting his research on the Branch Davidians, he was often confronted by colleagues with the charge of being 'too sympathetic' to their viewpoint because he did not attempt to disprove their belief system. He was accused of 'accepting' their conspiratorial view of the world by portraying them as anything other than cultists. Other academics expressed concern that he had become 'too emotionally involved' with the Branch Davidians who had died at Mount Carmel. This empathy created by the loss of human life, it was said, would taint the data and lead to illogical and inaccurate conclusions about the events at Waco. However, the emotions surrounding these incidents and images are difficult to ignore and to do so would invite a poor interpretation of the significance of the emotive aspect of human interaction. This is one of the reasons why we advocate a strong qualitative research design. The process of qualitative inquiry allows researchers to include interpretations and discussions of their emotional reactions after the research has been completed. While some researchers have clearly become too involved with their research subjects, we feel that the only way to describe accurately the social and cultural processes involved with these groups is to become, to some extent, involved in the meaning constructs of the members.

Research on 'Racialists' poses an acute problem with regard to academic dangers. Research on this subject is often perceived to harbor a prurient interest within the sociology of deviance and to hold little or no scholarly value. Jipson has been repeatedly questioned on the validity of conducting research that does not focus on undermining these social movements. It is interesting that many academics appear to assume that research on social movements has to be conducted by supporters of those organizations. It is quite possible, as we have repeatedly stated at conferences and in classes, that it is possible to study objectively a social organization that one does not support. In fact, we would argue that other academicians and policy makers ignore these social movements at their peril, as recent events in the United States and Europe have aptly demonstrated. If we comprehend the origins of these forms of association and behavior, then attempts can be made to channel the discontent associated with extremism into mainstream forms of protest.

However, with these groups as study subjects, researchers run the risk of being labeled as supporters or propagandists. For example, we have spent many years working to construct recognized and funded research around the concepts presented in this chapter. Yet colleagues at professional meetings continue to question the validity of any research on extremism that is not linked directly to official law enforcement agencies. The assumption being made is that these groups, individuals and movements are intrinsically different and problematic when compared to the majority of society; and therefore are of no value to the general study of humanity. However, social theorists and researchers have long maintained that there is no better way to understand one's own socio-cultural system than to enter into the study of other structures and meaning systems. As Geertz states, 'we must learn to grasp what we cannot embrace' (Geertz 1994: 465).

The second major area of academic critique comes from the notion that research will lead to a process of de-legitimizing extremist structures and beliefs. Our purpose as researchers is not to condone, validate, negate, glorify or condemn extremist beliefs. Instead our remit is to investigate and present our findings so that extremists can be reintegrated into the human community to the greatest degree possible. Others may respond that participants in 'Racialist' groups and NRMs are not deviant, while still taking the position that it is possible to say that the actions of some of these organizations (e.g. desecrating Jewish cemeteries, lynching, violent assaults, etc.) are illegitimate. While we understand that position, we believe that we must grasp the world view of extremists rather than judging action. Only in understanding the origins of the action(s) can we hope to address them adequately.

## Danger involving the wider community: dangers beyond the researcher and researched

Thus far we have discussed some of the dangers associated with the interactions between the researcher and the researched, as well as the researcher and the academic community. However, there are also perils involving extremist groups and the wider society, in terms of direct physical interaction, the emotional response of the larger community to this type of research, and the consumption of media images of these groups. The events at Ruby Ridge, Idaho (21 August 1992), Whidbey Island, Washington (8 December 1984), and Waco, Texas (28 February 1992 to 19 April 1992), indicate that a certain amount of peril is involved when extremist groups come into direct contact with law enforcement.

When there is social contact between extremist groups and elements of the larger society, such as during a supremacist rally, the interaction is often charged with strong emotions and a possibility for violent confrontation.

If a researcher is to become involved in a pre-existing context one must be aware of the potential dangers of the situation. Researchers often conduct their work in communities that are removed from their place of residence. It may become easy for researchers to distance themselves from a research site with which they have no immediate personal connection. Although the presence of a researcher may increase the level of tension among and between the members of an extremist movement and the larger community, an outside observer can benefit a community as well. Researchers may be able to offer mediation in certain circumstances but members of the extremist group may view the potential propaganda value of the situation as useful and consequently act in a more aggressive manner. The presence of the observer or researcher may indicate to the group that there is a greater legitimacy to their goals or ideas because someone is interested in them. This sense of 'new-found' legitimacy may be a catalyst for increased activities, recruitment and organization, which in turn may lead to counter-responses from the community at large. The nature of these responses, of course, will vary according to the composition, nature and history of the specific community. In Jipson's research on Ku Klux Klan rallies it was found that the researcher's presence at such events can actually lead to greater posturing by Klan and related organizations (Jipson and Becker 1997).

It is also possible for the researcher's presence to heighten the desire among the group to have a confrontation; the subjects of the research may become more convinced of the veracity of their beliefs and may build up a stronger sense of moral indignation. It is also possible that the subjects may begin to notice the gaps in their internal logic structures. Either of these results may lead to a desire to take a stand, to make a statement, or to participate in an event that may not have occurred without the researcher's presence, questioning and analysis. Thus, it is important for researchers to realize that they have an impact on the researched, the community and themselves.

In order to help prevent an escalation of tensions, the researcher must take care in the structure, organization and timing of the research. If a particularly important date or event for the group is imminent, the researcher should be aware of this. In order to deal with an already heightened emotional state, scholars must carefully choose the pattern of their questions and observations so as not to increase an already dangerous interaction. Taking greater care to document the preparation for an event, rather than pushing for detailed information on the structure or meaning of the event, can lead to strong observational information that the researcher can use to construct questions that will elicit good data and analysis in a *post hoc* atmosphere.

The emotional response of the larger community to these issues is important to consider. We are examining groups that actively define themselves as anti-systematic, isolationist and contrary to the larger society. The local community may see these movements as deviant, evil, 'brainwashed' or poorly educated. However, this interpretation can be dangerous. If the accepted view of 'Racialists' is that they are incapable of organizing and building networks, then society will be ill-equipped to respond to this threat. Therefore research in this area needs to recognize the feelings and anxieties of the wider community, whilst maintaining a research agenda that will gather important information about the beliefs of 'Racialists' and NRMs. This can be difficult given recent events in the United States and elsewhere. For instance, the people of the state of Oklahoma exhibit the symptoms of an assault victim when discussing the images and issues surrounding the Oklahoma City bombing. Both NRMs and right-wing separatist groups have been labeled as part of the cause, if not directly responsible for the bombing. The people of Oklahoma feel a sense of violation and carry a deep hatred toward extremist groups. When Litton has discussed with them the legitimacy of extremist groups as social entities, the response has been hostile. There is disbelief that someone would or could take these groups seriously. These interactions have given Litton a greater understanding of the issues involved with mass or collective trauma.

As we have illustrated, there are significant repercussions to participating publicly in this type of research. Beyond the scope of public versus researcher interests, there are also issues of media and academic exposure for these groups. By participating in research that becomes publicly visible, a group may gain coverage which advertises, and sometimes aids, their cause. While researchers are required to maintain the privacy of the people they are studying, the participants themselves are not bound to those same standards. Groups that are often labeled as undesirable or fringe are frequently excited about being the center of interest and this is particularly true if the group sees the researcher as a propaganda tool. In the longer term, a group may be forced into more public confrontations after the research is published or receives media exposure.

## Concluding comments on researching dangerous groups

Our research has been with extremist groups, which is a specialist area of social research that few readers will have encountered. However, our experience can be seen to raise broader concerns for anyone undertaking research on groups who are negatively labeled, who engage in threatening or dangerous behaviors, or whose belief systems challenge the norms of society. Three key issues around the risk of conducting research on dangerous groups have been examined in this chapter. First, we discussed the direct physical dangers to the researcher. Where groups are known to have the potential for violence the researcher, and those around them, are liable to be a target for reprisals if the group feels threatened by any aspect of the research process. As we and Calvey (Chapter 3 in this volume) have argued, taking a covert research role is not necessarily 'safer', as discovery could put the researcher in immediate and severe personal risk. Our position is that although some physical risks remain, the open study of these groups at least allows the possibility of honest interaction between researched and researcher.

Second, in this chapter we have discussed the subject of the career dangers associated with researching on extremist groups. Given the primacy of quantification in social research, qualitative research itself can be seen as a difficult career choice. However, the added dimension of a focus upon extremist groups as subjects makes one's position even more perilous. Extremist groups are often seen as illegitimate topics of study and the membership as 'mind-controlled zombies'. By re-conceptualizing extremists as part of an anti-systemic social movement, instead of following the standard deviance and collective behavior models available, we risk the alienation of the social science academy. The final area of danger we have considered in this chapter is the jeopardy posed to the wider community by researching dangerous groups. While the issues of liability to the researcher may seem obvious and, after some consideration, academic dangers from this type of research become clear, the broader issue of the effect on the public of researching dangerous groups is less obvious and can be difficult to predict.

In general, we would recommend that qualitative researchers studying extremist or potentially dangerous groups take three basic steps to prepare for, and deal with, these dangers. The first is to clearly structure the research agenda. A thorough literature review on the group you intend to study and careful examination of research on similar groups is necessary. Research on white supremacy, for example, is useful for those who study NRMs and vice versa. To avoid any misinterpretation of one's position in the social group, the stages of research should be designed carefully and the parameters and focus should be argued in an academic mode. This will help not only in explaining your position to academic colleagues but also in gaining entry and developing research roles among your subjects. We have found the best strategy is to use a pilot project in the early stages of conducting research with dangerous groups. This allows you to forecast what kinds of dangers may be experienced later.

Our second general recommendation is to maintain these research convictions at all stages of the project. This means that you need to continually reinforce your position as a researcher among the group you are studying. This will build a level of trust and honesty between your subjects and yourself and allay fears from colleagues or peers about the research focus. It is always important to establish and advertise the boundaries between what we study and who we are. By maintaining connections to your wider research agenda, you can clearly delineate the benefit and accuracy of your research. It will also help you to maintain a certain distance from the difficult emotions invoked by these topics. Our final general guideline is simple. There is no real legal protection for your research or your presence in these groups. If the dangers to your own person, to the group or to the community become unacceptably large you must remove yourself from the situation. It is because of this that, unlike Calvey, we do not recommend covert research. If discovered, the risk of physical harm to the researcher and those around is escalated.

Undertaking research with dangerous groups necessitates a careful consideration of the possible risks. One needs to be able to anticipate and deal with these issues in a contingent manner but this is no excuse for naivete. In preliminary contacts the researcher(s) can determine the suitability of the organization, site or event for the research. The benefits and potential for harm of the project can then be weighed up and considered within the wider ethical framework of the possible impact of the findings upon both participants and other members of society.

## Notes

1 This chapter is based on research conducted on New Religious Movements and 'Racialist' groups in the United States. While both authors have conducted research on both types of group, the material presented here is based primarily on Jipson's work with Racialists and Litton's work on New Religious Movements.

2 In his research, Jipson has noted the growing popularity of the term and concept of 'Racialism' as opposed to other self-identifying labels among white supremacists, white nationalists, racist skinheads and followers of 'Christian identity'. In an attempt to argue that the movement is not centered on hate but instead focused on racial and cultural preservation, this term has been widely adopted within the international white supremacist movement. For this chapter, rather than differentiate among these factions within the wider movement, the umbrella term of 'Racialism' will be used.

3 A caveat is in order here because NRMs do not accept or use the term to describe themselves or their activity. Instead most would refer to their organizations as churches. However, rather than clutter this chapter with several references to distinct churches the general term NRM is used. Where the specific context and details of a church are useful to elaborate or illustrate an idea, a self-designated title or term will be used.

## Bibliography

Adler, P. and Adler, P. (1991) 'Stability and Flexibility: Maintaining Relations Within Organized and Unorganized Groups' in W. Shaffir and R. Stebbins (eds) *Experiencing Fieldwork: An Inside View of Qualitative Research*, Newbury Park, CA: Sage.

—— (1994) *Constructions of Deviance*, New York: Wadsworth.

Agar, M. (1980) *The Professional Stranger*, New York: Academic Press.

—— (1986) *Speaking of Ethnography*, Beverly Hills, CA: Sage.

Aho, J. (1990) *The Politics of Righteousness*, Seattle: University of Washington Press.

Barker, W. (1986) *The Aryan Nations: A Linkage Profile*, written and published by William E. Barker. Place of publication unavailable.

Barkun, M. (1994) *Religion and the Racist Right*, Chapel Hill: University of North Carolina Press.

Becker, H. (1963) *The Outsiders*, New York: The Free Press.

Bernard, R. (1995) *Research Methods in Anthropology: Qualitative and Quantitative Approaches*, 2nd edition, Walnut Creek, CA: Altamira Press.

Blee, K. (1991) *Women of the Klan*, Berkeley: University of California Press.

Blum, H. (1977) *Wanted! The Search for Nazis in America*, New York: Simon & Schuster.

Blumer, H. [1934] (1969) 'Outline of Collective Behavior' in Robert R. Evans (ed.) *Readings in Collective Behavior*, Chicago: Rand McNally.

Brightman, R. (1995) 'Forget Culture: Replacement, Transcendence, Reflexification', *Cultural Anthropology* 10, 4: 509–46.

Castells, M. (1976) 'Theoretical Propositions for an Experimental Study of Urban Social Movements' in C. G. Pickvance (ed.) *Urban Sociology: Critical Essays*, London: Tavistock.

—— (1983) *The City and the Grassroots: A Cross-cultural Theory of Urban Social Movements*, London: Edward Arnold.

Christensen, L. (1994) *Skinhead Streetgangs*, New York: Paladin Books.

Clifford, J. and Marcus, G. E. (eds) (1986) *Writing Culture*, Berkeley, CA: University of California Press.

Dees, M. and Fiffer, S. (1991) *A Season for Justice*, New York: Simon & Schuster.

Denizen, N. (1989) *Interactive Interactionism*, Newbury Park, CA: Sage.

Dobie, K. (1992) 'Long Day's Journey Into White', *The Village Voice*, 28 April.

Ezekiel, R. (1995) *The Racist Mind*, New York: Viking.

Flynn, K. and Gerhardt, G. (1991) *The Silent Brotherhood*, New York: Signet Books.

Gabriel, J. (1998) *Whitewash: Racialised Politics and the Media*, New York: Routledge.

Geertz, C. (1994) 'The Uses of Diversity' in Robert Borofsky (ed.) *Assessing Cultural Anthropology*, New York: McGraw-Hill.

George, J. and Wilcox, L. (1996) *American Extremists: Militias, Supremacists, Klansmen, Communists and Others*, Amherst, NY: Prometheus.

Glaser, B. G. and Strauss, A. L. (1967) *The Discovery of Grounded Theory*, Chicago: Aldine.

Jipson, A. and Becker, P. (1997) 'Protesting Klan Rallies: Community vs. Non-Local Organizations', paper presented at the American Sociological Association Conference, Toronto, Canada, August.

Jorgensen, D. L. (1989) *Participant Observation: A Methodology for Human Studies*, Newbury Park, CA: Sage.

Katz, W. (1986) *The Invisible Empire*, Seattle: Open Hand Publishing.

King, M. and Hunt, R. (1990) 'Measuring the Religious Variable: Final Comment', *Journal for the Scientific Study of Religion* 29, 4: 531–35.

Kox, W., Meeus, W. and 't Hart, H. (1991) 'Religious Conversion of Adolescents: Testing the Lofland and Stark Model of Religious Conversion', *Sociological Analysis* 52, 3: 227–40.

Le Bon, G. [1895] (1960) *The Crowd*, New York: Viking Press.

Lee, A. M. (1970) 'On Context and Relevance' in, Glenn Jacobs (ed.) *The Participant Observer,* New York: George Braziller Publishing.

Liebow, E. (1967) *Tally's Corner*, Boston: Little, Brown & Company.

Litton, C. (1994) 'Creation of a Cult: Media Representations of the Branch Davidians', unpublished Master's thesis, Bowling Green State University.

Lofland, J. and Lofland, L. (1984) *Analyzing Social Settings*, Belmont: Wadsworth.

Luhrmann, T. M. (1989) *Persuasions of the Witches' Craft: Ritual Magic in Contemporary England*, Cambridge, MA: Harvard University Press.

McCarthy, J. and Zald, M. (1973) *The Trend of Social Movements in America: Professionalism and Resource Mobilization*, Morristown: General Learning Press.

—— (1977) 'Resource Mobilization and Social Movements: A Partial Theory', *American Journal of Sociology* 82: 1212–39.

MacLean, N. (1994) *Behind the Mask of Chivalry*, New York: Oxford University Press.

Miles, M. B. and Huberman, A. M. (1984) *Qualitative Data Analysis*, Beverly Hills: Sage.

Richardson, J. T. (1985) 'The Active vs. Passive Convert: Paradigm Conflict in Conversion/Recruitment Research', *Journal for the Scientific Study of Religion* 24, 2: 119–236.

—— (1991) 'Experiencing Research on New Religions and Cults: Practical and Ethical Considerations' in W. Shaffir and R. Stebbins (eds) *Experiencing Fieldwork: An Inside View of Qualitative Research*, Newbury Park, CA: Sage.

Rockwell, G. L. [1967] (1977) *White Power*, National Vanguard Books.

Scarce, R. (1990) *EcoWarriors*, Chicago: Noble Press.

Shaffir, W. and Stebbins, R. (eds) (1991) *Experiencing Fieldwork: An Inside View of Qualitative Research*, Newbury Park, CA: Sage.

Smelser, N. (1962) *Theory of Collective Behavior*, New York: The Free Press.

Snow, D. and Bedford, R. (1988) 'Ideology, Frame Resonance, and Participation Mobilization', *International Social Movement Research* 4: 197–217.

Speier, M. (1973) *How to Observe Face-To-Face Communication: A Sociological Introduction*, Pacific Palisades, CA: Goodyear Publishing Company, Inc.

Spradley, J. (1979) *The Ethnographic Interview*, Fort Worth, TX: Harcourt, Brace, Jovanovich.

—— (1980) *Participant Observation*, Fort Worth, TX: Holt, Rinehart & Winston.

Stanton, B. (1991) *Klanwatch*, New York: Grove Weidenfeld.

Staples, C. and Mauss, A. (1987) 'Conversion or Commitment? A Reassessment of the Snow and Machalek Approach to the Study of Conversion', *Journal for the Scientific Study of Religion* 26, 2: 133–47.

Thompson, J. (1988) *My Life in the Klan*, Nashville: Rutledge Hill Press.

Tilly, C. (1978) *From Mobilization to Revolution*, Reading, Mass.: Addison-Wesley.

Touraine, A. (1981) *The Voice and the Eye: An Analysis of Social Movements*, trans. Alan Duff, London: Cambridge University Press.

Turner, R. and Killian, L. (1987) *Collective Behavior*, 3rd edition, Englewood Cliffs: Prentice Hall.

Whyte, W. (1955) *Street Corner Society*, Chicago: University of Chicago Press.

Wolf, D. (1991) 'High-Risk Methodology: Reflections on Leaving an Outlaw Society' in W. Shaffir and R. Stebbins (eds) *Experiencing Fieldwork: An Inside View of Qualitative Research*, Newbury Park, CA: Sage.

Zellner, W. (1995) *Counter Cultures*, New York: St Martin's Press.

Zeskind, L. (1986) *The Christian Identity Movement: Theological Justification for Racist and Anti-Semitic Violence*, The Division of Church and Society of the National Council of the Churches of Christ in the USA.

# 10

# WHITENESS

## Endangered knowledges, endangered species?

*John Gabriel*

### Introduction

It is a challenge, even a hazardous one, for a white, male academic to write reflexively about the dangers of research into questions of racism and ethnicity. However, *not* to confront such questions is arguably more, not less perilous. Being a white researcher in this field has been the norm for too long and taking the powers and privileges of 'whiteness' for granted has only served to secure its legitimacy. The political dangers of not addressing such questions thus outweigh the emotional costs of problematizing and deconstructing one's own research practice.

Accordingly, the purpose of this chapter is to use my research experience to explore five different kinds of danger. The first is that of representation. Who gets to define and select research problems; in whose voice are the results written up and analyzed; and for whom is the research written? If the research draws on the accounts of others, for example through interview, then their words are framed, prompted and edited by the researcher. The problem of representation also poses numerous risks for the researcher. Amongst those of particular significance in this context are the dangers of silencing, misrepresenting and pathologizing some ethnicities, whilst normalizing others. I shall return to this below.

Second, there are what might be termed professional dangers, linked to the idea of what is considered 'safe' research. For example, the relative lack of studies of higher education might well reflect such risks. Research that is considered too close to home might well be seen to threaten the standing of the very research bodies and institutions which sponsor such research in the first place. The idea of the researcher as piper playing the funder's tune may be an oversimplification but must go some way to explain the dearth of research that takes university funding bodies, professional associations, trade unions, research centers, administrative and academic departments, etc., as its focus. Ideas of value-freedom, academic freedom and the protocols of 'good research' also serve to protect researchers from admitting the hidden bias in their work and even their unwitting collusion with dominant values. Reflexivity encourages a more open engagement with such questions, although safety first might well advise their avoidance.

Third, there are the consequences and uses of research which, though difficult to anticipate in advance, can pose risks for both researchers and researched. Even well-intentioned liberal research can indirectly put people at risk and hence has been viewed with justified suspicion by minority groups. We live in a surveillance age in which new technologies and increasingly sophisticated information systems are used to control and regulate marginal groups. The on-going debate regarding the collection and potentially conflicting uses of ethnic data in the British census is one of many examples.[1] Research can feed such systems of control depending on how it is taken up and by whom. Under these circumstances it can be argued that the physical as well as moral dangers faced by those being researched pose a set of ethical dangers for the would-be researcher.

Studies of neo-fascist groups clearly pose a fourth, this time perhaps direct physical danger to those observing such groups at close quarters (see Chapter 9 in this volume). Such research begs a number of questions. Should researchers conceal their values and/or research credentials in order to gain access to the group and win its trust, and is this strategy, considered unethical in 'normal' research circumstances, legitimate because of the exceptional nature of the research? Moreover, could it not be said that research on the 'far right' might actually serve to enhance the status of extremist groups in some circles, or at least aid would-be sympathizers in their search for contacts and other kinds of information? Finally, it is worth asking to what extent such research serves 'white interests', both by confining discussions of racism to the practices of some lunatic group rather than rooting it in mainstream culture and by projecting fantasies and desires on to others, thus regulating and defining the norms of white behavior.

A fifth danger is that of unreliable knowledge. This is not uncommon in any field of research but it is all the more acute in an area as sensitive as the study of racism and inequality. Unreliability can take a number of forms. For example it is more than likely that qualitative researchers of different ethnic backgrounds will elicit different responses from the same respondents asking the same questions (Song and Parker 1995). 'Unreliable' can also mean that survey responses may be 'adapted' by anxious or cynical respondents. Finally there is every chance that 'officials', for example civil servants, politicians, managers, etc., may well espouse an official, 'politically-correct' rhetoric in response to probing questions, which bears little relation to institutional practice or individual behavior. The last of these examples poses a further set of ethical dilemmas for researchers when they try to get around such institutional ploys. Research strategies might be called for which include the use of hidden video cameras or cassette recorders, covert observation and/or the need to 'dress-up' the research in order to gain access.

In what follows, I shall refer to two research projects in which I have been involved, entitled 'Local Politics of Race' and 'Whitewash'. The former examined the role of local politics in combating racism and promoting racial equality in Liverpool and Wolverhampton in the United Kingdom. It ran from the late 1970s through to the mid-1980s (Ben-Tovim et al. 1986). The latter was a research project undertaken in the mid-1990s for a book on whiteness and the media in England and the United States (Gabriel 1998). The research process in each case will be examined in terms of the strategies used to confront and negotiate the different kinds of danger identified above. Sandwiched between the two projects is a discussion of the changing vocabulary of 'race' and ethnicity and the emergence of whiteness as a key concept. These are changes, I will argue, that reflect emergent dangers in the politics of 'race' and ethnic relations research from the mid-1980s onwards.

## Project one: the Local Politics of Race

Some of the background conditions shaping the development of the 'Local Politics of Race' project were particular to the UK. Because the 1976 Race Relations Act had placed a statutory duty on local governments to promote equality of opportunity, anti-racists were encouraged to concentrate on activism in local government. This trend was further bolstered, from 1979 onwards, by the election and re-election of a series of right-wing Conservative governments under Margaret Thatcher. Growing evidence of racial discrimination combined with a relative lack of research on the institutional processes that limited the impact of anti-racist and race equality politics prompted us to focus our research on this locality.

Broadly, the project explored differences between Liverpool and Wolver-hampton in terms of the limitations of local politics in realizing racial equality and eliminating racism. Regarding research methods, the idea was to combine participant observation of community organizations and groups with more formal interviews with key officers and politicians in the respective town halls. As it turned out, the Chief Executives of both authorities refused access to the research team for these purposes. The risks associated with such denials are commonplace in research but no more so than where the researcher's agenda relates to highly sensitive questions of institutional racism and racial equality policies, the results of which are likely to cast the institution in an unfavorable light. Even when access is given, researchers are still faced with the problem of penetrating what has now become a highly sophisticated rhetoric of 'politically correct' institution-speak. Under such circumstances 'formal' evidence of current good practice might belie disturbing yet unearthed continuities with an inadvertently (or not) racist past.

All research set-backs have their silver linings, however, and in our case, the failure to establish formal ties with the local authorities forced us to put an even greater emphasis on the role of participant observation and, as I shall explain, action research. The Chief Executives' decision not to permit access proved decisive, both in re-orienting the research and arguably in enhancing the reliability of our findings. The research group agreed that another and perhaps more foolproof way of exploring institutional processes was to test them directly through our involvement in local organizations such as Community Relations Councils and Anti-Racist Alliances. In other words, instead of, for example, inviting Chief Education Officers to recite the Local Education Authorities' (LEAs) commitment to equal opportunities and anti-racism in semi-structured interviews, we were able, as members of local organizations, to put forward proposals and demands directly to them via community consultative fora in which we participated. Arguably the data from these meetings proved a more accurate measure of the LEAs' 'beneath-the-rhetoric' commitment to equality and anti-racism and hence of institutional obstacles.

The research 'findings' were of two kinds. There were those that were fed into our respective organizations and included local research studies of housing policies in Liverpool and youth provision in Wolverhampton. Linked to these were the strategy and position documents discussed and written collaboratively with fellow organization members and used as a basis for negotiation with the local authorities. The second kind of 'finding' was more an analysis of the obstacles and limitations of local politics. In our study, these included an ideological emphasis on class inequalities within local Labour ruling groups, the bureaucratic structures of local government and the constraints imposed by central government. This formed the core analysis of the book and developed out of research team meetings.

Inevitably any research is both selective and in some ways 'representative' of its subjects whether these be town hall officials or members of local community organizations. The question of representation is particularly fraught in this kind of research where who gets to speak for whom has rightly provoked controversy. To some extent researchers always speak for someone else; published interview findings inevitably entail processes of selection and 're-presentation'. To suggest otherwise only serves to invest yet more power in the hands of the researcher. A more productive research strategy might be to try to take this subjective aspect into account in the initial design of the research. In our case the first type of finding distinguished above sought to represent the collective views adopted by those ethnically mixed but black-led organizations of which we were members.

We did not intend nor did we ever claim to represent anything beyond this constituency and certainly not 'the black community'. The second type of finding, the analysis of the limitations of local politics, reflected the views of the research team alone. In these findings we represented ourselves.

It is very difficult to gauge the impact of research after it has been published. To this extent, minority groups and organizations have rightly been suspicious of research as it rarely benefits them and/or is seen as part of an information-gathering exercise on the part of public bodies. The periodic yet heated debates around the collection of census data has been one example of this. Whilst social scientists were keen to use such data to measure patterns of disadvantage, many minority organizations were concerned that the police, social service and immigration authorities could make more sinister use of it. The surveillance of minority groups, which is based on information gathering and data collected from a variety of sources, poses an important ethical dilemma for researchers. In our case, the Local Politics of Race project was intended above all to be of interest and use to community activists and students. Its overall aim was to explore different grassroots political strategies in the light of local institutional resistance. However, at least one local activist suggested, not unreasonably, that the research might be of equal use to local authorities, local police forces and central government in their efforts to gain better understanding and hence greater regulation and control of community politics.

## From dangerous blackness to endangered whiteness

Political vocabularies change over time as concepts and labels take on different connotations, often as a result of being appropriated by one set of interests over another. Throughout the period of our local politics project, there was a broad consensus amongst those community groups and organizations in which we participated that the biggest problem was convincing the all-powerful public and private bodies of the pervasiveness of institutional racism. 'What about the Poles, Jews, women and the disabled?' was a typical institutional response, not for a minute because local politicians or officers were committed to eliminating racism and inequalities across a wider spectrum but rather in order to fragment and undermine the collective voice of anti-racists. Under those circumstances, the signifier 'black' was used as a way of pre-empting such divisive tactics. It served to present a unity as a strategic device in the struggle against racism. It was never intended to exhaust other sources of identity and forms of cultural expression.

Nevertheless, from the mid-1980s, anti-racist political discourse began to come under attack, not only from the new right for whom it came to symbolize 'loony leftism' but also from intellectuals from diverse ethnic backgrounds who saw it as monopolizing and hence suffocating diverse gendered, classed and religious groupings and identity markings. It was argued that the term anti-racism itself had become institutionalized, that it had reduced diverse ethnic groups to all-encompassing identity labels such as 'black' and all individuals to victims of 'racism'. Anti-racist discourses of the 1970s and 1980s were thus dislodged from their dominant position by those embracing a wider set of categories including 'new ethnicities'. These stood for new dynamic, hybrid formations rather than old, static, ethnic boundaries. One effect of such conceptual and political shifts was to broaden the parameters of politics beyond town halls and Westminster to include cultural sites and the politics of representation as expressed through film, photography, television, theater and music. These more inclusive concepts and sites provided opportunities for research to expand and diversify. Equally relevant here was the growth in the number of researchers from divergent ethnic backgrounds that in turn opened up opportunities for ethnographic research originating not in the white, anthropological, male gaze but from a range of diasporan perspectives.

This brings me to the emergence of whiteness as a conceptual category. I would distinguish here between being or passing for white and the 'discourse of whiteness'. The former refers to an ontological state; the other to a body of dominant knowledge. The relationship between the two is neither one of direct correspondence nor of complete independence; people who appear white to some are not to others and this seemingly fixed attribute changes over time. The case of the Irish in the United States in the nineteenth century is a good example (Ignatiev 1995). Moreover, you do not have to be white to express white values. In fact, spokespeople from diverse ethnic backgrounds have often proved politically invaluable in espousing white values through the media (Gabriel 1998).

On the other hand, being a white researcher carries a symbolic significance whatever the political direction of the research. Being white and in a position to define the research agenda and hence produce new knowledges can only serve to enhance the authority of whiteness and hence sanction the privileges associated with being white. The Local Politics of Race project was undertaken by four white researchers at a time, as I have suggested, when radical discourses of race were preoccupied with institutional racism and 'black' politics. That particular focus, combined with an analysis that effectively privileged the role of white researchers as knowledge producers, served to reproduce whiteness, albeit in one of its less virulent, arguably more benign forms. I shall return to this below.

The emergence of whiteness as a legitimate object of study in part related to some of the intellectual developments outlined above. The idea that whiteness was an endangered knowledge and that whites were fast becoming an 'endangered species' in some cities in the West prompted a political backlash that has been expressed variously in: the bombing of the United States Federal building in Oklahoma in 1995; National Front demonstrations at the UK's main channel port, Dover, in response to the arrival of Roma refugees from the Czech Republic and Slovakia in 1997; proposals to cut benefits and rights of appeal for asylum seekers/illegal immigrants; increased policing and surveillance of minority communities; moves to reverse affirmative action in the US, and ridiculing and stifling anti-racist initiatives in the UK from the late 1980s onwards. These developments have in turn inspired a new research interest in the phenomenon of whiteness, which brings me to the second project.

## Project two: Whitewash

What kinds of research has this recent interest in whiteness generated? I have already referred to research into organizations, parties, etc., that promote an explicit ideology of white supremacy. The physical hazards facing researchers doing this kind of research are discussed elsewhere in this volume (Chapter 9). However, whiteness has not just been defined in terms of white supremacist politics but also in the mundane, everyday culture of white ethnicity. To this end, the study of white men's groups, societies, festivals and a myriad other cultural practices has become a rapidly expanding area of academic inquiry, particularly in the United States.

It might reasonably be asked whether studying the minutiae of white men's lives is not just a convenient excuse to turn attention from racism and minorities toward a narcissistic celebration of whiteness, at least for white researchers? Perhaps so, but with two important qualifications. For once whiteness is being recognized as an ethnicity rather than being equated with the 'universal' and/or treated implicitly as the norm. Nor are constructions of 'otherness' used in this discourse to define, sanction and prioritize whiteness, a process Edward Said powerfully illustrates in his study *Orientalism* (1978). Nevertheless, the more we research white culture, the more we potentially marginalize representations of diasporan cultures, new ethnicities and forms of representation. Furthermore, to treat whiteness as just another ethnicity runs the risk of ignoring or even concealing very real differences in terms of institutional power between it and other racialized ethnicities.

The research for Whitewash emerged out of these concerns. At all costs I wanted to avoid a celebratory treatise on whiteness. The premise of much of this latter kind of research, that 'it's OK to be white' and to research about whiteness, can and has formed part of the backlash referred to above. On the contrary, I wanted to focus on the politically strategic role of whiteness in bolstering an allegedly beleaguered ethnic group. I also wanted to avoid the pitfalls of a media analysis which leaves little or no room for anything other than theorizing the role and impact of dominant ideology. My project thus included a number of organizational/campaign case studies in both the United States and

Britain, around which the principal aim was to mobilize against expressions and manifestations of whiteness.

In his book *Towards the Abolition of Whiteness* (1994), David Roediger makes a powerful case for retaining a socially constructed concept of race against those who argue that just to mention it draws attention to difference and makes racial violence and discrimination more likely. Arguably, a similar case can be made against the use of whiteness. If we accept the view that whiteness is an invention, an act of contrived selection, the aim of which is to construct and defend a unitary ethnic/national identity, then research on whiteness can only help to reify a flawed notion. Would it not be preferable to look at the ways in which whiteness is in fact a product of varied cultural influences, many of which are African and south- and east-Asian in origin? In other words whiteness is not 'white' at all but the product of cultural syncretism; of multiple comings and goings; of diasporas of people and products; of accumulations, fusions and extinctions over the centuries. Better to work on diversity, it could be argued, than to reify a concept fit only for the historical archive.

One way out of this dilemma is to hold on to the fact that whites and whiteness, like race, are socially constructed rather than fixed or essential categories. This being so, research into the processes responsible for the construction of whiteness and research that illustrates the diverse origins and syncretic character of whiteness would complement each other rather than appearing to offer mutually exclusive lines of investigation. The reification of whiteness is only possible if a reality is conferred on it beyond its status as a social construct. Nevertheless, to research whiteness is to research a culture that, by definition, already dominates mainstream institutions, including those owning and controlling the means of information. One might ask, why saturate the public media realm with more research into whiteness at a time of heightened levels of mobilization and cultural expression on the part of hitherto subordinate ethnic groups? In response to this, I would make a distinction between ethnicity which takes its knowledge for granted, treats it as the norm and offers it up to global culture as universal, and that which problematizes that knowledge and explores the particularities of its production. So long as this latter kind of research does not define or dominate the field of inquiry then arguably it has a legitimate role to play. At least this was my own rationale for undertaking the research for Whitewash.

There is a further risk in such research. On the one hand whiteness is expressed through public discourses, including the media, and at key symbolic moments, for instance national sporting events, royal weddings and funerals, wars, etc. On the other hand, whiteness is defined through numerous, more private and mundane discourses, structured around routine daily events, including an array of domestic and leisure-based activities as well as paid work

175

settings. These seemingly neutral public and private spaces are where the hitherto invisible ethnic dimensions of whiteness are reproduced. The importance of such narratives lies in their proximity to everyday life and meanings. They do not derive exclusively from public discourses or highly symbolic events. However, examining such public and private spaces does not necessarily provide ready access to the institutional mechanisms that act as primary definers and modes of exclusion both in terms of cultural identity and access to an array of citizenship rights such as work, education, housing and criminal and civil justice. Whilst not wishing to detract from the case to study the more innocuous, seemingly innocent sites of white ethnic identity formation, my research for Whitewash made processes of exclusion, public discourses and key institutional sites, such as policing and immigration, its priority. In fact more work is needed that bridges the gap between the more mundane routine expressions of whiteness and those sources of institutional power and primary processes of exclusion.

At one stage in my research for Whitewash, I had intended to carry out face-to-face interviews with members of US militia groups and to track down Resistance Records in Detroit, home of the fascist music scene in North America. The latter was of particular interest because of its considerable links with UK and European distribution networks via the Internet. As is often the case with net surfing, hypertext can provide numerous additional contacts. On this occasion, details of the fascist music scene led me to a terrestrial address for Underground Resistance Records, also in Detroit. My research thus took me (physically, not virtually this time) to a downtown building standing almost alone on derelict land. I pressed the intercom button and was ushered upstairs into what turned out to be a distribution base for an African-American techno and dance music company. The enhanced anonymity of groups and individuals on the Internet can lead to relatively innocent yet interesting encounters (in my case including an hour-long lecture on the differences between Detroit and German techno music) of this kind. On the other hand, if fascist net surfers were to make the same mistake as me and journey to Detroit thinking they would find an underground distributor of racist music, who knows the possible repercussions for groups like Underground Resistance?

In the end I also decided against a project which entailed ethnographic field-work with white supremacists, thus avoiding the more obvious physical dangers associated with this kind of research. Rather, I was more interested in the relationship between the ideas of the far right and more coded versions of whiteness which run across the political spectrum from conservative to progressive. A study of the far right, on its own, might have exaggerated its discontinuities with mainstream politics and thus arguably served to legitimize the latter in ways which ran counter to my intentions. Moreover, as I have suggested, the tactic of both exposing and, in more academic contexts, explaining the fascist right not only puts researchers at considerable potential physical risk but can also act as a data base for those already active or aspiring to be active in far right organizations. In other words the research could put others at risk too. The Internet is a good example of the potential hazards in this area. The anonymity of authors, coupled with their lack of accountability, can work to promote freedom but it can also be used to peddle ideas and information that threaten the rights and freedoms of others. Moreover, ethnographic accounts that present a human side to fascist politics can help to legitimize, if not glamorize, the activities and personalities of the far right, depending on who gets to read such accounts and how they are interpreted. Violent life styles can be repugnant to some or fascinating and even pleasurable to others.

Thus my research on the far right was not based on interviews with its activists but took its lead much more from interviews with those involved in anti-fascist organizations and campaigns in New York, Louisiana and Alabama in the US and London and Birmingham in the UK. My interest in anti-fascist mobilizations with particular reference to their use of the media gave me insights into the far right whilst at the same time access to groups whose activities I was keen to document. Furthermore, as I have suggested, I also wanted to use this part of my research to establish continuities between politics that wore its whiteness on its sleeve and expressed and defended it unashamedly and those more conservative, coded versions of whiteness, whose ethnic 'outing' was uneven and in its early stages.

In making these connections between far right and mainstream political discourses my intention was not to gloss over real differences either in ideology or outcome. Nevertheless, I argued that at one level there was a strong synergy across the political spectrum. The political mainstream in the US and Britain may not advocate violence, yet, hiding behind a thin veneer of respectability, its stance on issues like law and order, immigration, and more generally its discourse on rights and responsibilities arguably have helped to legitimate different forms of exclusion, discrimination and even physical violence. Had Whitewash concentrated exclusively on the far right it might have served unwittingly to weaken rather than unmask these continuities across the political spectrum. David Duke's 'transformation' from white-sheeted member of the Ku Klux Klan in the 1970s to Republican senator in the Louisiana legislature in the 1990s personifies the kinds of connections and continuities between the racist right and the 'legitimate' mainstream which I was seeking to explore.

As I have suggested, part of my research looked at a number of case studies of local anti-racist organizations and campaign groups in both the US and UK. With one exception, I found remarkable uniformity both in terms of the profile of their members and their approach to campaigning, including their use of the media. The groups and campaigns were predominantly white in terms of their founders, leaders and many of their key activists. In the United States in particular their anti-racism was based on the rationalist premise that racist myths could be debunked by anti-racist facts. This often, although not always, went hand-in-hand with legalistic strategies based on the assumption that the judicial system could be made to work equitably. White spokespeople were often used to front campaigns on the grounds that they would enhance the credibility of the campaign. Similarly white interests were appealed to in campaign publicity for equally expedient reasons even if this meant forgoing an explicit critique of racism.

## Conclusion

The research was thus forced to acknowledge a more benign but nonetheless important version of whiteness expressed through liberal progressive discourse. Whilst the purpose of this kind of politics was to deconstruct and challenge white supremacy, the practice, if not the assumption, was that whites were/should be at the forefront of the assault on whiteness. This brings me back to my own whiteness. I need to ask whether my own political background attracted me to some groups and forms of anti-racist politics more than others arguably less 'conventional' and/or 'familiar', at least to me. Was it a coincidence that I interviewed so many groups/organizations with a white leadership and a legalistic, rationalist approach to campaign politics? There are obvious professional and emotional risks in confronting my own perspective and in pursuing this line of reflexivity about my own research. Only at moments such as this, when forced to confront and reflect on my whiteness, does it become uncomfortably clear that there may not be a 'right' side for a white researcher or, at the very least, their position will always be fraught and ambiguous.

Both research projects discussed above were committed to giving a voice to grassroots organizations. In the case of the Local Politics of Race project, these included organizations of which we were members. In Whitewash, the research relied more on qualitative interviews. Whatever the strategy, research inevitably involves a process of distilling, editing and interpreting information and views expressed by others, that is to say, representation. The danger of the latter is all the more acutely felt by researchers who are only too aware that the history of racist thought has been built on the power to define and thereby to possess 'others'. There are real dangers in professing and/or of being seen to speak for whole communities or even for a particular political constituency or body of opinion.

This last point relates to the question of who the research is for and to whom are researchers accountable? The very notion of accountability is increasingly said to threaten notions of academic autonomy and value-freedom. These days, research is being required to make itself useful and answerable to 'user groups', notably big business or government bodies. Such developments threaten those hallowed freedoms referred to above when what academic autonomy and freedom meant was the privileging of white, middle class, male discourse. Like other white discourses it hid its ethnic particularity behind a set of universal claims. Such research protocols ensured that white male academics were answerable only to their white academic peers who, not surprisingly, sanctioned their knowledge claims. Leading figures have thus been able to monopolize theoretical debate, research wisdom and policy options merely by being strategically placed within their research communities.

To resist both the trappings of academic freedom and deference to big business or government potentially puts researchers on a collision course with their profession. Few funding opportunities arise from making research accountable to grassroots organizations. The likelihood of disputes over 'representation', political strategy and appropriate language increases the more research is opened up to public, popular channels of debate. So too is the likelihood of rejection or dismissal by academic peers not least for breaking the ground rules of research. Arguably, the current focus on whiteness provides one opportunity to challenge those bastions of white academic and corporate culture.

The emphasis in research in the late 1990s on ideas of diaspora, hybridity and the end of racial binaries, it is to be hoped, will not promote a new generation of white academics holding forth on the grounds that they/we are not really white and anyway it's all one big melting pot of cross-cutting influences and syncretic cultures. Such 'hybrid' whiteness can serve as an essentialist gloss designed to protect an embittered and allegedly endangered white race. However, the fact remains that white skins continue to monopolize institutional positions, from Tony Blair's New Labour to Bill Gates's Microsoft and from Hollywood's Oscars to London's BAFTAs. Whites may feel endangered but in truth, and there is some kind of 'truth' here, they are not. The danger of researching whiteness is that it may serve to promote the very knowledges and careers of those it is seeking to deconstruct and displace. The long-term aim of research should be to marginalize and disempower whiteness and the given authority of white researchers. The pursuit of research along these lines for white researchers will be the most hazardous task of all.

## Note

1   The proposal to introduce a question on faith into the 2001 British census was met with mixed reaction. On the one hand it was thought by some to be an invasion of privacy and likely to be used to monitor the growth of Islam in particular whilst on the other it was welcomed as a way of providing more useful ethnic data than the old skin-based classification (*Guardian*, 4 January 1999).

# Bibliography

Ben-Tovim, G., Gabriel, J., Law, I. and Stredder, K. (1986) *The Local Politics of Race*, Basingstoke: Macmillan.

Gabriel, J. (1998) *Whitewash*, London: Routledge.

Ignatiev, N. (1995) *How the Irish Became White*, London: Routledge.

Roediger, D. (1994) *Towards the Abolition of Whiteness*, London: Verso.

Said, E. (1978) *Orientalism*, London: Penguin.

Song, M. and Parker, D. (1995) 'Cultural Identity: Disclosing Commonality and Difference in In-depth Interviews', *Sociology* 29, 2: 241–56.

# 11

# SHEER FOOLISHNESS

## Shifting definitions of danger in conducting and teaching ethnographic field research

*Jeff D. Peterson*

## Introduction

The notion of risk and danger as elements in ethnographic research have been discussed occasionally, but usually definitions have been fairly confined. Lee (1995) touches on many points that include physical and psychological danger and others have discussed their own dangerous fieldwork (Wolf 1991; Armstrong 1993). Others have focused upon the way risk is perceived by individuals (Douglas 1992) or within social systems (Friedman 1987). This chapter develops the literature to look at other issues around risk and ethnographic research that have not been sufficiently addressed. I have been particularly fascinated by the way in which teaching ethnographic field methods has caused me to consider danger more consciously than when blithely entering into such situations as a researcher. This chapter is, in part, concerned with the way directing and managing students in the field has affected and indeed enriched my understanding of risk and threat.

The chapter reflects upon three key areas in relation to risk and danger in the field. First, I suggest that there is a fluid nature to what is 'risky' and 'dangerous,' and that this fluidity is an important part of the nature of work in the field. The definition of danger shifts constantly and the researcher needs to be acutely aware of the transitions of his/her perceptions of danger. Second, I will examine the way in which views of what constitutes risk and danger vary with the position of the actor in a particular social context. Lastly, virtually all of the literature concerned with researcher-risk focuses upon the dangers to the individual researcher engaging in their own fieldwork. There seems a need to broaden this discussion to encompass danger and risk as valuable pedagogical tools at an early stage of social research training. I suggest that using risk and danger as pedagogical tools may be valuable in terms of focusing student research and in learning about the sociological perspective. Some may find this idea controversial, as teaching research methods has often been undertaken in a 'safe' classroom-based setting. My experiences of teaching students about research from within the field, working with them on projects, sometimes in remote areas, has encouraged my view of risk as an educational device.

I would contend that risk and danger are inherent in the ethnographic field process, and the evaluation and consideration of such issues should be overtly discussed and thought about. Indeed, it is precisely when we feel that we are at risk that perhaps we should pause to consider what that means, and why we feel this way. At the same time, I see little to be gained by evaluating who has done the most 'dangerous' fieldwork as a manner of determining what research is most genuine or cutting edge. In my view perceptions of threat and danger are extremely relative, and more importantly, these perceptions should be subjected to analysis as part and parcel of pursuing one's ethnographic research interests.

The basis for this analysis comes from a number of sources. Two years of fieldwork in Guadalajara, Mexico, studying urban social movements in low-income and squatter settlements, provided me with a number of interesting opportunities for examining the issue of risk and danger in the field. The fact that I was also doing collaborative research with my spouse, an anthropologist, also meant that we often discussed, and had discussed for us (by participants, other researchers, etc.), the idea of gender as it related to danger in the field. Shortly after finishing my dissertation I took a position at Linfield College, a small liberal arts college in Oregon. In my first semester a colleague introduced me to an advocate for the homeless who did 'urban plunges' in Portland, Oregon, and with whom she had also taught a course 'Down and Out in America'. Subsequently, I have used urban plunges in several of my classes (this involves students living on the streets for short periods), taught 'Down and Out in America', and have also taught an ethnographic field course in the coffee-growing region of Matagalpa, Nicaragua.

## The fluidity of risk and danger

It is not disputed in the literature on ethnographic research that there is fluidity to the nature of risk and danger in the field. However, there is room for discussion of what is meant by danger, as in many cases it is assumed that there is some inherent quality to the notion of dangerous fieldwork. Some topics for research can seem dangerous but this is misleading. For instance, Lee (1995) discusses research on mountain climbing. While statistically speaking, mountain climbing is considerably less dangerous than one would think, it is nonetheless perceived to be exotic, exciting and risky (Breyer 1993). Experienced climbers often suggest that it is the violation of fairly specific rules of safety, or ignorance of these rules, that land people in trouble.

Thus, danger is often seen as something exotic; it is because we don't know the rules or because we are out of our element that something may be dangerous. This too is a limited view of risk and danger, as it cannot be said that in every situation one can assume safety merely by getting to know the rules, the situation or the culture. For example, it is fairly apparent that one is at greater risk in Peru during the time of the Shining Path, or that there is a higher risk of certain diseases in the highlands of Nicaragua than in most places in the United States. Both of these ways of looking at risk and danger, and many others in the literature, seem to focus on trying to define what 'risk' and 'danger' are, in terms of some kind of inherent quality or set of experiences. My suggestion, however, is that what constitutes danger shifts constantly and, as I will discuss later, we should be paying particular attention to the notion of risk and danger as evidence of an increased opportunity to learn about the research concern at hand.

There are many ways in which the perception of risk or danger can shift, depending on physical contexts, the locus of the actor, and over time. When I am in the rural areas of Nicaragua in the province of Matagalpa, I am at a higher risk of disease, banditry, etc., than I am at Linfield College in McMinnville, Oregon. Initially, the concerns about risk have more to do with the transition at the nation state level (and considerable concern according to different actors, who I will discuss later). Further steps of immersion and adjustment took place as we (a group of students and myself) transitioned from Managua, the capital, to Matagalpa, a smaller, provincial capital, to the coffee co-operative which was twenty miles into the highland jungle of the Matagalpa province. The adaptation process covers many areas, ranging from general hygiene to knowledge of local customs to being aware of the possibility of banditry in the surrounding areas. An example of a non-threatening adjustment had to do with the issue of hygiene. Within four days we moved from a system with all modern conveniences (US), to one where there was no hot water or toilets that could flush all matter (Managua), to bathing out of barrels and pouring buckets of water down a fixture (Matagalpa), to going to the bathroom in the bushes and bathing several hundred yards upstream in a creek. Students discussed the transitions with incredulity as we 'descended' to each level. However, upon returning from each area (that is, 'ascending' the scale) they were equally amazed at what a luxury it seemed to have in turn 'a fixture and collected water' or a toilet that flushed and water that was piped, etc.

It is especially common as researchers 'enter the field' to experience this transition as one of going out of a specific area that is considered not to be dangerous into one that is dangerous, risky or at least unknown. Prior to going into the field, my sense is often one of leaving a geographical area that is familiar, where routines are established and self-chosen. The transition is one into a geographical space that is unfamiliar – the lack of familiarity often being due to class, subcultural or cultural differences and nation state differences.

An important initial aspect of my research in low-income settlements in Guadalajara, Mexico, was the sense of apprehension I had regarding my security in a different country. Once in Guadalajara for several months, however, and adjusted to the national differences and to the region, perception of risk focused around class differences as we (my partner and I) began to think of moving into a low-income settlement. Thus, I was used to life in general in Guadalajara and among the intellectual élite, but the move into low-income settlement life caused another set of concerns. In fact, several American and Mexican colleagues expressed concern about the idea of actually living in a settlement, as opposed to living somewhere less dangerous and visiting by day, doing interviews and attending meetings from a safer base. Often the fear has more to do with notions of danger as they are reproduced on the basis of class in society, to which members of academia are not immune. The idea that a supposedly homogeneous economic class occupies a certain area can be both a comfort and a cause for concern. Thus the researcher has to remain aware of the way that perceptions of risk are socially constructed and affected by mainstream ideas about participants, where they live and the risks which they encounter in their lives.

## Shifting notions of risk and danger

### *Physical versus psychological*

There are a number of ways in which risk and danger vary and should be considered both in the area of research and in pedagogy. I suggest that risk and danger should be discussed more overtly as a way of maximizing their positive aspects and minimizing the negative consequences. At present researcher risk is most usually understood in terms of physical risk to the individual researcher. However, there are a number of types of risk involved to the individual, and that risk also varies with the location of the actor in the social scheme.

Clearly, there are elements of physical danger in doing research and in teaching research in the field and these demand our full attention when discussing and planning research. Lee (1995) notes the implications of doing research in areas where researchers and graduate students have been killed. There is also the physical damage that comes from disease. For instance, I contracted Hepatitis A and was laid out for six weeks during my research, and during a course in Nicaragua most of my students spent time in a private clinic at one stage or another. One even lapsed into a coma state, and at one point we had difficulties finding a pulse. Thus, the physically dangerous aspects of research should not be under-emphasized, but as I will point out later, these events allowed us to have important insights with regard to the research topics we were pursuing.

Confronting one's personal ideological views and upbringing is also an important challenge that occurs in carrying out social research, and one that carries a certain amount of risk. The notion of 'going native' is often denigrated as merely identifying too closely with the group one is studying. I would suggest it is also part of a process of the individual having difficulties in reconciling his/her previous world view or self-image as a representative of a country, with intimate involvement with another people or group. As a graduate student working with a wide variety of groups in Guadalajara, Mexico, I frequently had to confront the fact that my status in the community was in flux, and at the mercy of forces that were often beyond my control. At one point I was participating in a rally protesting the death of Archbishop Romero and of six Jesuit priests in El Salvador. I went with a group from the neighborhood where I was doing fieldwork to downtown Guadalajara, where we met up with other groups. As the protest got under way, various chants broke out, including '*El pueblo, unido, jamás será vencido!*' (The people, united, will never be defeated!), and I felt comfortable chanting that along with the crowd. I was, after all, part of the people and felt a strong sense of social connection. Later, however, the crowd started chanting '*El que no brinca es yanqui*' (Whoever doesn't jump is a Yankee), after which the whole crowd would give a little hop. At this point I became uncomfortable and did not join in the jumping. While I felt that I could be one of 'the people' I was not sure I could presume *not* to be a Yankee. This also got me thinking about the embarrassment of my country's involvement in Central America and my lack of control over the actions being taken, supposedly by a government meant to represent me. As I walked along, several of the people around me noticed that I was not jumping and asked, 'Why aren't you jumping?' I responded with, 'What can I do? I'm a Yankee,' to which the response was a collective, 'No you need to jump, you're not a Yankee,' and 'We're talking about George Bush and all of those guys, not you.'

Thus, within this encounter, there was a concern on my part as to how far I could identify with the group. This was a situation that frequently arose. A sense of alienation occurs frequently when switching in and out of the field. Coming back from the field is even more alienating in some respects, and varies in relation to the types of previous life experiences and preparations a person has undergone. Aspects of physical danger are frequently of greatest concern to parents, administration and others when students are out on the streets studying the homeless or in a less-industrialized country like Nicaragua. However, my experience has been that I am most often dealing with the students' sense of alienation as they attempt to reconcile their previous world view with the ethnographic experience. One student who participated in the Nicaragua field

185

course had managed to maintain a rather detached point of view of global inequality in a class that she had previously taken with me. However, whilst in the field, the consequences of that global inequality became much more real, profound and troubling for this student. We spent considerable time during and after the class discussing the ways in which it changed her view of the poor in Nicaragua and in general.

Although some research is looked down upon for its lack of immediate and inherent physical risk, engaging in ethnographic research has different types of risk that should be thought through as part of the research process. The deeper involvement and understanding with participants that may be achieved through ethnographic research may mean that the research project may be more difficult to complete. The consequences of carrying out the research may affect familial relationships, individual relationships with members of the community that is being researched, and professional and academic relations as the researcher tries to accommodate the demands of each within one action framework. Ethnographic fieldwork is often used as a way of providing information about daily life in ways that convey the context, depth and the 'true' nature behind what can often become meaningless statistics. It makes sense that the methods effective in adding dimension and contextual grounding to quantitative information would also have a more significant psychological impact on the researcher. For example, knowing that over half of Nicaragua's population is in absolute poverty is a disturbing statistic, but conducting ethnographic research that details exactly what that means in the daily lives of a family is bound to be more psychologically distressing.

## The cultural construction of research risk

The psychological risks of ethnographic research are thus part of a cultural construction, as well as the outcome of taking those risks. I suggest that it is the same with physical danger. As Adams (1995) proposes, however, risk is culturally constructed and this way of viewing risk counters Armstrong (1993) who seems to suggest that somehow others are doing less genuine research because they are not willing to do the dangerous fieldwork. Breyer (1993) makes clear that the perception of risk is very different between activities constructed as risky (e.g. mountain climbing) versus activities that actually have high death rates (e.g. driving a car, riding a bicycle). Escaping this perception is difficult and ideologically driven, as Breyer shows in his comparison of 'expert' and 'non-expert' views of what is dangerous and what is not.

Adams (1995) also suggests that often a causal link does not exist between actions designed to decrease risk and the actual occurrence of accidents. His examination of the questionable linkage between safety-belt regulations for cars and the degree to which reduced deaths can be directly attributable to those laws is a case in point. I suggest that these studies also make the case for examining, and being up front about, the psychological nature of risk. Thus, it is not only the potentially damaging side of risk that needs to be evaluated, but also the advantages of engaging in risky behavior. The experience of mountain climbers suggests that it is not the physical aspect of mountain climbing that is so dangerous, but more frequently poor mental fitness and lack of decision-making skills that lead to problems. The element of physical danger, however, helps the individual focus on both the psychological and physical demands of mountain climbing.

## Danger and time

Notions of risk and danger in ethnographic research are also in flux, both psychologically and physically, along lines of the place and time in which you are engaging in research. As in mountain climbing, perceptions of risk tend to be heightened for the novice around the issue of physical danger. Having listened to novices ask questions of experienced climbers, they are generally in awe of the physical aspect of the act. The experienced climber conveys over time, however, that the notion of danger shifts. There is clearly a skill set that needs to be learned, and knowledge about the physical side of mountain climbing needs to be understood. However, the emphasis moves from physical skills to the decision-making process and the psychological aspects of mountain climbing. Similarly, the initial focus of ethnographic research varies over time. The initial stages of the 'Down and Out in America' class revolve around the physical aspects of danger. For example, fear of drug users/dealers, anxiety about sleeping under a bridge and whether that is safe, and generally wondering if they are liable to be attacked, are all concerns of the students. In time these physical fears recede and the psychological impact of the experience comes to the fore, as students begin to accumulate knowledge about what represents danger in the physical context that is the domain of homelessness.

I find that I am most often concerned with the psychological impact upon students, once they begin to understand the humanity of the people with whom they have contact on an urban plunge. The process of disabusing students of the view that homeless persons are dangerous and different has a strong, often alienating impact on them. The concern that 'real' homeless people show for their safety and their physical needs, and the discussions they are willing to have with the students, suggests a real *lack* of difference between the groups. In addition, students also come to see that the homeless population is not a single group, but a wide variety of subgroups. It is just as difficult to refer to the 'homeless' population as a homogeneous group as it would be to the 'housed' population. The discovery of this human texture produces some real quandaries for students when related back to the monolithic views of the homeless as conveyed through the media, family discussions, and even university classes. This means that a shift generally occurs from concerns about their own physical safety to the concerns they begin to develop for the long-term homeless. An acknowledgment of the short-term nature of their experience also signifies a shift from a present-oriented concern with their own safety to a future-oriented concern with the safety of those with whom they are working in the homeless population.

## Placement of the actor

The final way I will discuss how perception of danger and risk may shift concerns the situation of the individual in this web of events. As a researcher who has conducted fieldwork I have become aware of the ways in which I must confront the element of physical and psychological risk in my own research. Like most other researchers, there was a notable lack of focus on this issue during my training as an undergraduate and graduate student. As is often the case, it was during my initial attempts to do research that I acquired a set of skills that helped mitigate the possibility of physical danger. Most of us become aware of the ways in which we may be psychologically affected by experiences and we develop ways of dealing with the mental aspects of the research process, for instance the psychological difficulties and the potential sense of alienation. This is very different, however, from the way in which the new researcher, the student involved in experiential learning, the administrator, or even how I, as a teacher, view the notion of ethnographic research. To say that everyone experiences ethnographic research differently is to state the obvious. However, what is less often considered is the way in which these different viewpoints intersect at the point of risk and danger in research.

Having conducted my own research allows me to focus on the experiences of my students, but I have also come to see teaching ethnographic research as more than just teaching 'a method'. Students must learn about the risks of ethnographic research and the methodology of it, but I must also consider the risks to the institution, and even find myself considering the consequences that this activity might have on my career. Students are also responding to a number of concerns, including personal safety, worried family and friends, expectations of teaching staff, etc., alongside learning how actually to carry out a research project. Doing 'less risky' ethnographic field research, where students are navigating spaces with which they are more comfortable and familiar, would eliminate one major category of concern. There might be fewer consequences to the process, both physically and emotionally, if students are not forced into areas that have been previously unknown to them. I suggest, however, that it is not just acknowledging varying perceptions and contexts of risk and danger that are important, but these can also serve as markers for when we are truly about to learn something in our ethnographic research. Thus dangerous situations, however conceived, are not merely to be understood, but are necessary and important elements of doing research and in teaching how to do it.

## Danger as research (it's all data)

Drawing from the list of ways in which I suggest that notions of danger and risk may vary, I also suggest that it is precisely when we are sensing risk that researchers should be particularly attentive to taking notes. Evaluating danger in the context of research is not just a matter of warning individuals that ethnographic research can be physically or psychologically dangerous, or that it can be alienating. Instead, we should be stressing how important it is to be aware of the ways in which those occasions may allow us to learn more about the area in which we are interested. Renato Rosaldo (1993) relates one extreme example of this in his book *Culture and Truth*, where he discusses the loss of his wife Michelle Zimbalist Rosaldo in the Philippines. In the chapter 'Grief and a Headhunter's Rage', he looks back at the way in which we often describe people in our fieldwork in a distancing, impersonal way. While working through his own personal grief over the loss of his spouse, Rosaldo comes to understand the personal grieving of Ilongot headhunters.

The potential insights from dangerous situations need not be quite so devastating. Some of these situations arise with personal experiences of feeling at risk, and it may also be the case that the shifts in what seems dangerous are important. One example of this came from the fact that I conducted my fieldwork with my spouse, Judy Mohr Peterson, who was at the time a graduate student in anthropology. One element of our research in Guadalajara was going to meetings in our neighborhood and in other neighborhoods as well. An interesting feature of carrying out our fieldwork was the common saying that 'the home belongs to the woman, but the street belongs to the man'. This clearly reflects the strong gendered division of public and private within this society. Judy was often escorted back and forth from meetings; this was a practice that both of us accepted but did not really think about. The rigidity of this division was underscored for me following an event that occurred as I was walking home late from one such meeting.

I had attended a bricklayers' meeting which lasted until past midnight. Our neighborhood, Rancho Nuevo, was fairly dark, since street lighting had been installed but shut off shortly thereafter. As I was walking home a clearly drunken man, holding a knife, confronted me. Being in a bit of a daze from the long

189

meeting and the smoke-filled environment, my first thought was to just get past him. I decided that he was not able to move quickly, and that if I could just push past him with a shove I would be able to make it down to the safety of Don José's taco stand (Don José was the head of the household where Judy and I lived). There would be people and better light. As I shoved the man, he fell down, which actually panicked me more. I reckoned that he would now really be angry, added to which he still held the knife. As I began to back away, I realized that not only was he not getting up, indeed, he was snoring after having passed out.

Still a bit shaky when I reached the stand, I related the story to Don José. He laughed and shook his head. While I agreed that it was a bit funny that my supposed assailant had passed out, I was surprised there was not more of a reaction to my having been confronted with a weapon. I related the story a number of times to others in the community, and got a similar reaction. There was general amusement, but several times people also asked about Judy's safety and suggested that we needed to make sure she was accompanied when walking about. It became clear to me that, as a male, the street was considered to be my natural element and I was expected to be able to take care of myself. Furthermore, my being from the United States did not make me an exceptional category – *all* men should be able to take care of themselves in these situations. The concern was instead focused on taking care of the person who would *not* be in her element should she be accosted in the street. Thus, a situation I found physically dangerous turned out to be helpful in understanding some of the ways in which gender roles were perceived in this society.

Researchers in situations where they are vulnerable, physically or mentally, may also benefit from paying particular attention to how people react to those vulnerabilities. During my fieldwork in Guadalajara I contracted Hepatitis A, which left me in a debilitated state for a good six weeks or more. This period provided both Judy and I with some interesting notes on how people in the community viewed our relationship. We had interesting comments on how 'ustedes trabajan como un equipo' – how we worked as a team – more than couples in the *colonia* where we lived. We also learned a number of interesting facts about how people saw the healing process, with several intriguing cures being suggested.[1] Thus, listening to people as a result of my affliction helped us gather information regarding gender roles and the combination of healing techniques as viewed by members of the *colonia*.

Curiously enough, another long-term benefit to Judy's career resulted from this period. It was during this time (January 1991) that we were gearing up to do our survey of eight low-income settlements in the Guadalajara Metropolitan Zone (GMZ). As the sociologist, I was largely responsible for carrying out the survey, just as Judy, the team's anthropologist, was the lead in our fieldwork and semi-structured interviews. My hepatitis prevented me from being able to initiate the study, and I was relegated to editing the survey, collating the questionnaires and training our interviewers – all things that could be done while lying flat on my back. Judy was forced to begin the survey, and, with our interviewers, completed the first two and a half *colonias* before I was well enough to participate. This situation actually led to her being able to use these survey skills in obtaining positions later on in her career, since even after I rejoined the team, we were working more as partners in the survey research. Thus, just as it is all data when it comes to ethnographic research, one never knows when there may be benefit to taking risks in the field.

It is also important to examine those times when what appears to be the same activity moves in and out of the dangerous category. As I went into the field I remember having apprehensions about living in a low-income neighborhood, and some of the issues of safety. However, throughout our fieldwork we generally felt very safe in Rancho Nuevo and in most of the other neighborhoods. From time to time disconcerting events would occur, but these seemed largely insignificant to us. So comfortable were we that when we carried out our survey we walked through all of the neighborhoods almost regardless of the time. We were in *colonias* past midnight, often in areas that had no street lighting and had to be navigated by flashlight. While colleagues thought of this as foolish and dangerous, our experience in our own *colonia* and the responsiveness of our respondents led us to think otherwise. In fact, we finished our survey with nothing but minor incidents, and most of those associated with a temperamental Volkswagen Beetle that frequently left us stranded.

I found it interesting, however, that when Judy and I returned after several years of not living in Rancho Nuevo, my perception of our work was dramatically altered. I remember driving through one of the *colonias* selected for our survey and saying to myself, 'What were we thinking when we did that?' The neighborhood was the most hospitable of all, and because of this, the one in which we finished our survey the quickest, and yet it seemed foreign and alien as we drove through it six years later. I believe these experiences indicate a key contribution that ethnographic research makes regarding the issue of danger. Ethnographic research, while being risky at times, also establishes a context for evaluating risk and danger in ways that other methods may not. I also propose that this ability is not just a learned set of skills, although I can remember intellectually that there was little concern for safety. The ability to continue evaluating risk in the field is transitory and needs to be kept updated with further fieldwork. The advantage the researcher gains from the first experience is particularly useful if s/he applies the knowledge gained from this sense of risk and danger to future research and teaching, with the understanding that it is part of the process of beginning to do ethnography.

# Risk as pedagogy

If risk is an accepted element of fieldwork then it should be included as part of early instruction on research and students should be taught to evaluate risk consciously. By acclimatizing students to a continuum of fieldwork that may range from what they find 'slightly' risky to situations that approximate more risky environments I believe they are helped to recognize the ways in which risk can inform their understanding of the topic under study. It was not until I began to think more about how to teach social research methods that I began to evaluate the usefulness of risk and danger in research in a more comprehensive manner. Risk can be a part of pedagogy in at least the following ways. First it may be used as a short-term confrontation of personal ideas or beliefs. It may also be used as a vehicle for focusing the intensity of research. Third, it can function as a way of giving students (undergraduate or graduate) their first conscious evaluation of the risk and danger of ethnographic research.

Students who are engaging in social research too often come to think of research projects as something they are doing for Professor 'X', rather than a project in which they should be personally interested. While I encourage students to think of their research as the latter, I also suggest to them that one way in which they can focus on the research in question rather than on doing a project for me, is to choose something that involves some personal risk. I usually suggest something that makes them feel uncomfortable in that it may be unknown to them or forces them to confront some of their own personal biases, rather than physical risk, especially since they are going to be doing this on their own.

This is in part where the idea of considered risk versus sheer foolishness is salient. As opposed to the urban plunge or the 'Down and Out' and Nicaragua courses, where there is an element of supervision and working with students to understand and work through some elements of physical risk, the independent project should probably be oriented less in this direction. I suggest that using a degree of fear based on a challenge to personal belief systems is more appropriate, since my goal is to get students to focus on the project with more intensity and less casualness. Students too frequently choose ethnographic field projects that are convenient to them, where they are already participants or insiders, and where they are unable to see the subject in question as a newcomer would. My general experience has been that students who go outside of their own everyday experience submit projects of a better standard that they find more interesting. As with the urban plunge, students who are prepared to do this learn not just about another type of group or behavior, but also gain a greater appreciation for the phenomenon under study.

I have found the use of urban plunges, supervised weekend experiences of homelessness, to be a useful tool in two of my courses. The urban plunge, which definitely involves some physical risk, is especially useful in the 'experiential learning' context. What students get is more an 'experience' than an in-depth look at the lives of homeless persons. This enables them to evaluate their preconceived notions of homeless people and the way members of various institutions in our society, such as the media, schools and their own families, have portrayed people who are homeless. There is risk in my taking students into the streets, or as one colleague once commented, 'You know you're only one lawsuit away from never doing them again, don't you?' This is accurate in the technical sense, and something that I keep in mind at all times during such visits. Yet precisely because of its unconventionality the urban plunge is a valuable tool. Students generally understand the risk that I, as the professor (and others), am taking in doing this. However, like my colleague, they also overestimate the physical danger that is involved. I suggest that this is valuable if the trade-off is having them understand what it is like to freeze under a bridge along the Willamette River, or learn about the incredibly diverse ways in which individuals, couples and families in our society can become homeless. In reality, while their safety is a concern to me during the plunge, I find that I spend more time during and after the urban plunges helping the students to work through the new and different way in which they now see the world as a result of the experience. One student stated after going on an urban plunge in Portland that he had grown up in the city and used to 'hang out' on Burnside (a major thoroughfare and a main street for some members of the homeless population). It now seemed to him a completely different street than the one he had known before. The urban plunge can help students evaluate homelessness in ways that a lecture, a class discussion, or a movie simply cannot.

The use of risk as pedagogy should specifically be evaluated as part of the evaluation of ethnographic field methods in general. By using my own field research experience as a base for students, I feel that it is possible to teach them how to become more comfortable as field ethnographers by giving them as 'real' an experience as possible. The realities of carrying out research can be difficult to recreate in the classroom. Carrying out a door-to-door survey can seem quite straightforward until you try to visit homes in a tough neighborhood. For instance, you may have to weigh up your commitment to the integrity of your sample against the challenge of getting past a pit bull in a front yard. Similarly, the ethnographer learns first and foremost by being plunged into an area with which they have previously had little or no contact. I suggest, however, that students given a chance to experience the fear of first-time research in a population they might consider risky will make better insiders as they mature in their careers.

In the 'Down and Out in America' and Nicaragua courses, I have been able to assist students in evaluating the original, fearful process of going into the field. Furthermore, students can then learn about the ways in which 'dangerousness' is fluid and varying. One common element to these experiences is that I find myself conveying back and forth what the different actors or groups of actors may see as dangerous. In Nicaragua, for example, I found myself helping the students understand what the notion of threat meant in relation to working in the coffee fields. Students remarked that they found it interesting that every time they told local people about seeing a snake, the first thing they were asked was, 'Did you kill it?' I found out that many of the snakes were either coral snakes or poisonous green snakes that often lie in the coffee trees and bite pickers in the chest after falling out of a basket. Explaining the meaning of this threat was important for the students' safety, but from an ethnographic point of view was interesting in terms of the significance of the risk to local people. Such fears are much more crucial in rural areas as medical assistance is two hours' drive away. The idea of letting a poisonous snake slither away possibly to bite someone else is seen as putting at risk someone else's life, even if yours was spared.

On the other hand, on this same trip, many students began to fall ill. There was no drinkable water, indeed no latrines, and we bathed in a stream. After one illness, where a student slipped into a coma and we had difficulty finding a pulse, several members of the community wanted to know what they could do. I tried to explain the idea of little bugs in the water, and how we could purify the water.[2] The water was not usually dangerous to the local people but was a big problem to the students. This provided for some interesting discussions between the students and the families about notions of health and wellness, especially when I reduced some of the stigma they felt by explaining to the families that even in our country we have these problems when we go into the mountains.

During these field experiences, students got a chance to evaluate the ways in which their views and perceptions of threat changed. Even more importantly, this pedagogical approach also allowed me to help students in working through the psychological and alienating effects of the ethnographic experience discussed earlier on in this chapter. I suggest that discussing alienation as a conscious part of the research process maximizes the benefit of the learning experience. Students work through the culture shock that they experience; fear of perceived physical risks and difficulties reconciling some of their previous views with their current experience. Having support around them, in the form of their peers and professors, makes them better field ethnographers, and gives them a sound base upon which to build their future independent research.

## Conclusions

In this chapter I have proposed that risk and danger are an integral part of the ethnographic field experience. Notions of risk vary greatly according to the actor involved, time, space, physicality and in the social psychological sense. Also, risks and threats have traditionally been seen as obstacles to the research endeavor. Through being conscious of and evaluating how shifts in the notion of risk may occur, the researcher is prepared, not only to enter and leave the field, but also to maximize the potential for learning about their subject of study during their stay. However, the consideration of risk and danger has not usually been seen by social scientists as a proactive way of being able to frame experiences in the field. I have argued here that the researcher's feelings of threat or vulnerability may indicate that they are closer to understanding an important aspect of the field than perhaps when things seem to be going well. Often we find ourselves being caught so off guard by these experiences that we may miss gathering some of our most important data while we react to the risky or dangerous situations in which we find ourselves.

Finally, I suggest that one solution to this might be to include using the notion of risk as inherent to ethnographic research early on, when students are first learning about the process. The teaching of research methods is often carried out in the safe and sanitized setting of the class or lecture room, away from the realities of the field. I am arguing here that carrying out research projects and experiencing measured risks are an important tool in aiding students to develop as researchers and to prepare them for independent study. The experience or perception of risk during a research project may be understood as a continuum, whereby students gradually become acclimatized to the presence of some types of threat. At the same time they are working through the shifting nature of what feels risky to them as their time in the field goes on.[3] Understanding the nature of the fluidity of risk and danger may allow students to understand more systematically the psychological, social and physical processes that are inevitable as they conduct fieldwork. They should be encouraged to regard this learning process in a positive manner and this can be promoted through peer and teacher support. Thus, I propose that exposure to specific forms and situations of risk and danger may be advantageous in teaching, in producing better research, and even in creating better researchers.

## Notes

1   One of these came from a friend of mine who said that 'Tequila cures everything' and advised several large quantities to get rid of the problem. By not pursuing this course of healing, I fortunately avoided cirrhosis of the liver. Along these same lines, researchers often learn of the blurred line between so-called conventional and alternative medicines. A colleague of ours, Jonathan Amith, tells of a long and drawn-out search for a local cure for his headaches. Following a long story about the magical nature of a local cure, the shaman in the end provided him with two aspirins. My students in Nicaragua had similar stories about the powerful properties of Alka-Seltzer as a cure-all.

2 There were also some interesting and amusing results. One student reported how her housemother boiled the water for nearly twenty minutes and then used cold, non-boiled water to cool off the coffee for her. In another case one of the housemothers bringing us food decided that if a few drops of bleach in the water was good, a quarter of a cup would really do the trick. A few of us managed to drink some of it, and I had visions of my incredibly whitened innards as a result of the experience.

3 This is not to say that one cannot move back and forth along the continuum due to expected and highly threatening events.

# Bibliography

Adams, J. (1995) *Risk*, London: UCL Press.

Armstrong, G. (1993) 'Like that Desmond Morris?' in D. Hobbs and T. May (eds) *Interpreting the Field: Accounts of Ethnography*, Oxford: Clarendon Press.

Breyer, S. (1993) *Breaking the Vicious Circle: Toward Effective Risk Regulation*, Cambridge, Mass.: Harvard University Press.

Bronstein, J. M. (1987) 'The Political Symbolism of Occupational Health Risks' in B. B. Johnson and V. T. Covello (eds) *The Social and Cultural Construction of Risk*, Norwell, Mass.: D. Reidel Publishing.

Douglas, M. (1992) *Risk and Blame: Essays in Cultural Theory*, London: Routledge.

Fetterman, D. M. (1991) 'A Walk Through the Wilderness: Learning to Find Your Way' in W. B. Shaffir and R. A. Stebbins (eds) *Experiencing Fieldwork: An Inside View of Qualitative Research*, London: Sage.

Friedman, K. E. (1987) 'The Study of Risk in Social Systems: An Anthropological Perspective' in L. Sjöberg (ed.) *Risk and Society: Studies of Risk Generation and Reactions to Risk*, London: Allen & Unwin.

Hobbs, D. (1993) 'Peers, Careers, and Academic Fears: Writing as Field-Work' in D. Hobbs and T. May (eds) *Interpreting the Field: Accounts of Ethnography*, Oxford: Clarendon Press.

Lee, R. (1993) *Doing Research on Sensitive Topics*, London: Sage.

—— (1995) *Dangerous Fieldwork*, London: Sage.

Rosaldo, R. (1993) *Culture and Truth: The Remaking of Social Analysis*, London: Routledge.

Wolf, D. R. (1991) 'High-Risk Methodology: Reflections on Leaving an Outlaw Society' in W. B. Shaffir and R. A. Stebbins (eds) *Experiencing Fieldwork: An Inside View of Qualitative Research*, London: Sage.

# POSTSCRIPT

*Geraldine Lee-Treweek and Stephanie Linkogle*

Thirty years ago Howard Becker (1970) asked, 'Whose side are we on?' Out of this seemingly straightforward question have arisen complex debates about how we as researchers should see our roles in the field, how we should relate to participants and how far we should try to protect them. These kind of issues are now routinely discussed as part of social research methods courses and by scholars engaged in the research process. In contrast, with a few notable exceptions (e.g. Lee 1995), the issue of protecting researchers is often disregarded and has never been fashionable to think about or to discuss. In this book we have tried to redress this imbalance by outlining some of the concealed and/or ignored aspects of researcher risk. The contributors to this book have reflected on how they coped with various risks, many noting that sharing danger and threat with participants often facilitated deeper insight into their lives. In doing this we have not sought to negate risk to participants. In fact we would argue that researcher and participant dangers are often interconnected and difficult to disentangle.

Researchers and participants, however, are differently placed in relation to danger as recent debates on ethics have emphasised. One important distinction is that researchers are often employees of institutions and hence the risks they face can be considered within the framework of employment legislation designed to protect all workers. Yet ironically the changing research climate may work against researchers being seen as workers in need of protection. Universities and colleges across the world have become more oriented towards research, increasing the pressure on academics to publish. The use of contract and part-time staff for research projects has increased in many countries and these individuals usually lack the status and job security of tenured academics. These researchers may have less time to evaluate the risks and, because of their relative lack of power and status, they may feel unable to ask for support or to demand basic safeguards in the field. As Jamieson notes in Chapter 4, research managers or more senior staff are not necessarily aware of the problems of researchers in the field. To put researcher safety on the agenda is essential to developing safer research practices and protecting everyone involved in the research process. However, this also requires a change in the mindset of everyone undertaking research, from established academics to students carrying out research for undergraduate or postgraduate degrees.

## Is social research worth the risks?

Risk is a part of all our lives. As noted in the first chapter, lay people are becoming increasingly aware of the risks of everyday living due to health and safety legislation, media interest and large-scale safety scares around such topics as food, work and the environment. Although many of these public scares have focused upon risks to physical well-being, more recently there has also been concern with the threat of long-term psychological distress. For instance, there is greater public awareness of the damage that catastrophic one-off events can cause and terms such as Post-Traumatic Stress Syndrome have entered everyday phraseology. Moreover, the general effect of sustained stressful work situations has been the focus of popular, media and medical interest. This broadening awareness of risk has impacted upon the social sciences and, in particular, great interest has been shown in protecting participants from harm. However, the nature of qualitative social researching is that it involves immersing oneself in the experience of participants, and, as a result, coming into contact with the dangers that participants themselves negotiate. Furthermore, it is clear that some topics of research, such as the observational study of potentially dangerous and threatening groups, can put researchers in danger for extended periods of time.

As so much effort in 'post-industrial' societies is geared towards risk avoidance, it is pertinent to question whether the research enterprise is really worthwhile. Most researchers would say that on balance it definitely is, and we can identify a number of reasons behind this belief. For instance, we can argue that social scientists are interested in the full breadth of social life and want to understand how it operates. In particular, qualitative researchers wish to get close to a phenomenon in order to understand fully the way participants experience it. We wish to unravel the meanings that are used in a setting by the participants themselves and uncover the alternative ways that experience can be considered. In some cases that world may be completely inaccessible to most people. For instance, David Calvey in Chapter 3 of this volume has argued that his research as a bouncer provided an authentic account of 'doing bouncing', a world which is concealed to non-bouncers. Part of his rationale for using covert observational methods was to understand the work as bouncers did themselves, by observing the work in as natural a setting as possible. Calvey's chapter is vigorous in its defence of the serious risks which he took in order to carry out the study. He argues that ethnography requires engagement, commitment and 'living' the field

– whatever that may bring. In other situations risk may be experienced by chance rather than calculation, as in the case of Jeff Peterson's account of attempted assault in Mexico (Chapter 11). As Peterson makes clear, these experiences enabled him to understand participants' attitudes to their own personal safety and provided insight into the highly gendered notions of risk that were prevalent in the field. Linkogle in Chapter 8 also reflects on encounters with physical danger in the field and concludes that when risk is an intrinsic part of an event, as in the case of the Nicaraguan Santo Domingo festival, the researcher must be willing to expose themselves to such dangers. Thus encountering danger in social research is 'worth it' in the sense that risk is often a composite part of the social life we are studying. To exclude threat would lead to a merely partial account of the participants' social world.

To this claim we would add the caveat that the researcher can never completely share the experience of participants, which begs a set of ethical questions. Thus far we have considered a range of serious threats faced by the researcher, broadening the concept of danger beyond immediate physical risk. Yet clearly researchers must be mindful of their responsibilities to participants and this includes an awareness of the possible harm that they may cause them. Research ethics is a theme that is increasingly central to discussions of social science research. Here, the idea of informed consent predominates to the extent that any form of covert research is widely considered to be unethical. Whilst debates on this issue have been fraught (Humphreys 1970; Wax 1980; Bulmer 1982; Homan 1991), disclosing the nature of research to participants and securing their agreement to participate in it is the basis of most codes of research ethics.

Our inclusion of Calvey's chapter, which reflects on his experience of covert research, is intended to stimulate debate on this topic. Given the secretive and often criminal nature of 'bouncing', Calvey argues that his research would have been impossible had it not been covert. Is covert research justified under such circumstances? In terms of many formal statements of ethical practice the answer would probably be no. However, there may be grey areas where even overt studies stray into not being as open as they could be, and in which not all participants have been fully aware of the implications of research.

Representing others is another issue which is fraught with ethical danger. Above and beyond fulfilling an obligation to obtain informed consent, an important ethical consideration which researchers must address is their power to (mis)represent social groups and the possible consequences of these representations. To this end, John Gabriel (Chapter 10) traces the shifting arguments on the ethics of research on 'race' and ethnicity and his own attempts to undertake anti-racist research. In contrast, Jipson and Litton's research on white supremacists (Chapter 9) is concerned to move away from a perspective of 'deviance'. They present participants as acting rationally within the terms of their own belief

199

systems. Does such a 'neutral' approach, to what are clearly repugnant groups, serve to legitimate their activities and provide them with the 'oxygen of publicity'? A vital issue to consider is the effect that the publishing of your research may have on their credibility. This is especially important in relation to groups who may hold ideas about other people in society that are inflammatory or potentially dangerous. Accounts that are perceived to present such groups in a positive and everyday light can sometimes be used to promote their case for acceptance. In these cases researchers need to be prepared to justify their position and explain the utility of their work to the development of knowledge on such groups. Jipson and Litton contend that excluding particular social groups from the research agenda is perilous. Policy makers, law enforcement and society in general need to be aware of how such groups operate and the way they construct their identity in relation to other groups. Here, issues of public safety, and the possibility of reinforcing aggressive and anti-social behaviour, have to be weighed up against the need to know about and understand these belief systems.

The research process is an emergent and exciting enterprise. It can take you in a variety of directions and the kinds of threats that may be experienced can be difficult to predict or plan for. The example we presented you with in Chapter 1 was the case of Rik Scarce, the first sociologist in the US to be jailed for refusing to divulge information on research participants (Scarce 1994, 1995). Scarce refused even to admit to the authorities whether he had interviewed particular individuals and consequently was held in contempt of court and imprisoned. We asked him to consider, in retrospect, whether any topic or data was worth the risk of imprisonment. He notes that his imprisonment was less an issue of data than the principle of the right of academics, as professionals, to protect sources of information (Scarce in personal communication). Where a statement of ethical practice binds us, the only professional way to act in the face of pressure to release information would indeed seem to be to refuse. It is interesting to consider that, because qualitative research is so reliant upon the flexibility of human interaction, we cannot tell what kinds of material may be divulged in an interview or may be witnessed whilst observing. Therefore, we could be called upon to protect such principles at any point.

## Can we make research safer?

As we have argued earlier, it is not always possible to eliminate threat from either everyday life or social research. Danger has an emergent quality which means that we may not be able to foresee how risky a situation may become. Rik Scarce (in personal communication) notes in relation to his own experience of research danger in the form of imprisonment:

... you have to keep in mind that, in ethnographic research, discomforting or even dangerous things fall into our laps sometimes. I never
sought out perpetrators of crimes and destructive behavior was not central to my research by any means. But part of the thrill – as well as the
danger – of ethnographic research is the uncontrollableness of it all.

It is the case that risks arise out of the blue and cannot always be planned for;
however, we do have the responsibility to try to predict and think through the
possible risks of research in relation to participants. As mentioned in Chapter 1,
ethical statements created by professional organisations, such as the British
Sociological Association, the American Sociological Association and the American
Anthropological Association, can serve as guides to research practice. Although
there are some differences in the detail of these statements, they all share a
concern with potential harm that might affect research subjects.

At the same time as being responsible to participants we have a duty to ourselves to mitigate the dangers that we might experience. This accountability
should also be taken up more vigorously by the institutions to which researchers
are tied, such as universities and research institutes. One of the main ways in
which they are supposed to do this in many countries is through risk assessment of
work tasks. This involves assessment of the possible dangers of activities and
planning to make the activity as safe as possible. Traditionally risk in universities
has been seen in terms of threats from physical work and from accidents on
campus; academic and research staff have not been 'risk assessed' in relation to
social research activity. Notions about academic work as a pen-pushing middle-
class pursuit contribute to the under-recognition of the risks of social research.
Furthermore, as Jamieson argues in Chapter 4, when dangers are experienced
they are often dealt with in situ. The research continues, sometimes without
colleagues or funding bodies knowing what has happened. It is very likely, given
the fear of litigation currently exhibited by institutions of higher education, that
risk assessments will become commonplace for all research work. When this
happens, issues such as lone working, support of workers in the field and physical
safety, will become central to planning and justifying research procedures.

A problem for all social researchers is how to ensure their own safety and the
safety of others whilst at the same time undertaking fresh and challenging work.
The contributors to this volume have all suggested informal means by which one
can make research safer for all involved. Thorough scrutiny and planning is
essential to every research project, on the part of both researcher and ethics
committees and/or funding bodies. Unfortunately, the well-being of researchers
is often not considered in this formal process and researchers are left to think
through these issues on their own. There are a number of practical steps that can
be taken to evaluate risk, including literature searches that may identify potential

threats encountered in a particular field, visits to research sites and careful use of pilot work. This basic physical risk assessment may also require the modification of plans to make sure that the research is as safe as possible. Changes to the timing or site of data collection and the exclusion of evening interviewing can minimise both felt and real threat to the researcher. Likewise, developing practices, such as getting lone researchers to telephone back to base regularly, can make data collection safer.

Just as with physical risk, emotional threat requires the development of coping strategies. Researchers of all levels of expertise should be aware of the possible personal and emotional effects of research. In Chapter 1 we discussed a job advertisement for a researcher needed to interview dying patients and their kin. This kind of work would not be suitable for all and indeed a researcher who had been recently bereaved may have found this topic extremely difficult to cope with. A high degree of self-awareness and honesty is needed when choosing a study topic. As Lankshear and Letherby note in Chapters 5 and 6 respectively, personal experience can both aid our understanding of participants' lives, but it can also be self-destructive. In the case of postgraduate students, who may be committing themselves to three or more years' work on one research project, these kinds of issues are particularly pertinent. Postgraduate research is often a lonely enterprise and the issue of maintaining boundaries between oneself and one's topic can be difficult at the best of times. If you are in doubt about your ability to cope with a topic it may be best to put your initial project aside (as something to return to in the future) and select another area of interest.

As a number of contributors to this book have noted, the support of peers is particularly important in helping researchers to work through difficult issues encountered in the field. In some cases, research team members and students working independently, but concurrently, on dissertations or theses can provide informal support. However, whether supported by peers or colleagues, all researchers can benefit from other sources such as specialist study groups within their own discipline. Joining one of these groups can have numerous benefits. They bring researchers with similar substantive issues together and facilitate the informal discussion of coping with fieldwork. Moreover, these groups can also provide a supportive forum for presentations of your findings added to which members often have knowledge of suitable publishing outlets, which is of great importance to new researchers. Overall, such informal networking is useful both in terms of personal support and professional development. As Lee-Treweek contends, where such backing is not available and where research is emotionally stressful, it can be helpful to use a personal counsellor as a sounding board or to help cope with particular difficulties. Emotional dangers are very difficult to predict or eliminate from the field. Therefore, strategies for dealing with emotional dangers challenge us to look outwards to others around for help when it is needed and to be honest about our limits and capabilities when under stress.

## Conclusion

This collection has highlighted some of the numerous dangers experienced by qualitative social researchers. It has noted that in research accounts danger has often been visible solely as physical threat, and that even in these cases, there has been little acknowledgement of the impact of physical danger upon the researcher. The aim of this collection has been to begin to develop the notion that qualitative research is often very risky for researchers. At the beginning of the book we presented our framework of dangers – physical; emotional; ethical and professional – as a starting point for thinking about social research and risk. The contributing chapters have developed these themes and illustrated the complexities of risk and danger in contemporary settings. Furthermore, these accounts have indicated how risk informed the analysis and understanding of the social settings under investigation.

It is of use here to summarise the approach we have used in this book. As noted in the first chapter, we do not seek to conflate danger with difficulty. We have highlighted serious dangers that impact on a researcher's physical state, their sense of self, their social relationships and their careers. Throughout, we have sought to provide a considered discussion of risk but not to put readers off carrying out their own qualitative research. At the same time, we would not want readers to think that we are arguing that danger and risk are merely obstacles to get around, or perhaps through. As Westmarland notes in Chapter 2, when we share dangerous experiences with participants it not only bonds us with them but allows us to see more clearly how social groups think about and mobilise against threat. Danger can therefore be a pathway to insight and can facilitate our understanding of research settings. However, it is also important that risks should be anticipated as far as possible in order to reduce the occurrence of situations in which the researcher is forced to deal with danger alone, in an *ad hoc* and unsupported way.

Finally, because we have chosen to present danger in a framework of distinct and discrete types, it may also seem we are positing an uncomplicated view of researcher risk. However, as the preceding chapters have illustrated, research risks are fluid and often experienced together in a variety of permutations. It would have been impossible to illustrate all the combinations of risk that could be experienced in the field, the preceding chapters merely serve as illustrations of the key issues. Similarly, the strategies discussed should function as a basic set of suggestions that can be modified according to your own circumstances. It is to be hoped that this collection will encourage the recognition of, and discussion about, researcher safety. We began the overview of this book with the question, 'Are you in danger?' We hope you will now be able not only to answer this question, but also to identify and respond to any threats you might encounter when researching the social world.

## Bibliography

Becker, H. (1970) *Sociological Work: Method and Substance*, London: Allen Lane.

Bulmer, M. (1982) *Social Research Ethics*, London: Macmillan.

Homan, R. (1991) *The Ethics of Social Research*, London: Longman.

Humphreys, L. (1970) *Tearoom Trade*, London: Duckworth.

Lee, R. (1995) *Dangerous Fieldwork*, Qualitative Research Methods Series, Vol. 34, London: Sage Publications.

Scarce, R. (1994) '(No) Trial (But) Tribulations: When Courts And Ethnography Conflict', *Journal of Contemporary Ethnography* 23, 2: 123–49.

—— (1995) 'Scholarly Ethics and Courtroom Antics: Where Researchers Stand in the Eyes of the Law', *The American Sociologist* 26, 1: 87–112.

Wax, M. (1980) 'Paradoxes of "Consent" to the Practice of Fieldwork', *Social Problems* 27, 3: 273–83, February.

# INDEX